'Sarah Thomas' lyrical, thoughtful prose takes us on a journey, both physical and emotional, to the far north – a region about which stories are increasingly essential, especially from those who live there. One senses her filmmaker's eye in her crisp visual imagery, and in her careful portraits of both people and place.'

Cal Flyn, author of *Islands of Abandonment*

'*The Raven's Nest* asks what it means to belong to a place from which we do not originate. It considers Icelandicness and proximity to it. Both anthropological and tender in detail, Sarah Thomas recalls an immersion that sometimes feels like drowning, at others a rush on swell to the shore. Her skills as an anthropological documentary maker come across on the page, but she is a participant in this story, present and implicated in what it means to dwell between tongues, cultures, landscapes and geological timescales.'

Abi Andrews, author of *The Word for Woman is Wilderness*

'*The Raven's Nest* is a story of many stories, nested together: the making and ending of relationships. Those chance meetings across wide unlikely spaces, how they spin for a while and how we can bear to let them go. But boil that down further and I would say it has much to say about chance, and taking chances, and being open to chance – and also the chance trickery nature plays on us. And that feeds into where stories come from, and whose stories we can tell. Sarah Thomas evokes characters and the culture, a sense of time and the landscape in beautiful prose which makes my brain do cartwheels.'

Nancy Campbell, author of *The Library of Ice*

Sarah Thomas is a writer and documentary filmmaker with a PhD in Interdisciplinary Studies. Her films have been screened internationally. She is a regular contributor to the *Dark Mountain* journal and her writing has also appeared in the *Guardian* and the anthology *Women on Nature*, edited by Katharine Norbury. In 2020, she was nominated for the Arts Foundation Environmental Writing Award. She was longlisted for the inaugural Nan Shepherd Prize and shortlisted for the 2021 Fitzcarraldo Essay Prize for the proposal for this book. This is her debut.

THE RAVEN'S NEST

SARAH THOMAS

Atlantic Books
London

Published in hardback in Great Britain in 2022 by Atlantic Books,
an imprint of Atlantic Books Ltd.

10 9 8 7 6 5 4 3 2 1

A CIP catalogue record for this book is available from the British Library.

Hardback ISBN: 978 1 83895 668 4
E-book ISBN: 978 1 83895 670 7

Printed in Great Britain

Atlantic Books
An imprint of Atlantic Books Ltd
Ormond House
26–27 Boswell Street
London
WC1N 3JZ

www.atlantic-books.co.uk

To the ravens, for making, unmaking and remaking the world.
And for the light; always the light.

Contents

CONTENTS

Breaking Up

August 2014

I am sitting in the kitchen of my old, corrugated-iron-clad house. Underneath me, 800 kilometres to the southeast, the earth has been breaking up since the evening I parked up out front, one long week ago. I arrived as the day dimmed, relieved to have the hours of rock and sea and fog behind me – months of anticipation giving way to reality. Then, 8 kilometres under the ground, below a distant glacier, unseen but detected by geologists and their myriad instruments, a tremor swarm began. I heard about it on the radio the next morning as the late summer sun poured in through the large windows. There had been 250 earthquakes during the night.

When the news broke, I laughed at the consistency with which my comings and goings between England and Iceland seemed to coincide precisely with weather changes and volcanic activity. The eruption of Eyjafjallajökull – the Icelandic volcano that nobody could pronounce, which closed European airspace in 2010 – was preceded by a lesser-known smaller eruption on Fimmvörðuháls. That had begun the day I arrived in March 2010 and ended the day I left, with the eruption of Eyjafjallajökull. I had been on one of the last flights for many days, separated from my husband by a cloud of ash.

Now, each day, there are more earthquakes, and a crack has grown to 50 kilometres long in a week – still invisible as it rips below Vatnajökull, the largest glacier in the country. Every day, almost every hour from 7 a.m. till 10 p.m., the radio news announces the latest earthquakes, usually in the region of 1,000 per day now, the strongest recently reaching 5.7 on the Richter scale. I hang on every word, pretty sure an eruption will follow, and not knowing whether I should prepare myself to leave before I risk getting stuck here.

The first few days of this trip were difficult. My destination – clarity in an uncertain marriage – is far from guaranteed. I have mostly been here alone. Well, with my cat. And a brief but intense lifetime of memories of this place to process – some dark, some joyful.

This house and I felt asynchronous when I walked in. It looked much the same as it did when I left, all those months ago. I had asked my husband, Bjarni, for our cat to be here when I returned. He made sure he was at the house when I arrived and was cooking lamb in the kitchen, almost like nothing had ever happened. The only visible evidence of time passing was a few kind notes from tourists who had come and enjoyed this 'thing' we had created, while we did not live in it ourselves – this 'bohemian Arctic hideaway', this 'romantic retreat' – while we had tried to figure out how and where we could live together, and failed.

I feel the need to do something physical, and aesthetic, to mark the change. In front of me, I peel decades of wallpaper, hessian and old newspaper from the walls in my study, to get back to the bare bones of this place – this wooden kit-house from Norway, erected in 1902. We know the name of the person who erected it, and that his son's wife lived in it for 70 years before we became the current owners. It may be that couple's history I am peeling away now, to reveal the time-darkened honey-coloured pine panelling it was made with, before it became fashionable to mask it with paper: a well-travelled wood, for there were no trees here big enough to build with. The final layer is *The Weekly Scotsman* from 19 June 1909. How did that newspaper end up in this house just below the Arctic Circle?

Old news, which one day mine shall also be. Trees, wood, paper, words – they vanish as they form.

Old news, which one day this imminent eruption shall be, whether it happens or not. For now, I try to embrace the Icelandic way and take each day as it comes. To stay put and do what I came here to do.

The international news recalls the 'chaos' caused by the 2010 volcano that nobody could pronounce. Júlíana, my old boss from the flower shop, dismisses these tremors as a 'media sensation'. I enjoy her humanizing of this seismic activity; the suggestion that somehow it is a protracted form of attention-grabbing, like a celebrity affair. My neighbour Mæja tells me, 'There's nothing you can do but wait and see. It's the same as driving a car in a big city. Sure, something might happen but that doesn't stop you from driving.'

Bjarni and I find each other much easier to get along with than we expected. The connection is heartfelt and strong, but we still know we must go our separate ways in order to become ourselves again.

It is like living inside a dream sequence: the backdrop is the same, he is there, he is calm and almost happy. The cat is curled up on the chair. It's like it used to be, but it's not. Neither of us can live in this house anymore. He cannot bear the reminders of our broken union hanging on every picture hook and in every colour we painted the walls. I cannot bear the long months of darkness and the separation from the rest of the world – a crucible for unreconciled pains. I have returned to live in my own country, where at least I know that the sun will rise above the horizon every day. I have not stood in this house to be prodded by these hooks and these colours, until now. I have traversed rivers of grief to arrive here, and now we must make new memories.

I still love him and yet I cannot smell him anymore. I try, but I find nothing. It disturbs me. It is one of the foundations on which I committed to this unlikely path. Have sorrow and distance altered our chemistry?

'Can *you* smell *me*?' I ask him.

'You smell like a distressed mink,' he says, without irony or insult. For him, it is simply a fact. Like an eruption will be a fact. And a divorce. There is nothing I can do but accept our fate.

* * *

I accept it and we go together to initiate proceedings. On that day, of all days, there is a region-wide phone and internet drop-out, apparently nothing to do with the tremors. The majority of administration at the Sheriff's office, which handles such proceedings, is done online.

For as long as this drop-out continues, there will be a shutdown of the region's bureaucratic processes. There is nothing we can do. I leave tomorrow. I shall leave still married.

As I spend my final hours in Reykjavík, the news breaks that the crack has become visible, and the glacier is collapsing. I make my flight back to Edinburgh.

As I trundle my bulky luggage – much of it chattels from my Icelandic study – along North Bridge in the city dark of 1 a.m., across the tracks of Edinburgh Waverley station, my eye is caught by the gold up-lit stone lettering emblazoned across the façade of an imposing turn-of-the-century building: *The Scotsman*. I slow to a halt as I realize that it is in *this* building that those words were created – the old news that I had been peeling off my walls – before they made their way across the sea to my house, and my study.

The next day I receive an email from Bjarni:

> The volcano erupted at two minutes past midnight the night you left.

Landing

May 2008

My neck aches as I react to the 'bong' prompting passengers to fasten their seat belts. My face has been pressed against the oval window for thirty minutes straight, turning only briefly to say, 'tea, please'. Beyond the condensation of my breath and the delicate ice crystals forming on the outside of the window, I have been looking out at a translucent blue sky that seems stretched thin by the weight of profuse sunlight. Beneath it, the sea is a choppy teal blue as if painted by a stippled brush and the shoreline meets the mountains frankly. Their opaque indigo bulk rises sharply and they are flat on top as if a giant has taken a sword to them. It is an Arctic palette, an infinite blue, and the landscape appears as wild and unsullied as Earth does from space. Though I know pristineness is an illusion in our times, for the moment I am enrapt. I am heading the furthest north I have ever been: sixty-six degrees latitude. Even in late May, snow swirls on the mountaintops and rests in shaded hollows. Since lifting off from Reykjavík I have not noticed any other cities or even aerial towns; only settlements I would describe generously as villages, and no more than three of them.

Having started the journey in London, I am on my way to the small town of Ísafjörður – the 'capital' of the Westfjords – in the top northwest corner of Iceland, which for reasons none of the delegates will fully understand, is the unlikely and awe-inspiring location for a conference of visual anthropologists. I will be presenting my MA graduation film *After the Rains Came: Seven short stories about objects and lifeworlds*, an observational documentary I made in Kenya, where I spent the latter part of my childhood and adolescence.

Observational documentary: the 'fly on the wall' style where the footage works to suggest that the filmmaker is not there at all. A film shot on the Equator, brought to the Arctic. The view from the plane's window could not be more different to the world of my film: the cracked earth, coloured beads and giant euphorbia trees of Kenya's Samburuland that will soon be projected on a screen down there somewhere.

I have been invited to stay with some friends of a friend, and as I gaze out at the wilderness, I feel fortunate to have connections in this remote place. I wrote to them a while back thanking them for their kind offer of a bed, and in response received 'directions': a photograph taken from the side of a mountain, looking down onto a long narrow fjord flanked on the opposite side by another steep-sided mountain – a trough of rock filled with sea. A spit curled out from the foreground to part way across the mouth of the fjord, forming a sheltered harbour. Brightly coloured houses were clustered on the spit and the few other flat surfaces of land. Their spread was contained by the clutch of the landscape, as if gravity itself pulled the houses towards the sea. Where construction ended, wild nature abruptly began – loose boulders on tussocky heaths and funnels of scree sloping up to terraced cliffs of basalt. This was altogether different from the patchwork of green squares and vast masses of concrete that is England from above. Over on the far shore at the bottom of the fjord they had drawn a yellow circle, and the word 'Airport'. Towards the foot of the spit was another yellow circle: 'Salvar and Natalía'. Their house was oxide red – I could see that from the photograph. My rational city brain was slightly wary of the lack of further information, but my intuitive self could see that this was the only information I would need. I liked these people: visual and concise.

As the twin-propeller Air Iceland plane suddenly banks sharply left, I recognize that this is *that* fjord, that spit seen from the other side. I imagine my hosts standing there taking that photograph, as I align its viewpoint with what I can see. I realize I might even be able to spot the house I am going to. My search for it is quickly replaced by alarm at the proximity of the wing tip to the mountain. It is a very close shave indeed, and a good thing they are standing there only in my imagination. I briefly look around at the other twenty passengers on this packed flight and cannot fathom how some of them are *reading a newspaper*. This moment is both frightening and phenomenally beautiful. We descend to the bottom of the fjord and bank steeply again. Somebody has mown a large HÆ into their hay meadow – a greeting to be seen from the sky. We land and bounce onto the airstrip facing towards the mouth of the fjord, from which we have just come. 'How is that even possible?' I think to myself.

I would later learn that Ísafjörður is one of the most challenging airports in the world in which to land.

We disembark into the miniature single-storey terminal where passengers are waiting to board the same plane back to Reykjavík. We mingle. There are two flights here a day, cruising back and forth across this lava, these mountains and these fjords: Reykjavík – Ísafjörður – Reykjavík – Ísafjörður – Reykjavík. Passengers departing Ísafjörður don't need an app to tell them if the flight is running on time. They just look up in the sky when they hear the engine rumbling and hop in their cars to curl around the bay to the airport, playing plane chase. I would later learn that the radar tower operator is also a carpenter in town, and simply cycles over to the airport when a flight is due, then returns to work when he has seen the plane safely off again.

It turns out that several fellow delegates are on the same flight and there is a coach waiting for us outside. White-bodied birds I have not seen before wheel, combative like throwing stars, above the car park showering the air with cries of *kriiiia kriiiia*. The passengers wrestle their black luggage into large four-wheel drives. The mountains tower above us and insist that we are small. You can spot those who do not live here: their mouths hang agape over the necks of their Gore-Tex jackets, and their luggage has lost all its importance. The locals seem to have developed an immunity to the landscape's power, but I imagine it is more complex than that.

We board the coach and a tall frowning man with a grey side parting and a shiny face fusses and breaks intermittently into nervous laughter. '*Hæ*. I'm Valdimar,' he greets us repeatedly. He is clearly the one in charge, but it looks like this is the most people he has had to organize in a while. It is hot, and I have come only with jumpers. The sun feels near. It is bright and beats on me through the large glass window, as if curious and eager to illuminate everything it can. I drink in the scene through squinted eyes and feel both sleepy and enormously awakened.

We round the bottom of the fjord, passing on our left a grid-like housing development and a supermarket with gaudy signage of yellow with a bright pink piggy bank: Bónus, it is called. Behind it all is a long, lush valley lined with lupine and speckled with brightly coloured wooden cabins. Midway up the valley I can make out a large waterfall that in another place would be reason enough to come here, and a small square plantation of some kind of pine that Valdimar refers to as the local 'forest'. There is a long, man-made sharp-edged ridge separating that valley from the buildings along the fjord's edge and he tells us that it is an avalanche guard. In the harbour lagoon to our right, flocks of eider ducks bob among reflected impressions of the sun-glowed mountains – morphing orange and green fragments floating leaf-like in the black glassy water. We pass a scattering of houses, then the town proper seems to begin. Valdimar takes the microphone again and points out in quick succession a kindergarten, a school, an old people's home, a hospital and, across the road, a church and cemetery.

'I suppose they have to be ergonomic with town planning here!' an Italian academic in the seat behind me chuckles. 'Look, a whole life in 500 metres.'

10

As we approach the spit on which the oldest part of the town is built, I see that the houses are all clad in brightly coloured corrugated iron, with differently coloured iron roofs. In just one street I see cornflower blue, deep red, egg yolk yellow, black. It gives the town an air of playfulness – I imagine the people here to be happy and daring. The coach slows to a halt by the church and I take my photo directions to Valdimar. It is a map made for a bird or a hiker at height. I am at the wrong angle here.

'Do you know where this house is?' I ask him. 'That's where I'm staying.'

'Whose house is it? Salvar and Natalía? Ah yes, I know them.'

He reaches for his mobile phone and scrolls for their number. He doesn't have it. He inspects the photograph a little more closely. '… Sólgata, Hrannargata, Mánagata, Hafnarstræti… Ah, that is this one.' He points at the street we are on. That was easy.

Twenty metres later I am standing in front of an oxide-red house, conjoined with a leaf-green house painted with a mural of giant dandelions. From what I have seen of Icelandic homes from the outside, it seems to be typical to make displays of ornaments in the windows, to delight those walking past on the street, and perhaps to give an inkling of the people who live inside. In the moments between my knocking and the door being answered, while I imagine what Salvar and Natalía might be like, I notice on their windowsill a tall glass jar filled with strangely shaped birds' eggs I have never seen before, each a different shade of aquamarine, green, duck egg blue, turquoise, ivory: an exquisite non-tessellation of otherness. For reasons I cannot explain, they touch me deeply. Can you be reminded of something by an entirely new form?

Salvar and Natalía have warned me by email that, though they are happy to put me up, they are extremely busy preparing to leave for the highlands, for their summer job running a 'mountain shop'. This titbit of information has made me curious about their lives. The idea of a seasonal existence makes so much sense to me. I am prone to get into deep conversation when something interests me, but in the circumstances, I prepare to drop my bags and make myself scarce as quickly as possible. I am greeted at the first knock by two smiles and a welcome large enough to fill the reception room that seems to be dedicated entirely to this purpose, and to the storage of a sizeable rail of coats, hats and scarves. After putting down my bags and exchanging greetings, the blue eggs are one of the first things I ask about.

'Ah, *svartfuglsegg*,' says Salvar. 'Yes. They are *very* beautiful.'

He gives me one to hold. It has been drained and has a hole at either end.

'*Svart-fugl* means "black-bird" but it's not your kind of blackbird. It's the word for the seabirds that are black. There are several kinds. This one is *langvía*. "Guillemot", I think you call it.'

I turn it in my fingertips and hold it up to the light. It is at once strong and fragile, pointed and round, simple and infinitely complex – a collection of paradoxes in ovoid. A thick strong shell the colour of turquoise, a perfectly rounded base that sits so naturally in the palm of my hand. Sides that rise gracefully like the steepest of volcanoes into a sharply rounded point. An archipelago of burnt umber marks speckled over an ocean of delicate blue. It is as though it has been clutched excitedly by a tiny-fingered beast covered in paint. Holding the egg in that moment, I feel within me a tectonic shift so deep that only the most perceptive would notice.

I have been back in England for ten years, but I find my childhood in Kenya bubbling unexpectedly to the surface. Our lives were porous to wild creatures. I was often immersed in the textures, scents and soundscapes of savannah or scrub or ocean. Even at home in the then forested suburbs of Nairobi, Sykes' monkeys would descend on our garden, and the most audacious would sneak into our house to steal pineapples and mangoes. I was taught never to smile at monkeys because bared teeth are a sign of aggression. Once, on a school camping trip, I woke to pee in the night and unzipped my tent onto a galaxy of buffalo eyes reflecting my headtorch.

But, having moved to Kenya from England, that wild had always remained exotic to me – other. Or perhaps it is I who remained other to it. It was the nature seen in wildlife documentaries, not mine. The potential dangers posed by the wildlife – from megafauna to malarial mosquitoes – meant my relationship with it was often about protecting myself from it. I could be in awe, but I could not bring it close. Here, all of a sudden, I am holding the wild in my hands in a front room on an island in the North Atlantic, an ecology continuous with the UK's, where I have so far spent my adulthood. This is a wild to which I can relate: somehow familiar though not yet known. It is not trapped behind glass, or enclosed within a national park: it lives in the world. And for better or worse it is in my hands because it is used. The eggshell is hollow because the egg has been eaten.

'*Kaffi?*' Natalía offers.

It will be the first of many cups drunk around the large table in their triple-glazed conservatory; their Vetrarhöllin ('Winter Palace') as they proudly call it. Today, there is enough time only to make a quick life-sketch of each other. They tell me they are artists. Natalía is from Moscow and Salvar is an Icelandic farmer's son. They met at art school in Germany. They had noticed each other and Natalía asked shy Salvar out for a cup of tea. 'It is the longest cup of tea in history. We are still having it!' Natalía giggles. They came to the Westfjords to live alone on Æðey, a small island near here, having heard on the grapevine that a job was going reading the weather instruments which served the region. They knew they would be inspired by the solitude and the nature and have time to develop their artistic practice.

After seven winters of living that life, alternating with their summer job in the highlands, they decided to be part of a community on the mainland and chose Ísafjörður, this regional capital of about 2,600 people. From the island, Salvar came 'shopping' one day to find a house. 'Get something cheap and outside the avalanche zone that we can make nice,' was Natalía's only instruction. He found this modest red house on the spit across the fjord, the sea at either end of the street. They got such a good deal, they believe, because the locals were so grateful for the 'hardships' they had endured living alone on an island. Salvar chuckles. 'Oh the "suffering"! We *loved* it.' After months of renovating, the neighbour put the adjacent house up for sale, which they also bought.

'This house is our life plan – as long as the rising sea levels don't get us first,' Salvar says with a healthy dose of realism. 'So, there is plenty of time to renovate slowly. We are not rich, but we are happy.'

'We won't do anything with the next-door house for ages. But one day it will be our studios.' Natalía's voice is like a song. 'That's why we've painted *huge* dandelions on it, so at least it looks beautiful. First flowers of summer. Look!'

There is a hummock in their back garden, overflowing with dandelions in the long grass. 'That is an elf hill,' said Salvar. 'Isn't it beautiful?'

Between June and September each year, Salvar and Natalía tell me they go to the highlands to a place called Landmannalaugar to run a shop, housed in two vintage American school buses, which provides food, essentials and, of course, coffee to hikers and day trippers. That is why they are particularly busy now, packing and ordering supplies before going south in two weeks' time. That is as far as we get for now.

I show them the programme of films for the conference – documentaries from all around the world. '*Æi!* Why do they never *advertise* these things?' says Salvar. 'It is so frustrating. It's not often we have something so interesting happening in our town.' They promise to come to my film and will try to find time to see some others. We drink coffee and chat for at least half an hour before I realize it is time to go and register at the conference, and Salvar and Natalía remind themselves that they are busy preparing for the summer.

I sense immediately that we delegates are interlopers in this place, this life; that visitors' affairs are very separate to local ones. The visitors arrive, mostly once winter is over, with the star-shaped birds. They are equipped with their global perspectives and their brightly coloured waterproofs, feeling, as I do, that they have made it to the edge of the world. But for the people here, this is not an edge. This is their centre. If you were to stand on the pebble beach at the end of Salvar and Natalía's street, looking out across the mouth of the fjord to the mountains and glacier beyond, you too would feel that the rest of the world was somewhere very far away, and of seemingly little relevance – but undoubtedly having an impact on this fragile island. I feel privileged that, by staying with Salvar and Natalía, I may get to stand at the shore's edge and listen to the tide a while; to stand where the subtler levels of Here and Elsewhere mingle, not visit Iceland through a window.

Shift

May 2008

Over the course of a few days, as the sun didn't set until around midnight, my late-night conversations with Natalía and Salvar took me deeper into this world and their place in it. Their version of 'busy' was quite different from mine. There was always time for ambling conversation. When I am busy, I barely have time for myself, let alone others. And especially not for the kind of thinking that curls like smoke from a low fire. Even in their busyness, life seemed to be about meeting the day to see what it had in store for them, rather than imposing plans on it. Of course there was a 'to do' list, but it was mutable, shaped by what else presented itself.

In a different, much busier way, growing up in Kenya had shown me that planning was almost futile. Our life was chaotic and never 'on time' because of our resistance to what presented itself; because of a misguided sense that life was controllable, regardless of the consistent failure of this approach. My parents and other expats, hardwired by their conditioning, seemed to find this intensely frustrating at times. The Kenyans I met seemed more inclined to improvise their existence than design it – some of them out of necessity. And a disregard for modern Western timekeeping was commonplace. Both made a strong impression on me. This idea that we get to decide what the day is for; that we can plan and control everything; that we run to a schedule: I can see now that it is a behaviour I have learned in England or through Englishness. It is an extractive mindset. But for a brief period during my childhood, a glimmer of another way to be became visible.

As a child in Nairobi I noticed, too, the expat community of which I was a part would go to great lengths to create an island of 'home' in spite of the context: furniture made from African hardwoods in the style of European antiques, Women's Institute mornings, country clubs. At that age I found it surprising. I had imagined that if we were moving to Africa our lives would look and feel more African, whatever that meant. I suppose the impulse to replicate the rhythms, habits and aesthetics of home in a strange place is a natural one, perhaps as a way to anchor oneself. At first, I simply felt uprooted. Because I had just turned eleven when we moved there, I did not yet have a sense of who I was. I was a sponge.

Looking back, my parents' ambitions to create a stable home life were impossible to achieve in the way they might have wished, underpinned as they were by the inequality embedded within our situation. We and other expat families certainly enjoyed a better quality of life than we would have back home, but the question 'at whose expense?' wasn't one that was asked.

Once things had settled down and I felt safe enough, teetering on the cusp of adolescence, I was thirsty for influences and wanted to drink from the pool I was in. My home life was somewhat at odds with that adolescent self who was becoming an adult – this adult. I was so curious to peer over the walls of my privileged 'island' – a beautiful house with bars on the windows in a walled compound patrolled by a night-time security guard – to mingle with the place itself. But I grew up being told that what was outside those walls was dangerous.

I had wanted to learn Kiswahili at school to feel the place in my mouth at least. But in a quirk of the British education system under which I was taught, only those who had failed French, which was compulsory, got to learn Kiswahili. I was never immersed in it. It wasn't essential because 'everybody' spoke English. I did not understand back then the histories and forces of colonialism and neocolonialism which play out in these facts – Kiswahili relegated to the bottom of the pile in its own country by a private education system which is a legacy of the former colonizer. A system in which, in Geography, we learned the names and locations of UK motorways and not the dazzling topography of the Serengeti on our doorstep.

I found the segregation between expat life and the country in which that life took place infantilizing, disempowering. By twenty, I had travelled much of the world alone and thrived on building relationships with the people I met. But in Kenya I felt afraid to travel and encounter people in the same way, mainly because of the narratives of danger that had been a staple of my upbringing. No doubt the danger existed, but there was much else I was missing. Making the film that I had come to Iceland to show had been a turning point. It was the first and only attempt I had been able to make to meet Kenya as I wanted to meet it. Returning as a twenty-six-year-old visual anthropology student, ignoring warnings from other expats, I had taken a bus alone with my video camera to Samburuland, a region in north central Kenya, to shoot my MA film.

I had arranged to spend two months living with a Samburu family with whom a friend of my parents had a long-term connection. I happened to arrive with the first heavy rains in four years, which for a cattle-keeping people means everything. In recognition of this, I was given a Samburu name by Nkoko, the matriarch of the household: Nashangai – 'the one who came with rain'. This status, fortuitous as it was, softened the barriers to our connection that existed because I didn't speak Kiswahili, or their own language, Maa. I learned what Maa I could, and hired one of their sons, Lkitasian, as an interpreter. And we all learned to relate in other ways: joking, mime, storytelling, making.

I'm not sure I will ever completely understand the complexities of my discomfort around my family's presence in Kenya, but in Samburuland I never felt unsafe. Utterly confounded, sometimes. In complex relations because of whiteness, gender, age and marital status – always. In danger, only once, when we stumbled upon an elephant – a mother with calf – and had to run away as she charged. Alive to the world? Very much so.

There was something in this corner of northwest Iceland that reminded me of that aliveness: a life unmediated by... what? Power? Expectation? A direct relationship with one's surroundings, in this case free from the weight of potential threat or feelings of inequity. With time and light untethered, immersed in a more reciprocal way of being with the world, it was as if I was being made aware of a former and potential self all at once, and of how much I had been sculpted in the meantime by capitalism's numbing agendas of progress and productivity.

For Salvar and Natalía, life was evolution and improvisation: a matter of cause and effect with a philosophy grounded in experience, blended simultaneously with an acceptance that you never know what is going to happen. They were clearly quite self-sufficient but welcomed new ideas. The way they talked about life made me feel there was something about this place that nurtured experiment. Ideas were tested out and approached playfully: something might not work but it wouldn't be deemed a failure. It contrasted with the well-planned output-driven culture that I was a part of, which was reluctant to admit when something was not working, let alone change it. This approach to life landed in my stomach, not in my head, and it fluttered.

Their former role on Æðey – 'island of eider ducks' – an otherwise uninhabited island 25 kilometres off the coast, had required living on a small farm. They took weather readings five times a day and fed the animals. Once a week, provisions would be brought by the post boat, and that was, for the most part, the only human contact they had. Theirs was an important role – the safety of the local community depended on it: everyone's lives were ruled by the weather here, not least the fishermen on whose catch the economy largely depended.

Yet finding anyone who wanted to live alone on an island had become increasingly difficult. The last man to do the job had been using the role as an opportunity to sober up. But a friend arrived with a box of alcohol, and heavy drinking ensued. It ended in the host trying to shoot his guest for tempting him to fall.

The island had been Natalía's first experience of living in Iceland full time. Apparently, it was not uncommon for foreigners, and even Icelanders, to come to Iceland only in summer to do 'summer jobs'. Staying year round was a different act requiring a particular mentality, and it was an expression of commitment understood by everyone who did it. She learned Icelandic from Salvar and from watching television. And, thinking she would need to diversify her skills to live in this region, she taught herself first how to use a computer, and then how to do graphic design on it. Their arrival had coincided with the beginnings of the internet becoming mainstream. The world was now at her fingertips, and one thing they had a lot of was time. That is how they lived for those seven winters until moving to Ísafjörður.

I had been put in touch with Natalía and Salvar by my friend Hugh, a volcanologist. Every summer he travels from Lancaster University to the highlands of Iceland to study obsidian, a black volcanic glass found only in a few places in the world. A place called Landmannalaugar is one of his field sites. Hugh is the kind of person that, when you are round at his for a cup of tea, will place a lump of obsidian in your hand and enthuse about his latest discoveries. He told me that it is called *hrafntinna* in Icelandic: 'raven-flint'. It has the dark lustre of a raven's feathers and is superficially similar to flint in appearance, although flint is not found in Iceland. Specifically, Hugh studies how obsidian is made by breaking and then healing again, breaking and healing – in cycles. He is captivated by how its apparently perfect sheen 'hides a history of repeated failure and recombination'. It is this history that makes it so strong and sharp – one of the earliest materials to be traded by humans, invaluable for tool-making.

Hugh met Natalía and Salvar at Landmannalaugar, where their provisions shop is the only one within a 60-kilometre radius. He uses the campsite as base camp and the shop is a godsend. Landmannalaugar is in a national park. There is barely any infrastructure, but every summer visitors descend in their thousands as it is the beginning, or end, of a famous hiking route: the Laugavegur ('way of the pools'). The eponymous *laugar* are hot springs around which this campsite has established itself over the years, and Salvar and Natalía's business has expanded to meet the demand. Hugh is one of those rare creatures – a regular visitor with a deeply informed relationship with the landscape. He has a perspective on it that Natalía and Salvar could not have no matter how much they walked in it or lived in it. They, in turn, have local knowledge that has enriched Hugh's understanding of the country and the place. Each summer had seen the continuation of an ongoing conversation, and they had become friends. It was a fortuitous coincidence that my conference was taking place in this town that Natalía and Salvar called home in winter, as most international events took place in the capital, Reykjavík.

One night they told me the story of their mountain shop. It began in 1996 when they were still art students in Hanover. That summer, Salvar brought Natalía over to Iceland to show her the landscape and to earn some money fishing. The local municipality had recently issued permission for local residents – mostly farmers – to fish as much as they wanted in several mountain lakes near to the Landmannalaugar campsite – then still only a small gathering of tents. Some short-sighted thinking had seen Arctic char introduced to the lake with no competing species. They had grown large for several decades, but eventually they over reproduced resulting in an excess of smaller fish. The char population needed reducing quickly. For several years following, Salvar's brother Sveinn and his family had been net-fishing the smaller fish and selling it to tourists irregularly – tent to tent, or to order. When Natalía – the enterprising foreigner – arrived she organised the fishermen's daily appearance at the campsite with their catch to supply the growing number of tourists.

In a highland desert the offer of fresh food was like a dream, and the fish were bought up willingly. Some tourists during that first season had asked if there was butter or oil to fry it with. Natalía and Salvar gave them some of their own. The next season, Natalía suggested, to Salvar and Sveinn's bemusement, that they should sell butter and oil for more than they bought it for. The idea of making a profit was an alien concept to the brothers. Under Natalía's guidance they broadened their provisions supply and within a few years they needed a vehicle from which to sell it. The first was an old army Hanomag truck. They would park it up on the campsite and tourists would come to them. Every season thereafter, their stock was added to according to tourists' requests. Twelve years and several vehicles later, their enterprise has become a perfectly adapted organism – adapted both to the constraints of the location and to the needs of the people coming there. They showed me a photo of its current iteration: a mobile off-grid empire called Fjallafang – 'Embrace of the Mountains'. Two green long-nosed vintage American school buses parked head to tail, painted with Arctic char dancing along the sides. One where customers could sit and drink their coffee out of the wind and rain, and the other filled to brimming with everything a hiker might need – *and* fresh fish.

I was taken by the idea of a business growing slowly and adapting to fill a niche, rather than moving in suddenly to occupy a space as many other businesses seem to do. Salvar and Natalía's main objective seemed not to be to make a lot of money, but to provide a service and valuable information to visitors to this special place; to help protect it through their love of it. As tourism was on the increase now, they were enjoying the job less because they no longer had time to have real conversations with people.

The highland landscape is incredibly delicate, they told me. Salvar brought out astonishing photographs of its undulating bare mountains – ochre, purple, rust, teal and indigo, punctuated with opaque turquoise tarns and steaming hot springs, the tops pocketed with snow. It looked like the beginning of everything. They told me the ground was only exposed, largely free from snow, for three months a year – June, July and August. Any damage caused during summer by excessive footfall, the puncturing effect of walking poles, or off-road driving would be locked in and exacerbated by the elements for the nine months of winter.

There was barely any infrastructure in Landmannalaugar. Being in a national park, building was not permitted, although Salvar told me the main petrol company and convenience store chains were working hard to have the regulations changed. Before the Fjallafang fleet drove in each June, and after it departed each September, all that existed was a mountain hut and a shower block. A warden would stay on in the hut into the white expanse of October for the few Icelanders who came with their winter jeeps. 'She loves that time of year, because she can step out of the hut in the morning and just scream,' Salvar said, without comment.

Our long conversations, sat around the table in the 'Winter Palace', would sometimes continue until 2 a.m., when the sun had dipped just below the horizon and cast an outrageous pink all over the sky. The sea and sky were visible in a gap between houses, and I found them irresistible. As my hosts made their way to bed, I would head out onto the quiet empty street to meet the sea, to smell its sighing tidings, to listen to the murmurs of eiders and bask in the glow of the small hours. To have my private moments with this time, this place, this light – and this fluttering in my stomach.

One morning, as I wolfed down some muesli in the kitchen and exchanged a few words with Salvar over coffee, the fridge shook momentarily. Salvar lifted a finger and froze as if waiting for something.

'Earthquake,' he said.

'Do I need to worry?'

'*Nei, nei*. The Westfjords is not a very active region. That must've been quite far away, in the south country maybe. I'd better call my mother.'

The shudder had been so brief and Salvar's reaction so relaxed that I continued with my day. This was not how I would have imagined my first experience of an earthquake.

The conference became an afterthought; a place I would go to during the day to sit in a dark room. I listened to PowerPoint presentations and watched ethnographic films about other places in the world. But, increasingly, Here beckoned much more strongly. And when it did, I would go outside. I wandered the backstreets of the town, enjoying the abundance of dandelions in people's gardens and on the verges and the roundabout. They seemed not to be considered weeds. A smattering of bright colour after a long spell of whatever it is that winter looks like up here was probably quite welcome. There were tents up in most of the tiny gardens, which had low picket fences. I was excited by a culture that wanted to sleep outside as soon as the weather was good.

The sun seemed closer to the Earth here. It was much hotter than I had come prepared for, but still I wanted to buy an Icelandic jumper. Fortunately, in a small hand-knitters' co-operative run by women, I found out that there was such a thing as a summer jumper: a thinner knit and sleeveless. I pulled one I liked from a pile on a shelf. 'What size is this?' I asked the woman at the counter. 'Why don't you try it on?' was her excellent reply. I liked these people. The jumper fitted as if it were made for me, and I bought it.

Natalía and Salvar took time off from their summer preparations to take me to a swimming pool in a neighbouring fjord. 'We've seen how much you like to look at things and take pictures,' said Natalía as I climbed into their car. 'So we've cleaned the windows.' Ironically, to get to the pool we spent much of the journey inside a mountain. We drove through its single-track tunnel, which had a junction in the middle, my first encounter with Icelandic road planning.

'Why is it single track?' I asked.

'It was a lot of work digging through bedrock in the 1990s,' Salvar answered. 'It saved money. But happily they accidentally dug into a new water supply – an underground waterfall, which is what serves the town now.'

Interspersed along the tunnel were several lay-bys marked by a blue road sign with the letter M. Salvar told me it stands for *mætingarstaður* – 'meeting place'. A meeting place, not a passing place. Somewhere you'd take the opportunity to catch up with a friend or relative coming from the next fjord who you might not have seen for a while. Even a tunnel can be convivial.

We arrived in the village of Suðureyri and pulled up outside the only tall building. A mural spanned the end wall and Natalía and Salvar told me it was their handiwork, a renovation of an old work by a local artist. Between them, they seemed to be the public art people. The building turned out to be the school and the outdoor pool was attached to it. Natalía and I entered the women's changing room.

'Shower first, naked,' she told me.

On the wall was a poster: a map of the human body, showing me where my dirty parts were, in case I was unsure. One button turned on all 8 showers. It seemed rather wasteful.

'It's spring water... plenty of it,' said Natalía from under the steaming flow.

'Geothermal?'

'Yes.'

I wasn't used to guilt-free abundance. The shower was powerful and hot. I lingered there long after Natalía had gone outside and the shower alone would have left me satisfied. But I stepped out to a crystal-clear swimming pool, no smell of chlorine. A mountain rose directly behind the fence. Better still, the pool was flanked by three hot tubs of varying temperatures. I joined Natalía and Salvar in the hottest one and we floated in silence, letting the sun onto our bodies and the heat into our joints. Behind my ears the pool's overflow gurgled. The other side of the fence a cascade of water trailed down the steep mountainside; a white noise finding a route through the scree. I turned on my front and noticed a flask of coffee.

'Do we have to pay...'

'Help yourself,' said Salvar.

Free coffee. In a hot tub. Spring-fed. On a mountainside. I wondered at how life could be this blissful. I wondered if there was a catch, and what it was, but then soon forgot I was wondering.

'I love that everyone is camping in their gardens at the moment,' I said, finally breaking the silence.

'Camping?'

'Yeah. I was walking around Ísafjörður and there's tents in almost every garden.'

'That's because of the earthquake. In case it's just the beginning of something. It's not safe to stay in your house if there's a stronger one.'

I felt stupid. 'Where was the epicentre?'

'In the south country near to my mother.'

'Is she alright?'

'Her house is fine but the road to it has a large crack in it now.'

Perhaps that was the catch – the knowledge that the ground beneath your feet is shifting all the time; that the only thing you can know is what is happening now. Is that a catch?

My memories of that week, spent shifting between the films inside the conference and the constantly surprising reality outside, are a series of hyper-real luminescent images. They cut between close-ups of lichen-scribbled rock and the urgent shoot-growth of many species of tiny plants I had never seen, long shots of walking through broad vistas of a seemingly newborn landscape that felt all mine, and mid-shots of faces engaged in conversation. The conference is a series of fade-to-blacks where sleep should have been, but often was not.

Rising above all the other plants in late May were the umbrella-like fronds of wild rhubarb – large, waxy, dark green leaves atop stout pink stems. It was everywhere: on the hillsides between residential streets; out in the valleys. It was as if it had broken out of a garden one day and decided to take up residence somewhere freer. I decided to pick some and make a rhubarb crumble for Natalía and Salvar.

I did this the next bright evening, after another day in a darkened room. They let me loose in their kitchen and we ate it after dinner, the sour-sweet flavour titillating our tongues for the evening's long conversation. That particular evening, it was to be life-changing.

Natalía stretched her arms above her head, cat-like, and let out a moan of pleasure as seemed to be her after-dinner gesture. 'Sarah,' she said, as if it was a question. 'We've noticed how well you managed a strange kitchen; making this... how do you say... *krrrömbel.*'

'Would you like to run Fjallafang next summer?' Salvar interjected. 'We've been doing it for twelve summers and we need a break.'

'Yes,' I replied without so much as a second of hesitation.

I am not sure why so little rational processing went on in that moment, other than I felt that exactly what I had been seeking, but had not yet known the specifics of, was being offered to me on a plate: space. An absence of abstraction. A self-willed landscape. An antidote to the academic London life I had been living. Just me, the mountains and a load of people passing through. As they came and went, I would be staying. Watching the weather change, the meltwater course, the light remain – day and night – until the darkening of August.

'Yes. I really would,' I said almost to myself, sensing I was accepting an invitation to something much greater than a summer job.

Tónleikar – Concert
(*tón* – tone; *leika* – play)

Late June 2008

I had lifted from the lava fields of Keflavík International Airport to
return to London with wet eyes, pooled with images and a longing
that took me entirely by surprise. Three weeks later, I am back. It
is Midsummer – the exquisite balance point of the year where the
night is filled with daylight, and sleep comes when it decides to.
I am revelling in my inexhaustible energy and the need for food
seems to have been replaced by a direct photosynthesis. The light
is bright and Northern, and the air is so clear as to bring great
distances close. I can perceive the world in sharp focus – a field is
no longer a field but thousands of individual blades of grass.

My first visit felt strangely like a homecoming of sorts. There was
nothing especially familiar in the architecture or the culture, but the
immediacy and rawness of the landscape had engaged in an inspiring
conversation with my temperament. 'We need to talk,' it uttered.
This time around the feeling is reiterated in the material, by my fresh
knowledge of the streets and character of Reykjavík; by knowing that
the airport bus actually drops passengers off outside their respective

hotels, for no extra cost; by understanding the swimming pool changing room etiquette; by being reminded that life really can be this simple. My movements on this visit are fluid, sure.

I don't need to stay in a hotel this time. Filippo, an expat Italian film-maker I met at the conference, has offered me the use of his apartment, though he is not here himself. He has been going through a divorce from his Icelandic wife, and at the conference I had given time to listen to his pain. He seems glad of the opportunity to help me out now.

A celestial light floods generously into the open-plan apartment. Each face of the building has an expanse of window glass, smudged with salty residue. Although it overlooks the sea, we are still at some distance from it, and the smudges hint at the strong winds that whip at the building on days that feel a million miles away from this one. Each window frames a differently spectacular view: a volcanic mountain here, a sparkling rippled sea there, punctuated by the silhouette of a lighthouse. And this is Reykjavík, the capital city. 'Downtown' is really no larger than a village. I have come with a friend this time, and she is equally awestruck. Filippo has a taste for retro furniture and a fine collection of electronic music. We put on a CD – loud – and dance. It feels like freedom.

My companion on this trip is my London flatmate Uli, a German architect. She has witnessed how changed I was by my visit last month. When I got back, I told her about the magic of this place and then about Natalía and Salvar.

'That Russian artist... what did you say her name was again?' Uli had looked preoccupied.

'Natalía Mossolova.'

Her eyes lit up with an alchemy of joy and astonishment.

'You're not going to believe this, but I went to art school with her in Hanover. I remember that story of her marrying an Icelandic farmer's son. My mother has one of her artworks.'

She had been easily persuaded that coming with me seemed a fitting conclusion.

So here we are, in the third week of June. The three-month-long summer season is under way, and Natalía and Salvar have travelled the 650 kilometres southeast to go and sell fresh fish, coffee and anoraks to tourists on a campsite beside a natural hot spring. This is the job I have accepted for next summer, and I am beyond curious to see what I have agreed to.

It will take me some time to fathom the Icelandic distinction between summer and winter behaviour. Apparently, school holidays begin at the end of May and end in late August. Schoolchildren are given the opportunity to work by town councils and can be seen in high-vis jackets planting out flowerbeds on roundabouts and blowing leaves with a blower. It is not uncommon for employees' annual leave to amount to six weeks and during that time many take a 'summer job', which usually relates to tourism or the outdoors. Or they reunite with extended family at their summerhouses – not a luxury, but almost a given. This rhythm shift makes perfect sense to me, although I have never been to a place where the architecture of life and society so obviously supports it.

Summer is currently all I know, and my only destination.
The mountains, the light, the freedom, the elasticity of time.
The connectedness of a small population moving through a vast
landscape following a long hibernation. Uli and I are going to
the mountains to find Natalía and Salvar and this shop I have
agreed to run. But first we have a concert to go to. It was news of
this concert that drew me back to Iceland so soon. At the airport
on the way back from the first trip, I noticed in the local headlines that Björk and Sigur Rós – two of my favourite bands and
Iceland's best-known musical exports – were giving a free concert at
Grasagarðurinn, the botanical garden in Reykjavík, in three weeks'
time. I could not miss it. And more than that, my relationship
with this other-worldly place had clearly just begun.

Held under the night sun in Reykjavík's botanical garden, the
concert is the bands' effort to raise awareness of the environmental
devastation being wreaked by the construction of American-owned
aluminium smelters and the hydro-electric power infrastructure
necessary to supply them. I have been reading about it: a huge dam
was built in the east flooding a vast area and creating a dustbowl of
the region around it. Hugh will come too. He has just arrived for his
annual obsidian adventure. So, too, will 30,000 Icelanders. So, too,
will a man I have not yet met, who will one day become my husband.

Uli and I meet up with Hugh and we join a steady stream of music
pilgrims that can be seen walking from all corners of downtown
Reykjavík to fill the park, basking and squinting in the nocturnal
sunlight. They seem energized by the formation of a large crowd. I

guess it is unusual for a small population on an island a little smaller than England.

The concert is a time outside of time, made of light, joy and abandon. Sigur Rós's lead singer Jónsi's pure falsetto forms lyrics which belong here. Whether they are Icelandic, English or a language of his imagination does not matter. They seem born from the ground we stand on and the sound penetrates me the way great stories do. His voice is ushered by a heartbeat of marching drums played by an eccentric troupe of women. Some are elfin; others like warriors. All of them are beautiful. Björk emerges cloaked in ballooning silken technicolour, her forehead painted with triangles of orange, green, blue. She prowls and leaps a visceral dance across the stage. Her voice is limber and uncompromisingly committed. Her body hurls it around like a kite, trailing out and looping back again.

We have a good spot near the front. The evening progresses, presumably to night, and the sun continues to beat white gold. We are a little drunk on overpriced beer, and very drunk on all of it. I feel expanded, as if everyone in this park is a part of my body. We dance with the Icelanders standing next to us; one lifts me onto his shoulders for a better view. It is magical to witness these two bands together on home terrain, performing as Icelanders more than global superstars, enjoyed by a tenth of the country's population dancing in one park in the capital. The bands are clearly having a blast. Björk chants 'Náttúra, Náttúra, Náttúra!'. But there are no calls to arms, no mini-lectures on the plight of the pink-footed geese whose breeding habitat was flooded when the dam was built. For a concert to raise environmental awareness, there is surprisingly little mention of the environment.

From somewhere, perhaps naively, I have Icelanders down as green and progressive. It's probably the magma-heated swimming pools or just how clean everything seems – the air, the water, the streets. I was hoping this concert would give me the lowdown on this country's environmental credentials. From what I have seen, it is a place where ancient and modern co-exist, or at least different timescales are simultaneously visible – like the airport in the middle of a vast lava field, or the old parliament at Þingvellir being a cleft in the Mid-Atlantic Ridge. And it feels like a place where the dearth of man-made layers allows me to see more clearly the effects of my presence and how I might respond: a place I could learn from.

Is it un-Icelandic to put a downer on a joyous occasion by talking about the state of things? Why the silence?

I know from reading *Dreamland: A Self-Help Manual for a Frightened Nation* by writer and activist Andri Snær Magnason, a book that inspired this concert, that it is not only the highlands that are at stake, but a way of thinking about and valuing nature, here as elsewhere. There are plans mooted to harness the energy of most of Iceland's great rivers through an extensive damming programme. Not to supply the population – they are already well catered for – but for more American aluminium smelting plants. The argument for the plants is creation of jobs in rural areas. But how many jobs, and at what cost? Electricity is promised at rock bottom prices to attract investors. I don't get what is in it for Iceland. Given how central 'wild nature' seems to be to Iceland's identity, besides being crucial in its own right, I wonder if the population is about to sleepwalk into an irreversible mistake. So far it has managed to avoid becoming a heavily industrialized nation. In an era in which the fallout of the industrial revolution is thrumming ever more forcefully at every thread of the web of life, I am not sure what could be more precious than that.

A confetti of white paper squares is raining on the stage now. Jónsi communes with his guitar and almost the whole ensemble, including Björk, is beating on drums around him. The pulse is electric, and my pulse is synching with it. Though my idea of what environmental engagement looks like has been challenged, I am having one of the best nights of my life. I will have to dig much deeper to find out about this place.

I am only one sleep away from tomorrow, when we will take a coach to Landmannalaugar, a part of the highlands, to find Salvar and Natalía. There I will find out what my future plans might look like, and encounter this beautiful, fragile inland terrain for the first time.

Fjallafang – Embrace of the Mountains (*fjall* – mountain; *fang* – an embrace, armful)

July 2008

It is reassuring somehow that there is a coach to this place I need to go. It is a geographical location, but it also feels like a state of being that I am heading towards, one that I have dreamed of but never reached. As nobody knows I am coming – nobody who might rescue me if I lost my way – I am glad I can sit tight and be transported there. In the photos that Natalía and Salvar showed me, it appeared to be a technicoloured highland desert in the middle of nowhere, not somewhere that would be served by public transport. Though this isn't exactly public transport. Reykjavík Excursions seems to be a private company ferrying passengers to 'the sights' and the airport, and as such is mostly full of tourists. Icelanders don't seem to take coaches. They prefer to drive around in their 4x4s. These vehicles are enormous to my eyes, and their drivers clearly feel invincible.

The coach journey is – a surprisingly short – four hours. It starts from the BSÍ bus station in Reykjavík – a small 1960s block of a building with a glassy white interior that is half-waiting-lounge, half-canteen. I have read that the canteen is legendary for being one of the only places in Reykjavík where you can buy takeaway *svið* (boiled singed sheep's head cut in half, with the teeth and eyes still present). I do not take up the opportunity.

The journey starts with the coach cruising out of the sprawling American-inspired suburbs of Reykjavík. Outside of the very small and older 'downtown', Reykjavík is not a place made for walking. We pass industrial estates with shiny car showrooms tempting the soon to be debt-ridden Icelanders to spend money they don't have. There are car mechanics, factories and supplies stores presumably stocking all the building blocks of developed life.

Filling the gaps like putty are pizza parlours and burger joints – also a cultural legacy of the Americans who kept an air base at Keflavík from which to monitor the Soviet Union. They did not completely withdraw until 2006 and the base, just outside the capital, is now used as Iceland's international airport. All these businesses are fronted in an Icelandic signage whose design does nothing to suggest to me what might be inside. An expanse of generic 'industry' is punctuated by the surging behemoths of familiar icons like IKEA and Toys "R" Us. Surely the whole of Iceland could fit in there, I think to myself as we cruise past the huge IKEA store.

As the right-angled concrete buildings peter out and give way to lava fields, we descend into a flat plain, passing vents of geothermal steam, screaming white against the dark grey brittleness. As we round the bend to Hveragerði, it is revealed how this heat is being put to good use: a sea of greenhouses glowing with yellow light from within, apparently to grow cucumbers, peppers, tomatoes, mushrooms; even bananas – the last more to prove it is possible than to supply demand.

We pass through green rolling farmland – the first crop of hay benefiting from the long days, and indigo swathes of Alaskan lupine in full bloom. My fellow passengers are as enthralled as I am by the view and twitter excitedly like a flock of misplaced parakeets in their colourful Gore-Tex jackets. There is a man on the bus who catches my attention. He is not wearing a colourful Gore-Tex jacket, but a collared shirt and jeans. He looks like I imagined an Icelander would look, or at least wanted an Icelander to look: stocky, with short dark blond hair and a ginger beard that has been left to roam around his chin. His kind nose and pink complexion suggests he spends time outside in the wind, sniffing what news it carries. He seems at once to be engaged totally with the landscape outside the coach – almost part of it – and absorbed in his own thoughts. His alive blue eyes drink deep from the scene and reflect his world back outwards. Uli notices him too. 'What a man!' she whispers.

I do not yet know that I will share so much of what those eyes see, and what that nose smells. I do not yet have an inkling of the complexity of the internal world belied by those eyes. I do not yet realize that the landscape we are passing through is where his mother was born and raised, and where his mother's mother still lives. I will try for years to fathom the many ways in which those facts are related, knowing it is true, and also that it is futile to try to understand it.

After an hour and a half, the tarmac ends and the dirt track begins. The next two hours are spent being shaken as a result of the too fast 4x4s – the ground an eternal washboard. When you have an enormous 4x4 with enormous tyres, you are impervious to the washboard you are creating, it seems. The bone shaking that results is saved for the tourists and those in smaller vehicles. Tourists who hire cars (reasonably) copy what Icelanders do, probably thinking they must know best, slicing the landscape into flumes of dust. Salvar will tell me that each year, the track must be regraded at great expense.

Through my rattling eyeballs I wonder what their rush can be, to get *there*, as if *here* wasn't worth savouring. All around us another world opens up – an expansive, curious highland desert unlike anything I have ever seen. We pass a volcano called Hekla, which has been over-due to erupt for some years – its soft dark grey slopes rising out of a flat plain, and covered tentatively in green, like a carpet worn thin. Tracing its downward profile are occasional rivulets lined with the brightest of green moss, fluorescent and soft against the wet black sand.

Our track winds around variegated knolls of scree that dance colours from dark grey to oxide red to pale ochre, as if still burning, like the glow of freshly tempered iron. We pass a lake, choppy and teal blue, cradled by the bare, coloured mountains. I can see one lone rowing boat and a handful of impossibly orange buoys glowing in the littoral light. We have arrived in the technicoloured desert I saw in the photos, but it is so much more: a landscape criss-crossed by a lacework of rivers, held by mountains in a constant state of flux. I feel I am on a threshold.

Mounting a final pass, a glacial river valley opens up beneath us into which we descend. Finally, the campsite comes into view and the coach fords a 50-metre breadth of deep, fast-flowing river – as if that is a perfectly normal thing to do. It is no ordinary campsite. There is not a blade of grass in sight. The ground is all gravel, on a tongue of the riverbank. The cacophony of tents is sheltered from behind by a jagged wall of lava the size of a three-storey building. It looks like something between a festival and a refugee camp, on the moon – if the moon was more colourful. When I follow through next summer with what I have agreed to do – to run the shop on this campsite – this place will become my first Icelandic home. Behind the campsite is a mountain that is blue; not in a far-off misty mountain way: the rock is *actually* blue. It is, unsurprisingly, called Bláhnjúkur ('blue peak') and it will become my neighbour.

We soon find Salvar and Natalía's miniature empire. It is in fact a collection of three vintage American school buses – two green ones parked top to tail right next to each other, and a third blue one a short distance away. The green pair are obviously the shop and café. One has a queue outside, and inside the other, tourists sit huddled around tables clutching their steaming plastic cups like passengers on a train going nowhere. In my excitement at springing this surprise on Salvar and Natalía I had not anticipated the queue and I will have to wait my turn.

Finally inside, catching the plethora of goods for sale out of the corner of my eye – onions, muesli, camping mats, toothpaste – I shuffle up to the counter.

'*Góðan daginn!*' I say to Salvar as he serves a cup of coffee to a camper.

Salvar always speaks with his eyes first, and voice second. His concentrated stare lifts from the coffee cup and does not register my identity at first. Those eyes cannot compute this person in this place: their recent English houseguest from their northern home, back unannounced three weeks later here in the southern highlands. When they accept it is real, they widen and stretch. He hands the coffee to the tourist carefully so as not to spill it. He tends to jump up and down when excited.

'Nataaalíaa,' he calls out to the back kitchen, jumping up and down.

In a blur of fondness and excitement at what is to come, we exchange hugs and greetings.

'I'm here for a trial shift,' I say, half-jokingly, but excited to have a go.

'Great. I hope you will stay with us? We're living in a little cabin at a lake near here. Our nephew has just arrived also, but I think there will be space. Did you meet Bjarni?'

Bjarni steps out from the back kitchen, tucking his shirt into his trousers ready to start a shift. Bjarni, that same intriguing man who caught my attention on the coach, is standing in front of me now as Salvar's nephew. His face still glows a healthy pink. The shop is quite possibly the busiest place in Iceland in this moment, but my reality slows and focuses. It has no sound. Something in the depths of me recognizes him, far beyond remembering his face from half an hour ago. It's as if I recognize a place I am supposed to stay; a hearth that has been waiting for me. We shake hands smiling shyly at each other, and fizz.

It may only be a few seconds later that I realize that three other coaches have arrived with ours and all the passengers want coffee and sandwiches, immediately.

I step out of the moment I am in, back into the collective, and shuffle out past the parade of Gore-Tex in red, mustard and acid green, towards the door where my eyes are drawn to the negative space of people – to the landscape beyond their profiles – rather than the people themselves. Everything in my world has just inverted. This place is no backdrop. It is an active character.

The shop is busy with Laugavegur hikers. Iceland is being picked up by the tourist radar and the wealthier and more intrepid tourists are making it a hot destination. 'The Way of Pools', I remember Salvar telling me. It was also the name of the main shopping street in Reykjavík, belying the geothermal pools bubbling under that part of the city. A financial collapse is also bubbling beneath the surface, though most Icelanders will remain blissfully ignorant for another few months. Soon, tourists will flock here to clamber around more affordably in the pristine rubble of a collapsed economy, and a fallen króna.

I know there will be plenty of time to explore the world of Fjallafang. For now, it is time to get to know my 'neighbourhood'. The sky is large and bright, but there is an ominousness; a sense that this is not a place to relax, but to feel energized by the dynamic forces of the mountains and rivers. I am a small creature at the bottom of this gravelly bowl and all around me coloured dust is whipped into the ether from the peaks.

Beyond the flapping triangles of rip-stop nylon is a large wooden hut, and beyond that a bank of steam drifting from an isolated patch of lush vegetation, curling sometimes towards the hut like a special effect, then suddenly swerving off on a different course entirely, carried on the whim of the wind. Outside the wooden hut, campers are using a lean-to of sheltered cooking areas to huddle over their Primus stove Pot Noodles, while others walk in and out of the hut holding towels and wet clothing. This is where all the catching up with reality happens, the basics of mountain-goer maintenance: eating, showering, and the washing and drying of clothes and camping gear.

A wooden walkway begins from this building and hovers across a hot wetland of algae-lined clear streams, rushes, grasses and birdlife to a platform draped in coloured towels like a wishing tree. The streams converge in the cloud of steam, which lifts from a large, clear, natural pool deep enough to submerge a human body to the chest. In the water there are at least fifty steam-pinked bodies doing exactly this. It's clearly the place to be: a place where you are buffered from the mountains' changeability. This pool is the reason for this campsite's existence – a punctuation mark along the Way of the Pools.

Uli and I decide to join them. My cells, agitated by a shaky journey, and excited by the reality that is unfolding, slow to a gentle bounce then merge with the water around me. I become liquid and utterly content, floating in this moment and the future that awaits me – unknown but steeped in a wildness that I crave. I rest my head on the tufty grass bank and wildflowers lean over my face as if to see what they make of me. A sheep perches delicately on a tiny hummock island in the hot water and nips at the fresh shoots of grass with bared teeth. It is not a place I expect to see a sheep, but this place has already forced me to leave any expectations behind. The sun comes out, and in doing so feels gracious. My core is warming, and my face is bathed in mountain light. All around me the summer sculpts instinctively with its raw materials – sunlight, snowmelt, wind blow, river flow, rock fall. And over it the ant-like crunch and chink of hikers and their Nordic walking poles – 'stick men' as I later found out Bjarni calls them.

Drying off with my towel, I notice the wind has returned and the sky is overcast for the moment, but my warmth is total. I stand here almost naked in the highland wind and glow from inside. Hot springs are a privilege of life on this patch of the Subarctic – a direct link to the inside of the Earth's workings.

I return to the shop to buy some lunch. What sits on the shelves is an unexpected treasure trove of both necessities and luxuries, from anoraks and camping gas to brie and fresh pastries. People who come into the shop are either cold, underprepared or have just done the four-day hike to arrive here and are visibly delighted with what they find. The most unexpected item – the Arctic char – is a surprise because it makes so much sense: a regular supply of fish from the nearby lake. Fresh fish caught the day before within a few kilometres is a treat wherever you are, but when your diet has been a variety of dried sachets it is especially welcome. Salvar invites Uli and me to the blue bus, which serves as staff quarters, to join in with their lunch – Bjarni and his two younger cousins, Jóhann and Einar, are sitting around a lino-covered table and we squeeze in. Lunch is literally a steaming pile of Arctic char, the origins of this humble empire, covered in butter and a lemon pepper mix that Natalía has invented to complement the fish. Bjarni engrosses himself in it, unsuccessfully attempting to conceal his shyness. I am glad I will have the chance to spend more time with him when he is off duty, back at the cabin. It sounds like a small space, so we'll all have to get used to being in close quarters. He says the odd word to his cousins. His voice is gentle and they and Salvar seem to find him very funny.

Salvar tells me the char are still caught by his brother Sveinn – Einar and Jóhann's father – and still causing as much delight as the day they were first sold. The latest development is that the fish is now available fresh, smoked *and* marinated. I realize that it must have been Sveinn that I saw in the rowing boat on the lake, from the coach. Those bright orange buoys were floats for *his* nets. This really is a family affair. The only demand Fjallafang has never responded to, Salvar continues, is alcohol. They could make a killing selling beer to people going to sit in the *laugar*. But experience has taught them that drunk people drive off road and rip up fragile terrain. And they don't have the capacity to care about littering. Cans and glass bottles do not mix well with hot springs.

Sated, Uli and I go for a walk in the nearby lava field. Natural sculptures loom above us – twisted spires of jagged rhyolite with tussocks of moss pooled in their hollows. Puddles of pink mud encircled with frills of crystallized sulphur surround steaming vents. It is alive and breathing. Around these delicate formations are

48

the gashes made by unbelieving Nordic walking poles. Our need as humans to probe the unfamiliar is all too apparent here and it troubles me. Yes, this landscape is vast. It is easy to tell yourself that a few prods are insignificant. But each hiker has two sticks. Each stick pierces the ground hundreds of times on a walk and is followed by another pair. This slow excavation is the advance party for erosion by the elements, and the act of appreciation inadvertently becomes an act of desecration.

Walking back to the campsite, my eyes more attuned to the details of the landscape now, I notice another unwelcome vestige of visitors – cigarette butts. This air is so clear and so generous. Anyone's preference to breathe nicotine smoke is a mystery to me. I report back to Natalía and Salvar as the shop is selling cigarettes, and therefore partly responsible.

'We're going to stop selling them this year. We'll just sell what we have and that's it. That's why there's only menthol cigarettes and snuff on the shelf. And no tissues either.'

The shop closes and we pile into Salvar's jeep to head to the cabin 15 kilometres away.

The green cabin and a neighbouring gutting shed sit in a black desert, beside a lake lined with fluorescent green algae. There is another bus parked beside it – a vintage US Navy vehicle, inhabited for the summer by Sveinn's eldest son, who helps him catch and gut the fish for the shop and for other businesses, including the rural hospital. This cluster of dwellings and a work station is watched over by a sheltering wall of sculptural lava towers. Our cabin is tiny and divided into two rooms: a kitchen, and a bedroom with bunks. We will all be in the same small room: Natalía and Salvar, Uli, Bjarni and I.

There is a tension, a curiosity, between Bjarni and me. His complexion makes it hard to tell if he is blushing. His surface seems sweet and gentle, but a blanket to untold depths. He imparts fragments of knowledge within his shyness that are witty and wise. He has an intelligence that is bound up with this place, not an intellectual abstraction. I want to know him.

After dinner the hut draws the evening closer around us. Outside it is still bright but the smallness of the space and the lighting of a candle conjures some dim, and the in-between state of evening. Natalía, Salvar, Bjarni and Sveinn play a game they have invented called *maður dagsins* – 'person of the day' – where each takes it in turn to tell a story of the most remarkable tourist they have encountered that day, for better or worse. Salvar translates the funniest: a German turned up at the campsite with a giant pack of bottles of mineral water. 'Not even Icelandic mineral water!', he says. 'We have water *pooourring* out of the mountains here!'

We all play cards until stillness settles upon us as it does on the lake outside. I have been fascinated by the words I have heard exchanged between everyone tonight – their sentences a melody, and of a flavour I have not heard before. I ask Bjarni to teach me something. We huddle around the candle with a pen and paper. He shows me the vowels and what they sound like – alone, then with accents on. I repeat after him, watching his eyes and his mouth. *A* ('a'), *á* ('ow'), *o*

50

('o'), *ó* ('oh'), *ö* ('euh'), *u* ('uh'), *ú* ('oo'), *e* ('eh'), *é* ('ye'), *i* ('ih'), *í* ('ee'). It is only when Natalía comes back inside from brushing her teeth by the lake, that I realize I have been entranced by Bjarni for some time. We are in a space 2 metres square and I had not noticed her go out.

Over the next few days, finding places to explore our blooming love in such proximity to others is tricky, but somehow we manage. Or rather, we forgo the imperative for privacy – Bjarni more successfully than I. Sometimes we take off for a walk up the blue mountain, or we hide out in the bed at the back of the blue bus staff quarters. One afternoon, I am lying with him in his lunch break, basking in the delicious feeling of his skin on mine, when a man appears in the doorway. Looking straight at us, he holds up a large bag full of tomatoes, and speaks to Bjarni.

'*Já takk!*', says Bjarni. 'Yes please.'

They continue to chat and I am aghast, pulling the duvet up around my naked shoulders. The man acknowledges me with a nod.

'*Hæ*' is the only word he says to me.

'Sarah, this is my uncle,' says Bjarni, then continues chatting.

When the man finally leaves, I question Bjarni's lack of discretion.

'But he brought us tomatoes!' he says. 'And anyway... he's my uncle.'

It is infuriating, funny and thrilling. My world is being turned upside down, and I love it.

Mataræði – Diet
(*matur* – food; *æði* – craziness)

25 December 2008 – Jóladagur (Yule Day)

In Iceland, the 'traditional' Christmas meal is eaten and the gifts are
unwrapped on 24 December, Aðfangadagur, which literally translates
as 'Resources Day'. Today, it is Yule Day, a day for visiting.

As is the tradition in Bjarni's family, we have been on a trip to visit
his favourite aunt, Yrsa. With me in tow for the first time, Bjarni,
his parents Gyða and Haukur, and his sister Súla are piled into
their Toyota HiAce van. His father Haukur is driving, of course. It
seems he is not a passenger kind of man. He does not speak English
apparently, and I'm told he is keen that I should learn Icelandic as
soon as possible. Súla tells me her name means 'gannet'; that she calls
herself Súla because she likes the birds, and it is easier for foreigners
to pronounce than her birth name.

Aunt Yrsa lives on a farm a short distance from where she and
Haukur grew up in Ísafjarðardjúp – the large deep fjord from
which all other fjords in the region branch. From this *djúp* ('deep'),
the smaller fjords reach their fingery depths inland, filling valleys
scoured out by glaciers from the mountains like a woodcut. From

Gyða and Haukur's house, where we are all staying, the visit to
Yrsa has involved a two-hour drive along a winding road that
follows the shoreline of these fjords, and we are now travelling
the two hours back. On this day, we are newly acquainted, these
fjords and me. It is a journey I will come to make many times, and
each time I will get to know each fjord a little better, by name and
character: Álftafjörður ('swans fjord'), Hvalfjördur ('whale fjord'),
Skötufjorður ('skate fjord'). I will learn that all of these creatures
can be, have been, food.

'We don't eat swans anymore though,' says Bjarni. 'During the
Cod Wars we promised your queen not to eat them in exchange for
a 200-nautical-mile exclusive fishing zone. It's her totem creature or
something, isn't it?' he says, smiling ambiguously.

'Something like that.' My face breaks into a grin. Bjarni's 'facts' are
plausible enough to make them, if not totally believable, then at least
amusing. I love that he makes me laugh so much.

The Westfjords is one of the remotest parts of Iceland. To me, it is,
by extension, one of the remotest parts of the world. No map, no list
of distances, can relate what it feels like to be here, and what such a
location yields as a cultural and culinary legacy.

I got to feel its remoteness with my body and my senses two days
previously when Bjarni drove me here from Reykjavík: the entire
eight-hour journey made in the dark. I had only ever flown to the
region before, to the tiny 'capital' Ísafjörður – the location of my
conference last year and of Gyða and Haukur's house. The spaces in
between remained unknown to me. This time, we had intended to

fly but our morning domestic flight was cancelled: high winds were blowing in the wrong direction at this end. We were supposed to be arriving in time for a party that Bjarni's parents host every year for family and friends on Þorláksmessa ('mass of St Þorlákur') on 23 December. It was to be the first time I would meet his family and neighbours, and Bjarni had made out there was quite a buzz surrounding my arrival. I suppose I am a curiosity. A foreign girlfriend, an *útlendingur* ('outlander'), despite the fact that everyone is a foreigner here if we go back only 1,200 years. He told me that we would eat *skata*: fermented ray wings.

Sitting at Reykjavík Domestic Airport wondering how we would make it in time for the party, I remembered the airstrip at Ísafjörður from my first trip, tucked at the bottom of a narrow-sided fjord; how the wing tips almost brushed the mountainsides. I could imagine that there was no room for variables: the criteria for safe landing were already in a delicate balance.

We did not drive away from Reykjavík until 3 p.m., at which point the narrow window of daylight was almost over. It had taken a long time to find an economical Plan B. Nobody Bjarni knew was driving up and able to offer us a lift. This had taken many phone calls to establish. Instead, we hired a car at great expense and tried to fill it with people he knew to share the cost of petrol. This had involved more phone calls and waiting for other people who had not yet made a Plan B, or even a Plan A.

'*Þetta reddast*,' Bjarni had assured me on several occasions – 'It will work itself out.' He did not seem at all bothered that we might well miss the party that he had made out was such an important occasion. Leaving so late revealed two things. One: that Icelanders, or perhaps just Bjarni and his friends, do not deem it worthwhile to find a solution to a problem before it arises. He tells me winter flights are regularly cancelled due to wind direction, but it does not seem reason enough to have a back-up arrangement. Two: I learned just how dark darkness can be when not perforated by the light of habitations or streetlamps at regular intervals. During the eight-hour journey, sometimes through snow, we passed perhaps three villages; three patches of luminosity. The rest was totally black.

While Bjarni drove, I tried to grasp some sense of reality from the spots of road illuminated by the headlights, as we passed over it, on and on. It was a strange way to travel through a country for the first time, imagining everything I was passing through based only on what I had read, or seen from the air on my first trip, or from what Bjarni was telling me. In the middle of what seemed like absolutely nowhere, Bjarni pulled over and asked if I fancied a dip in a hot spring. A light snow blizzard cross-hatched the view through the windscreen, the nearest snowflakes illuminated by the headlights, leaving trails in my vision like comets.

'Where?' I had asked, peering futilely into the darkness and snow outside.

'There's a hut just up there with a tiny pool in it.'

As tempting as the idea of hot water was, I could not see this hut. I was impressed Bjarni knew where it was so instinctively. After hours of travelling through total darkness, I had no inkling of the nature of the place and could not get my head around taking off all my clothes here in sub-zero temperatures. We were already late for the party. I declined and we drove on.

We passed his Aunt Yrsa's farm.

'Don't you want to say hi?'

'We'll come for a visit in a couple of days.'

In the absence of visuals, Bjarni fed me titbits of local knowledge. This road was only tarmacked all the way up here from Reykjavík in 2000. I could only imagine how long the journey took before that. Until most boats became motorized in the mid-1900s, the Westfjords was home to only the hardiest of inhabitants. Norse settlers had come with their Celtic wives and slaves from the ninth century on. Their legacy is everywhere, from the treeless landscape to Bjarni's red beard. Dedicated fishermen and whalers sailed from as far away as Spain and the Basque country for centuries, such was the catch to be had in the waters here. In the winter of 1615, Basque whalers were stranded here for several months when their vessels were destroyed by a storm. There was not enough food to go around, and they had been stealing from farmers – so the story goes. In response to mounting tension, the local Sheriff at the time issued a decree allowing Basques to be killed on sight, and residents at Aunt Yrsa's farm had been among the farmers who had murdered more than thirty of them. It is a law particular to the Westfjords, which to this date has not officially been repealed. My best friend in England is Basque.

'Tell her to be careful if you invite her here,' Bjarni chuckled.

Other encounters with Basque and Spanish seafarers were presumably more peaceful: the Iberian legacy is still manifest in dark hair and brown eyes, here and there.

The Westfjords is bypassed by Route 1, the ring road which circuits 'the whole country' according to my guidebook. The book indicates that most visitors to Iceland do a self-drive trip around this ring road. More intrepid travellers divert to the Westfjords where, like me, they must be patient as the orange light-pricks of their destination creep imperceptibly closer, as the road meanders up and down and up and down the shores of the finger-like fjords. The destination is typically Ísafjörður, which Bjarni's parents share with two-thirds of the region's population, and most of its services. The lights you can make out from a distance are a few streetlights on the coast road beyond Ísafjörður. The town itself is tucked inside a fjord. The distance to Ísafjörður is only 100 kilometres from the region's southernmost portal, Hólmavík, as the raven flies (if indeed the raven flew in a straight line, which, being playful and curious, it doesn't, and nor does the crow). But that 100 kilometres takes four hours to travel, along 220 kilometres of road.

We finally arrived at 11 p.m. Sitting in a car all day and scanning the darkness for sources of stimulation and orientation had left me exhausted. Suddenly, we entered a house full of light and people, fairy lights around every window, and tables set up throughout the living room, dining room and kitchen like a pop-up café. Bjarni was right: I had clearly been the talk of family and friends, and their curiosity upon my arrival was overwhelming.

Not quite as overwhelming as the smell that hit me as I crossed the threshold. Navigating the etiquette of embrace versus handshake versus kiss, I was entirely distracted by the fact that Gyða and Haukur's house smelled strongly of ammonia. Their curiosity did not relate to my background or my journey north. It was mainly about how I would react to the *skata*, which turned out to be skate fermented for weeks and then boiled – the source of the smell. What could I say? It was just-bearably disgusting. It burned both my tongue and a place at the back of my nostrils and throat of which I am usually unaware unless I accidentally inhale seawater.

Chatting to the guests, it emerged that many Icelanders do not enjoy *skata* either. 'So, my new family isn't typical?' I had asked one of them.

'Typical from before 1950,' he had responded with a knowing smile.

I realized that whatever they were I would have to love them, as they were already being referred to as my *tengdaforeldrar* ('connected parents'): a term equivalent to 'in-laws' that pays no heed to marital status – or, as it turned out, to whether we had been together very long. A serious intention for the relationship seems to be sufficient.

Bjarni was clearly pleased that I could hold my own in this context, and touchingly proud to introduce me to his extended family and his parents' friends, although the attention was slightly embarrassing. It felt very obvious from the way he moved with and between them all that he was so much a part of this place and this community, in a way that I don't think I have ever experienced. He didn't have to do or be anything. I, on the other hand, felt 'other', under the spotlight, albeit a warm and friendly one. At intervals Bjarni would blink at me like a cat from across the room – his way of saying 'You can do it.' It was reassuring to feel at least that I didn't have to prove anything to him. Our love was sure already, and had been since the moment we met. The recognition I had felt then was this quiet certainty.

Later in his room – his childhood bedroom with its bright yellow walls – we chatted quietly, me finally able to feel myself again. It had been a very long day and I had traversed miles of landscape, inner and outer. We sat up in bed, me perched between his knees with my back against his warm belly full of *skata*. He brushed my hair slowly and carefully into a braid.

'Mama is certain you are my wife,' he said.

'I know. She said that to me the moment she saw me... It was quite the introduction.'

* * *

'*Matur!!!!*' was the call to dinner.

The 'traditional' Christmas meal at my 'in-laws' took me further on my journey into new culinary territory. The tradition was particular to them, and a relatively new tradition at that. Apparently, on 24 December most families eat a rack of ham. It used to be roasted ptarmigan, but they are becoming scarce. Just after six o'clock, when, following fifteen minutes of silence, the state radio broadcast the ringing of church bells from Reykjavík Cathedral, and Bjarni's sister had finished lighting all the candles, the family gathered at the table, dressed up for the occasion. Onto it, Gyða placed a baking tray with five cows' tongues – one for each of us – side by side, the rough grey coating as appealing as coarse-grade sandpaper. To my eyes, a tray of body parts was incongruous with everyone dressed in their finest. It was a scene from a *noir* film. But I tucked in with everyone else and the tongues were tasty, I had to admit.

I had eaten tongue before in England, but not *a* tongue. When I asked Gyða about the unusual choice, she told me that one year, a farmer had been getting rid of some cows' tongues. My 'in-laws' are renowned for their unusual tastes and resourcefulness, so he had rung to alert them to the potential haul. They could not bear good food going to waste, so they drove to the farm – not a small distance away – to collect the tongues. The great unveiling happened for Christmas dinner that year, baked in the oven whole. They enjoyed them so much that the tradition continued.

Today has pushed me still further. Two days after arriving, I am travelling again on the same road that brought me to Bjarni's parents, to that *skata* party, to the Christmas dinner of tongues. This time, at least, I can see what I am travelling through. The landscape is silenced by a thickness of snow. The sky glows a pinkish blue, the colour of something cold ripening, as it is shortly before dusk at three. We drive with the fjord on our right now, rough snow-covered fields descending to it, and just a few scattered summerhouses closed up for the foreseeable future. Steep basalt cliffs rise to our left, the dusting of snow picking out their dark crumbling terraces. On several occasions we pass frozen waterfalls: vast columns of ice suspended until warmer weather, like mute organs in a glacial church. It is a beautiful still day, and the calm sea mirrors the colours in the sky.

'*Hvað þetta er fallegur spegildagur!* (What a beautiful mirror-day!)' delights Gyða, clasping her mittened hands together in the front passenger seat. A 'mirror-day', Bjarni needs not explain, is when the sea is so calm that visible reality is perfectly doubled in it. I infer from Gyða's excitement that it is not a common occurrence. I don't know if it is a term she has just made up, but a person or culture that came up with such a metaphor is clearly one that lives day in day out with the vicissitudes of water and wind and feels fortunate when the weather is benevolent. I wonder if a mirror-day also implies a greater capacity for internal reflection, but that is an abstract topic of conversation for a Christmas family trip and I don't know her well enough to ask.

The road strikes through Haukur's family land at Kálfavík ('the bay of [whale] calves'). The land is mostly snow-blanketed tussocky fields sloping down to the fjord. There is a white concrete farmhouse with a red roof, standing stoically and alone. The road traces its path between the farmhouse and the steep cliffs which shelter the farm from behind, aloof and majestic. When he was a boy, Haukur told me through Bjarni's translation, the farm was accessible only by boat. On a Sunday evening, he and the other children in the *djúp* and surrounding fjords would be collected by the school boat and taken to the weekly boarding school two fjords away.

His family kept sheep and cows, and everything they ate they produced and preserved, or the sea provided. Among these foodstuffs, lamb was smoked with sheep droppings or birch twigs, and *skata* was fermented for several weeks by leaving it in a sealed box. Faster boats and faster roads changed everything for farmers and fishermen. They were, willingly or not, exposed to the ways and goods of the outside world. But despite that and despite the enormous fridges now in every kitchen, people still eat both smoked lamb and *skata* – especially the Westfjordians and especially at Christmastime. The birch-smoked lamb is delicious, but I doubt I will ever be persuaded by the *skata*. For Haukur, his early years remain the Glory Days, and 'foreign food' like pizza and hamburgers is an aberration that he outright refuses to eat.

The silence in which he grew up is punctuated now and then by a passing car. These cars are probably carrying younger Westfjordians, just like Bjarni and Súla and most of their cousins, back south to Reykjavík after their Christmas family visits, or older Westfjordians back north, having visited their children who have moved away. Or rather back 'west' as Gyða corrects me. So distinct is the Westfjordian identity that when they are travelling south towards Reykjavík, they say they are 'going south'. But on the journey home – an identical journey in reverse – they are 'going west'. Occasionally the lapping of waves and the steadfastness of the cliffs is criss-crossed also by the rumble and scanning headlights of refrigerated Eimskip lorries, transporting the latest fish catch to Reykjavík for export, or coming back with goods *frá útlöndum* ('from the outlands').

'*Hvalskurðará.*' Haukur points to a foaming river issuing from the largest waterfall we have yet passed, right beside the road. This one has not frozen. The water is too powerful. It is spectacular, but he doesn't stop the van, or even slow down. He has seen it many times, even if I have not.

'It means Whale-cutting River,' Bjarni explains. 'It's the boundary of my father's family's land. The water flows reliably year-round and back in the day that was useful if you were butchering a whale.'

We round the head of the fjord in which Haukur's cherished way of life played out and died. He drives the van like somebody who has served a long apprenticeship with this landscape, who instinctively knows all of its bends and gradients. I am still adjusting to his concession to modernity, if one can call it that – an obsession with the radio which has two main characteristics: loud and constantly on. He mostly listens to Rás 1 – Radio 1 – thank goodness, the better of the two national stations. The other is called Rás 2. Rás 1 is the original station of the state public service broadcaster RÚV, which must have caused a stir when it came on air in 1930. 'Orrriginal,' as Haukur would put it, with rolled 'r's and a hard 'g', to describe those things he finds 'proper'. I find it touching that, even now, the day's broadcast ends at 11.30 p.m. and doesn't resume until 6.45 a.m. In between, during the night, there is just silence. The first news bulletin of the day is announced with the repeating chime and clockwork whirr of a grandfather clock in a hallway. I don't imagine he'd change habit at this point to listen to any of the newer private stations.

On a peninsula he slows to a halt and looks to his right. It is a perfect panorama; an Arctic palette: a backdrop of corrie and glacier, a foreground of dark boulders silvered by the sighing sea and caressed by tendrils of dulse. Economical with conversation at the best of times, not one member of my Icelandic family thinks to point out that we are looking at something more specific than the view. Apparently, it is obvious. Haukur turns off the engine but the radio barks on. Suddenly, as my eyes adjust, I wonder how I could not have seen them straight away: a colony of recumbent seals lolling on the boulders, their skins shining with the day's reflection, looking up at us with the minimum of exertion.

'*Shhhh.*' I press my finger to my lips, as if that would make the radio quieten of its own accord.

The seals' heads lift but their bodies remain resolutely slumped. Their stare is intense: a liquid black, and somehow disarmingly human. It is the first time I have seen so many seals, so close, and I am enchanted. Rás 1 does not seem a fitting soundtrack for this moment.

'*Góður matur!*' Haukur remarks. 'Good food.'

Shocked, I climb out of the van to get closer to the enchanted version of this scene, joining Bjarni at the shore. I am not ready for what Haukur has just said.

Bjarni is making a low polyphony from pursed lips – a hum and a whistle simultaneously. It is beautiful and strange. Time stands still, becomes sound. The seals watch him, intrigued. One even dislodges itself from its perch and plops into the water, emerging closer to us with a blast of air from its nostrils, a twitch of its whiskers.

The silken sea reflects the sky and sighs, slicks the seal's grey neck with pearlescence, as it cranes for a better view.

'Good food,' I mutter, dismayed.

Gíslholt

June 2009

I am back for the summer to fulfil the promise I made a year ago. Salvar and Natalía are handing over their business to Bjarni and me for a season, so that they can have their well-deserved break. Perhaps I ought to be more intimidated by the fact that I am about to live and work full time with Bjarni for three months in a bus on a campsite in a mountain desert where there is no 'out', but I am delighted. Having only spent a week at a time in each other's company so far, I am excited by the prospect of making a home with him, no matter how temporary; of being free to get to know him all day and all bright night.

When he came to visit me in London a couple of months after we met, I saw then how well we would navigate the world together: both playful, curious and up for trying new things, although the new things we were willing to try sometimes varied wildly. In my flat one morning he made me breakfast: scrambled eggs and a herb I couldn't quite identify.

'Mandarin leaves,' he said when I asked. 'Your fruit bowl had some and I thought it's nice to have something green with it.'

It wasn't really. Rather tough, in fact. But I loved that nothing seemed to be off limits to him, and that he seemed to discover the world through his mouth and nose as much as through his eyes. With him, each day the world felt truly new. Perhaps it was him; perhaps that's just what love does.

We have come to Gíslholt to prepare. It feels like base camp: this is where the buses are kept all winter, and supplies converge here. I've heard Salvar refer to this part of Iceland as 'the flatlands', which it is, relatively speaking. As you turn onto a dirt track from Route 1, a blue road sign is scribbled with white lines forking ever outward like branches on a tree. Each line leads to a small white square with a name. It is the kind of sign you can only make sense of if you already know the terrain, and it is refreshingly free of angles and simplification. Gíslholt is the only word I recognize, but I have heard it many times already – referred to as the centre of the origin myth of Bjarni's mother's side of the family. As we drive the tracks the sign represents, undulating green hills shelter scattered farmsteads: these squares and names I do not yet understand. They are close enough for community, distant enough for a kind of personal space that seems to me like an Icelandic birth right.

The light is bright, and the sky is white, but it is not warm. Clouds hang like proffered blankets, not threatening rain, but reminding me that, although it is almost Midsummer, this is the Subarctic. To reach the farmhouses at Gíslholt, we have crossed a short grassy causeway between two small lakes like cataracts, reflecting the milky sky. The houses are on raised ground. *Holt* means 'hill'; I know that much.

But the 'flatness' of this region is brought into sharp relief by the edifice of the Hekla volcano. Hekla is also an Icelandic girls' name, I have noticed – one of Bjarni's many cousins bears the name. Hekla the mountain stands sturdily and alone behind these hillocks, like a matriarch in an old family photograph where she is the only remaining elder. Her shoulders are mantled in cloud, made blue by the distance.

Gíslholt is the farm in the south country where Bjarni's mother and her six siblings grew up. His grandmother, the matriarch of this family, has remained here since her husband's death. One of her sons, Sveinn, who fishes the lake near Landmannalaugar, has taken on the sheep farm and lives in a house built next door to hers. In one of the hay barns, he stores and maintains the three buses that comprise the Fjallafang Mountain Mall empire. I ask Bjarni to remind me what Fjallafang means. 'The embrace of the mountains,' he smiles proudly. We have come to check the buses are in working order, fill them with all the supplies mountain lovers may need, and drive them out into the highlands. Our journey will take us around the base of Hekla, and on across rivers and lava deserts into that land of colour which in the intervening year I have only seen in pictures. It continues to defy belief even though I have been there. Were the mountains really ochre, purple, russet and green; milky meltwater rivers charging between valleys; slopes venting the sulphurous exhalations of the Earth? This other-world is about to become my home and place of work for three months.

Nothing at Gíslholt begins before *kaffi og kökur* – coffee and cakes. After greeting Sveinn, we go to visit Bjarni's grandmother Amma

Sigga, Bjarni knocking on the door and walking straight in. He removes his shoes and pads through to the kitchen in his thick woollen socks. I follow suit. She is already laying the table with a spread that involves far more than coffee and cakes. The treeless landscape allows incoming visitors to be seen from some way off, mobilizing Icelandic hospitality in good time. The kitchen is compact and cosy – the units a shade of mustard yellow that looks unchanged since the 1970s. I wonder how she used to fit all her children in here. Appearing on the table are *kleinur*, a knot-shaped doughnut; buttered *flatkökur*, a flatbread, topped with *rúllupylsa*, sliced spirals of pink lamb flank and fat; *rúgbrauð*, a treacly dark rye bread; and *kæfa*, a pâté derived from some part of a sheep that I can enjoy if I don't ask too many questions.

She greets us with a kiss and beckons us to sit around the spread. 'How long have you two been together?'

'A year… ish,' Bjarni responds.

'Ah. You'll still want to look *at* each other, then.' She gestures to seats on opposite sides of the table. 'One day you'll want to look in the same direction.'

Being both a new couple and imminent colleagues, the feeling is unusual. We are two planets circling one other but held close by a strong gravitational pull, by a common purpose and responsibility for the shop. We are a team, with crackle. Our socked feet entwine under the table. Bjarni and Amma chat away in Icelandic and I enjoy listening to the tunefulness of the words, picking up a fragment here and there. But mainly I partake of her love through sampling the spread and watching the two of them – Bjarni sweet and tender with his favourite and only remaining grandmother. She is a short woman with cropped grey hair, and glasses, whose body isn't quite keeping up with her lively mind but is close behind. Her face seems to communicate anything the rest of her body cannot: her features dance above and below her glasses in constant motion, like a sheep dog rounding up a flock. Her expression seems always to be seconds away from kind amusement at somebody's expense, and dangly earrings swing either side of her face in accord with the excitement. Amma is clearly enjoying seeing Bjarni in a relationship – this shy boy she once knew becoming a man, having a sense of purpose. Love reinvents families as well as the individuals that make the couple.

Finally, Bjarni, realizing that I have been silent for a while, thinks of a point of shared interest. He knows I make jewellery.

'Sarah! Amma collects earrings. Would you like to see them?'

Of course I would, and she leads us through to a bedroom where there are about twenty pairs neatly displayed in a wooden box with a glass lid. In another country and another century, they would have been butterflies. Some of the earrings are made of recognizable materials like wood, and ribbon.

I notice a dangly pair with small globes of dark brown hanging from the hooks. 'What's that?'

'*Lambaspörð*,' she smiles, darting a humorous glance at Bjarni.

I can figure that out: lamb-shit earrings. This woman is crazy, and I love it. 'And those?' I point to a pair made of small, frilled ovals of bone the size and shape of a wood louse.

'Those are cod otoliths,' Bjarni informs me nonchalantly.

'What's an otolith? And Bjarni, how do you *know* these things?'
Not for the first time, I'm impressed by the breadth of his vocabulary.

'A bone in the inner ear of the fish. I think it helps them balance.'

I'm not sure what to make of this. Is this what Icelanders are like,
or what Bjarni's family is like? All I know is that their eccentricity and
matter of factness about shit and body parts, their ability to see them
as objects of beauty, makes me ring with excitement at the world
revealing itself anew.

'Bjarni... do you need any clothes?' Amma Sigga asks, stepping
back into the kitchen and making her way to the hall.

'What have you got?'

She pulls a ladder down from a trapdoor in the ceiling.

'Everything.' She nimbly climbs the ladder up to the loft, and we
follow as far as the opening. It opens onto several rooms, but each is
filled to the ceiling with bulging black bin bags. There is barely room
for one person up there. Amma Sigga begins untying them one by
one and pulling out items of clothing.

'*Nærbuxur?*' She throws an enormous pair of greying Y-fronts at
Bjarni, laughing.

'Awesome.'

'Bjarni, you've *got* to be kidding...' I say.

'What?'

'Old man's underpants...' By now, he has climbed down the
ladder and pulled them on over his corduroys. It is clear that he is
not going to part with them, especially now he's seen how fun it is to
wind up his woman.

I hear my name and Amma Sigga throws me a beautiful sage-green dress with buttons down the front flanked by a fine trim of lace. It is practical and pretty, and exactly my size. '*Takk*,' I smile.

'Why does Amma have all these clothes, Bjarni?'

'She collects them for the Women's Institute. But they don't have sales that often.'

Uncle Sveinn suddenly appears at the bottom of the ladder. 'Come around for dinner later? My friend has been fishing in Ölfusá river and he's brought me a salmon. He's big. Enough to go around.'

'*Já takk.*'

He's big. I enjoy that these nouns I live alongside have a gender, even when Icelanders are speaking English. 'It' is easier to commodify, but 'he' and 'she' become beings I must acknowledge a relationship with. I realize it has been a while since I have traded any money for anything. As soon as we are off the 'main road' it seems money is not required. With such a big family, life with Bjarni is intensely abundant. They are all resourceful, hard-working folk – not rich. But somebody has always got the thing you need, and food and generosity are plentiful. Though it is an expensive country, with this alternative economy pulsing underneath the official one, it seems that with time, kindness and intimacy this could be a very sustainable place to exist.

With this family, I certainly do not feel at the centre of a financial crisis – Iceland's reputed identity as of October last year. I realize it will be more complex than appearances show, but there certainly seems to be resilience in the fact that no one here is an island, even if they live on one. In the Icelandic sagas, the greatest punishment was to be outlawed, separated from kin and society, because it was those networks which kept people alive. Only two generations ago, most Icelanders were extremely poor and they depended on collaboration for survival. People today seem dedicated to making their realities at least *feel* like they comprise all the comforts their ancestors were deprived of, even if it is bought on credit. That is to say, the apparent wealth and people's enjoyment of it is often an illusion, propped up by bank loans. But still, I have not noticed capitalism having nurtured individualistic tendencies here, at least in the countryside. I suppose it's all relative. Despite a cultural memory of poverty, in this family I have noticed the *gamla daga* ('old days') always referred to with fondness – with a suggestion that it was a time of moral integrity that has been eroded with the arrival of wealth.

New clothes acquired, there's time for a walk before the next meal. I have been braced for hard work today but that is clearly not how this business operates. With Sveinn in the kitchen cooking his unanticipated bounty of salmon, he will not be in mechanic mode for the Mountain Mall buses today. Salvar and Natalía have not yet arrived to show us the ropes. So, all there is to do is reconnect with land and family.

Bjarni takes me first to an outbuilding beside Amma's house. At one end is a room that is home to a clucking vitrine of twenty white and auburn hens who peer at us through uneven single-glazed windows. Their red combs flash through the reflection of a pinkening sky. Bjarni talks to them tenderly: he seems to be as kindly with animals as with his elders. We enter the building through a peeling red door into a large bare room with a concrete floor.

'Slaughterhouse,' Bjarni tells me.

'Sveinn kills his own sheep?'

'Some of them. Just for family consumption. We come and help. And with the butchering. It's a nice time to see family. We'll come sometime.'

The home fridges I've seen are stocked full and it is possible to buy anything you would need from the supermarkets. But this ritual of families gathering around the processes of raising sheep for meat seems to be an emotional need as much as a practical one, especially as relatives are scattered around the country, and beyond. Icelanders and livestock arrived on this rock together, brought in boats by the settlers, and sheep eventually became predominant. The shape of family life would have emerged in concert with the lifecycles of their woolly companions, and as well as those traditions brought with them, vernacular flourishes would have evolved from farm to farm, household to household.

I look out of the window. These green rolling hills are now bathed in a low golden light and the sky is bleeding pink into purple. The sun is not going to set, but I have observed at this time of evening the air shifts – becoming windy for a while before settling into a cool bright night. I notice a silhouette of furry strips pegged to a string hanging across the window. It looks like some kind of ritualistic garland.

'What are those... in the window?'

'Mink tails. The state pays per tail.'

'What... is Sveinn a mink hunter as well?'

'Every farmer will kill a mink if they see one. They're destructive little bastards. They'll eat all the hens. They're not supposed to be here. Some idiot once thought it would be a good idea to start a mink farm in Iceland and some got out, so now we have them running around in the wild.'

'Right.'

I have a sepia-toned fantasy of a government inspector on horseback paying a visit to a farmer, travelling around the countryside with a logbook counting mink tails like beads on an abacus, and handing over a wad of notes. It is almost certainly not like that. But here it does feel like we are still in another era: pre-crisis, but *long* before. A time where 'problems' and 'solutions' were directly linked, and straightforward.

'Shall we go up the hill before it gets any colder?'

'It's not cold.'

'OK, I'd like to go up the hill before *I* get too cold.'

'Sure.'

I am becoming aware of how subjective my value systems are. And Bjarni, in his very gentle way, picks me up on it. I enjoy the challenge, but with everything being so new to me, it happens a lot. I feel, like I never have before, that I am going to be profoundly changed by this place.

Bjarni and I make our way up the hill – the *holt* – behind the farm-houses. The light is beautiful now, the hanging paleness of day giving way to an almost fluorescent sunset and a vista as expansive as our possibilities. We do not need much altitude here to be able to see all

74

around. At the top I feel like I am standing in the crow's nest of a tall ship sailing on a sea of green. In the distance, Hekla stands crisp and clear as a cardboard cut-out, the colour of a bruise. She is majestic.

'So, we'll be living beneath a volcano that is overdue to erupt?'

'We can make sure the van's always got enough petrol for an escape.'

Problem. Solution. Why is life in England so complicated? So full of prohibitions and protocols which do not allow for the cultivation of sense – of a feeling for handling oneself in danger, or with the land. I am quite sure I would never be allowed to put myself in the way of this particular 'problem' in England. There would be a pre-emptive restriction on travel within a huge radius of the volcano. But when the country you live in *is* a volcano, you have to keep on living your life.

Seal Wife

September 2008

The postcard Bjarni has sent me features a hand-painted seventeenth-century map of Iceland: *ISLANDIA* by Abraham Ortelius, Antwerp. Rendered in a gruesome, many-fingered form, like a tumour reproducing itself, the landmass is embellished with spines of mountains and the fire and brimstone rendition of Hekla as an active volcano. Though it was not erupting at the time the map was made, the imagined memory of the last eruption clearly burned brightly in the map-maker's mind. All around the shores, sea monsters swim, gallop, breach, prance, keeping lesser mortals at bay. Only those with true determination and faith would cross the waters to land on those shores. I am not yet one of them.

On the reverse is a smaller map, with a handwritten arrow pointing to a place on the east coast. In blue spidery letters:

The arrow points at Húsavík, the place where the seal tried to lure me into the sea. I have sent you 7 crystals from the shore.

Inside the accompanying package there are indeed seven crystals. Seven sea-rounded quartz pebbles the size of boiled sweets and the colour of translucent ivory. They click and grind melodically in my fingers, inviting a prolonged caress. Their smoothness is calming – the present chapter in a longer story of jagged crystals blooming into rock voids, then outliving them, rounded by time, polished by waves. Near to their surface, near to present time, they hold the story of Bjarni's seal wife.

September 2009

We are on the eastern leg of our round-the-country tour in our camper van – a month-long journey at the end of the tourist season, parking up wherever we feel like it. Bjarni wants to show me his country while we have the time and freedom to explore. He wants to take me to a bay where, not so many years ago, he had an encounter with a seal – a tale which he recounted when we first met, and which he has enchanted me with time and time again.

'Tell me how it happened,' I ask, like a child, as our van bounces down a heathland track towards the sea. A salmon-pink mountain, cross-hatched with dark striations as if drawn on by a charcoal pencil, recedes in the rear-view mirror.

'I was on a road trip around the country, a bit like this one, but alone. I went down to this shore, where we're going now, at night. The waves were gentle, and lapping. I noticed a sound, like, like a… singing. The waves washed over the pebbles and each time they drew back, I realized the stones *were* singing. *KIIIIIIIIIIIIIIIIIIII…* *KIIIIIIIIIIIIIIIIIIII…*' He looks at me and shimmies his right hand as he makes the sound with his tongue against his teeth, the delight of the memory washing across his face with each lap of a wave.

'I picked up a stone and realized it was quartz. The *whole beach* was covered in rounded quartz pebbles. I lay down to listen and before long I was lulled into sleep.'

'And then?' I press, knowing full well what next.

'When I woke up I was halfway up that hill... see how steep it is?' He points to his left. We are nearing the bay now. 'I couldn't understand how I got there. I tried to return to the beach and it was tricky even when fully awake. I had to scramble almost vertically down a cliff.'

I can picture the whole scene in my head. Whether his stories are true or not is irrelevant. They are absolutely believable.

'When I got to the beach the sun was coming up and it was turning into a *beautiful* morning. I sat contemplating what had happened in the night. Had I sleepwalked, shape-shifted, tele-transported? This beach had made that sort of thing seem plossible... is that... how do you say it?'

'Plausible.'

'Plausible, yes. And then, in the calm water, a seal appeared, and looked at me with these big, black, very *human* eyes. She locked my gaze. Then she turned her face to one side, again and again, beckoning with her head for me to follow her into the sea. A seal wife.'

This was not the first time Bjarni had been in a familial relationship with a seal. When we first fell in love, his mother Gyða had shown me an album of photographs of him as a baby and as a child, in that universal way that mothers seem to embarrass their children.

Though he was not embarrassed at all and I was far more curious about what was happening around the woollen swaddled bundle of his baby body. One photograph in particular had captivated me: Gyða lying on the floor, suckling Bjarni with the knuckle of one hand and bottle-feeding a baby seal with the other.

'It had been crying in the sea just below our house,' she told me. 'It had lost its mother we think, so we tried to feed it. But it became weak and died.'

It was a practical response to a problem on their doorstep – one neighbour trying to help another – but the lack of boundary between human and animal worlds moved me. The motto in this family, and indeed in general here, is *'bara prófa'* – 'just try'. In a sense, Bjarni had attained mythological status through that photograph, at least as far as I was concerned: a boy co-raised with a seal pup. But more enchanting still was how normal it all felt in this family. The unprecedented shapes of new realities would continue to slip out casually the longer I spent with them, like rough diamonds spilling out of a torn pocket, and paid no heed.

'I didn't follow her,' Bjarni continues. 'My road trip had grounded me, and I didn't feel like running away. But I would like to take you to meet her, if she is still there.'

The vista opens up as the bay comes into view. The water is an inky black but dances with the blue of the sky and the pink of the mountains that embrace it.

'And what was the part about your hands again?' I ask, recalling that there was a bizarre appendage to this tale.

'Oh yes. When I got out of this dream world where I climbed mountains in my sleep and got accosted by a seal, I went to the swimming pool in Reyðarfjörður to get clean. In the pool I looked at my palms and they had turned light blue. I thought I might be hallucinating, so I asked someone in the changing room what colour they were. They saw blue too. Something in my instinct told me it was to do with an electricity I had felt on top of that headland.'

He points again. We are snaking beneath the headland now. From here, I can gauge its steepness, and wonder how anyone could scale it in their sleep. I grin at the bizarreness of it all. The autumn air coming in through the half-open van window fizzes with the magic of the right story told in the right place.

'When I woke after teleporting, or whatever I did, something strange happened. It was sunny. The sky *all* around was clear and blue. There was a swamp and I decided to walk into it. As I did, a mist closed in around me – just at that place, just at the swamp. Inside the fog it felt as if electricity was... *crackling* through me. It felt like I could shoot *lightnings* out of my hands. So yeah... maybe that's what turned them blue.'

His story contorts time and reality. It's a good one, and I have spent long enough in Iceland not to be dismissive of things that sound improbable as I begin to see equally improbable things with my own eyes.

We pull up above the beach which has a bed of black sand. It makes the water at once so dark and so reflective – exactly like a mirror. The shoreline is a hem of pebbles scattering ever more sparsely up the beach. We climb out to explore our stopping place for the night, and this place of promised magic.

'Oh,' says Bjarni, with a tone of disappointment.

'What?' I wonder. It looks beautiful to me.

'Look. It's not covered in quartz pebbles anymore.' He bends to pick one up. 'There's a few but this is *nothing* compared to last time. And look, there's tyre tracks in the sand. *Huge* ones.'

The clues point to a reality far from the magic Bjarni had conjured in the van. Somebody has evidently come down with a truck and scavenged the beach, wholesale, for these treasures. I am still getting used to how pristine everything looks to my eyes, but what Bjarni can see is devastation. He is deflated. 'Looks like my seal wife is not here either.'

As the evening dims to night – a novelty for our eyes – we sit on the dry sand at the top of the beach and build a fire of driftwood twigs. We listen to the crackle of it, and the wash of the waves, though I hear no crystals singing. Bjarni feels for two quartz pebbles within his reach, weighing them up for appropriate shape and size in his fingers. Satisfied, he begins to strike them against each other. The smell of burning rock, not unlike an overheated gear box, hits my nostrils. Suddenly the quartz illuminates, and disappears again.

'Oh my god, that's *beautiful*,' I sing, quickly looking around for two pebbles of my own with which to play this game. This is pure delight: the discovery of something other-worldly in matter I may have walked over, ignorant of its qualities. Each moment like this opens me still further to the truths in these stories. Had I told someone about a beach covered in stones that glowed from within when they hit against each other, would it have been any more or less believable than a seal who tried to accost a man?

'People are probably buying these in magic shops all over Europe now,' Bjarni curses.

These stones will not sing on a shelf in a gift shop. They will never again be stumbled upon by a man trying to find himself, to be the soundtrack to his journey along the littoral of waking and dreaming.

The next morning, we explore the shoreline, focusing, as we tend to, on our own patches, and our own spheres of interest. I am taking photographs of the seaweed as it curls and plops around shells and pebbles. Bjarni has a foraging basket and is dangling his hand into the seaweed in deeper water to see if there are any mussels.

There is a wet puff of air 5 metres from us.

'*Halló kerling. Þarna ert þú!*' Bjarni talks to the seal like an old friend and continues looking for mussels. His casual reaction to her appearance reveals his belief that she would turn up. She swims closer and watches him intently. I watch from a distance and feel like an intruder. Though she could be considered my 'competition', in wanting to believe a story I sift the scene for visible facts which confirm its integrity and ignore the details that undermine it: seals are curious. This may be a male seal. It may well be a different seal to the last one Bjarni saw here which may also have been a male. But none of that matters. Here, now, they are having an encounter that transcends time and species, and swims to join all the other selkie stories that have ever been told. It is sad, and it is beautiful. But he has chosen me.

Að smala og að slátra –
Gathering and Slaughtering

October 2009

The summer has been silenced. Outside the sheephouse the snow is deep for miles around. Its whiteness heaps at every vertical intrusion in the landscape. The farm buildings, the smokehouse, the old tractor, the plough wheel, the knife grinding stone – all are reduced to a bare suggestion in monotone, like a quick charcoal sketch. It is only at the back door of the sheephouse that this pervading blankness is punctuated by a daub of deep, wild red.

It is the first week of October. We are back at Ögur, the farm where Bjarni's best-loved aunty, Yrsa, lives. With her husband, Hallgarður, she has raised six children and many hundreds of sheep since she moved here as a young woman from the neighbouring farm, around the headland at Kálfavík. It is a week since we gathered the sheep from the mountains, and now we are back for the slaughter. In this short time, winter has come like a full stop to a lyrical sentence.

It happened by chance that Bjarni and I had been able to participate in the round-up of the flock. It was a fitting end to the road trip we had embarked upon; our end-of-summer wanderings and the bringing in of sheep both determined by a change of weather. At the beginning of the trip in early September, I had stood in a bikini in the south of the country, seeking solace in the shade of a cave. We had slept with all the doors of our campervan open that night, it was such a balmy evening. A week ago, on 27 September, we awoke in the north of the country, outside a town called Siglufjörður. I was fully clothed in woollen underwear, helmeted in a balaclava, and had slept with my head under the duvet. On waking I turned and drew back the makeshift curtain in a cloud of my own breath. Just when I had thought the mountains could not get any more beautiful, draped in blueberry ling and dwarf shrubs steeped in autumn colours, a dusting of snow had fallen overnight, highlighting every contour. September is a month of ambiguity, it seems: it can be fine; it can be cold. Although we had lined the cavities of the van's wall and ceiling with sheep's fleece from Bjarni's uncle, Sveinn, a month ago, that was the first time it had felt essential.

That day, we decided to call an abrupt end to our journey and do the remaining 500 kilometres to Bjarni's parents' house in Ísafjörður in a day. He called to let them know we were coming. It had snowed there too, they said. And when the snow comes, or preferably before, it is time to bring in the sheep, who roam free in the mountains all summer. Every year since they can remember, they have helped Yrsa round up her sheep to Ögur. Her farm is a two-hour drive south of Ísafjörður, so we would pass it on our way.

I had not expected to be any more than an observer at the round-up, and wished I was equipped to film it. I soon realized that, with two arms and two legs, I was expected to muck in like everybody else. Though I was nervous, as nobody seemed to think it necessary to explain the procedure, I relished the opportunity to participate in a practice the family had engaged in for generations, and upon which Icelanders had depended for food since settlement. I appreciated their apparent belief that the way to learn was simply by doing it.

Traditionally, at sheep gatherings farmers and their friends and extended families cooperate to gather sheep belonging to all the neighbouring farms. It makes sense: the sheep roam free all summer, the flocks mixing, and all but the most stubborn sheep begin to descend the mountains of their own accord as they smell winter in the air. They are gathered into a central enclosure – the *réttir* – and separated according to their ear tags to be returned to their respective farms.

This one was a two-day affair, and the weather on the first day was awful. The night before we started, Bjarni and I slept in the attic room of his parents' summerhouse, halfway down the fjord along which the gathering would take place. It shook with gusts of wind. The next morning, we looked out of the kitchen window with slight trepidation over steaming cups of coffee. Snow whisked at the windowpane and the wind howled through the cracks in the house.

'This will be hard. The wind is blowing in the wrong direction,' Bjarni's mother said. 'The sheep like to have the wind in their faces.'

An advance party had gone out early. Fortunately, the news came in that the bad weather had compelled the sheep to make considerable progress down the fjord by themselves, which would make our job easier.

Our job was to drive the sheep down the steep and craggy-sided fjord, down to the road and around the headland to Ögur, on foot. The team consisted of: Yrsa and five of her six adult children and their families; Bjarni's mother and father, Gyða and Haukur; Bjarni and I; the neighbouring farmer, Aðalsteinn; and some locals from Ísafjörður, who rather enjoyed participating in this ritual and returned year after year. Yrsa's husband, Hallgarður – who had always been the *aðalbóndi*, the main farmer and the man who gives instructions to the gathering crew – was elderly and suffering from dementia, in the final stages of decline. He remained at the farm.

There are no sheep dogs here: the gathering is done just once a year, and it would be too costly to feed dogs for the whole year just for one weekend's work. The group formed a staggered line from the top of the mountain down to the road – the elders, women and children staying on or near the road, which had only an occasional passing car. The younger men, fit and intimate with the terrain, made their way up to the craggy heights and heathland on top of the mountain. Clapping and hooting occasionally to spur the sheep on, this line moved slowly down the fjord and throughout the day sheep began to gather on the road. The snow blew hard from behind us and the sun could not penetrate the clouds. Everywhere was dim. Although the sheep had initiated their own head-start, the daylight window was short and we could not make it all the way to Ögur. Cold and invigorated, we had stopped for the night near Kálfavík, but gone to

Ögur for *kjötsúpa* – meat soup – a reward for the helpers, made from last year's lamb.

On the second day, a generous sun reflected in the snow made the home run dazzlingly beautiful. I found it difficult to take my role seriously as I was distracted by the luminescent red of the blueberry shrubs in the low sunlight, and the blue shadows that clustered around them. I had my camera as I always did, and I wanted to stop and photograph every detail of this new landscape. Though winter had only just begun, this much snow was such a novel phenomenon to me. I could not simply walk on by. I stopped to snap off an icicle that dripped beside a stream and sucked on it. Of course, in that moment, two sheep decided to bolt back towards me. I had dropped back from the line, creating a larger gap than was ideal. As they ran towards me, I had a slow-motion fantasy about grabbing one in each hand, being the heroine of the round-up. Throwing down my icicle I stood ready, my limbs outstretched, my bent legs twitching, wondering which way to move. The sheep bolted either side of me. Thankfully, they were retrieved by a gatherer with much more experience.

As we neared Ögur, the sea of faces and fleeces – brown, white, black, grey – moved in a hypnotic undulation around the colourful uprights of the gathering crew. The children skipped excitedly towards the *réttir*. The bleating of six hundred sheep was cacophonous and the satisfaction of the gathering crew tangible. Another year's gathering was almost complete, and Aðalsteinn would write a poem about it, as he does every year, to be read out at Christmas. I wondered if my inexperienced antics would be immortalized. The hoots increased in frequency and everyone was together now, on the tufty fields either side of the road. We could see the gate to Ögur. A few sheep turned up the track into the farm, as they should, but the majority just carried on going, straight along the road.

'The *aðalbóndi* isn't with us!' I heard someone cry. Yrsa's sons, Frosti and Hallgarður junior, made a sprint. Every year that this group had gathered the sheep together, it had been Hallgarður, their father, who had stood by the farm's entrance to guide the sheep in. This year he was lying in bed, trapped inside his own mind and waiting to die. The ritual was so ingrained, and everybody's place in it so implicit, that nobody had been able to imagine Hallgarður *not* being there. The sons were too late. Too many sheep had passed the entrance. Through shouted messages and the continued forward motion, I deduced that it had been agreed to press on to Aðalsteinn's farm – the next one along – where half of these sheep were destined anyway, and to segregate them there. I was relieved that even after generations of practice, mistakes could still be made, and mine paled into insignificance.

After another hour of trudging along the almost carless road in the lowering light, we arrived at Aðalsteinn's farm, Strandsel. The sheep were herded into his *réttir* and separated out. A trailer was brought to drive Yrsa's sheep back to Ögur, where we had just come from. There was much laughter at the omission of an *aðalbóndi* replacement but I felt somehow that the hilarity masked the sadness of their recognition that this was the dwindling end of an era. Yrsa and Hallgarður's children all lived in Reykjavík and Denmark; they were not interested in being farmers. With Hallgarður's imminent demise, Yrsa would not be able to keep this flock. They had been her purpose, all her adult life. After a few runs with the trailer packed with sheep, we returned to Ögur for coffee and cake, Bjarni and I getting a ride standing in the back of the empty wooden trailer. I looked out across the sea, my down jacket hood pulled tight around my face in the cold blue evening.

*   *   *

Inside the sheephouse the sheep are skittish. Their hooves scuff the wooden slatted floor, which is matted with a fragrant mix of hay and shit. Penned in, they press against each other, awaiting their fate. In order not to make it too obvious to those beasts still alive, Bjarni and his father Haukur take a sheep out of sight to the back door of the sheephouse. Haukur straddles it to the ground, points a gun at its head and shoots. He slices open its neck with a knife. Deep red blood trickles out onto the perfectly white snow. It is exquisite and it is violent. I do not know how to feel. For a long time, the sheep's fleecy bulk continues to jerk beneath him. 'It's the death throes,' Bjarni explains, reading the concern on my face. I am impressed and a little disturbed that he knows this expression in English. When the body finally gives in, the head is cut off and taken inside. There it is placed alongside the others, upturned, and salt is sprinkled on the open neck flesh.

The sheep's body is brought in and placed belly up on a trough table to be worked. Gyða slices through the skin along its belly and hooks a rope to its front legs which feeds to a pulley in the roof. She moves to the other end of the rope with Bjarni, while Bjarni's cousin, Frosti, stays at the trough to grip the fleece. Mother and son heave, and Frosti pulls down. The fleece slips off like a jumper.

I was inspecting this winch a week ago, when we gathered the sheep into the sheephouse. I pulled down gently on the hook, following the rope up to the ceiling. Suddenly it yanked upwards, me still gripping it. Haukur was at the other end, chuckling. He embraces every opportunity to test my demeanour.

In the sheephouse the thermometer reads exactly zero. It is best to be working. We all wear thermal-lined overalls, or fishermen's rubber dungarees – bright orange and impermeable. This is messy work. We fall into a neat rhythm. Bjarni and Haukur grab a sheep, kill it, carry it to the trough. Gyða sprinkles salt on the neck flesh of its decapitated head, slices open the fleece, tugs on the rope. Yrsa hangs up the stripped carcass and slices along the length of its torso, reaching into its insides with her arms and scooping the glistening grey and pink innards into a wheelbarrow, aided by her five-year-old grandson Egill.

Frosti's wife, Steinrún, and I wash down the carcass with a hosepipe, and scrub at the blood spots with a brush. The carcasses accumulate on the rail, like a new line of visceral clothing in a factory. In this role my arms are mostly raised, and cold bloody water trickles under the elasticated cuffs of my overalls.

By the fifth carcass I scrub, I am no longer upset when I hear the gunshot at the back door. I see it for what it is: a process in which these sheep's lives and deaths have been overseen by the same family from start to finish. Though it is no longer 'essential' for survival, this gathering and slaughter connects them to something archaic, done this way since the settlement of Iceland. It is cyclical. It is a gathering of sheep and also a gathering of people in a sparsely populated land. I am going to eat this meat. I feel instrumental in the fact of my own existence and it is thrilling.

'We love these sheep,' Gyða had explained earlier. 'But when they're in this pen, they're meat.'

They had frisked around as she bent over the railings, touching their noses affectionately and inhaling their scent. I knew they had been given names and I could see they had been well cared for.

As the snow drinks up the last of the late afternoon light, the red blot at the back door expands, seeping into the whiteness. The sheephouse fills with pink carcasses and disembodied upturned heads – the eyes fixed now on an imaginary distance, clouding over. The plucks (the conjoined form of heart, lungs and liver) are nailed to a wooden beam suspended by their tracheae to keep them clean for later processing. They are wet, pink and burgundy like grotesque tropical flowers. Each of us who has helped with the gathering, and the slaughter, will be rewarded with meat. At each meal, which will also be a gathering of people, I will know exactly the life that I am eating and will know that I have walked across the land that sustained it.

The chill of evening pries at us. The cold carcasses are slipped into heavy-duty black bin bags, tied shut and loaded into a trailer.

Gos – Eruption/Gas/Fizzy Drink

25 March 2010

It is evening. A small portion of Bjarni's extended family are gathered
around the television in Gyða and Haukur's living room after a dinner
of boiled haddock and potatoes. This tends to happen when there is
something interesting to watch. The seven o'clock news tonight is
going to be special.

Bjarni and I are visiting his parents over Easter. We are between
lives. We have been in a long-distance relationship for more than
a year, and, since gathering in the sheep last autumn, we have
travelled together for six months in Kenya, Spain and England
on the proceeds of our stint in the mountain shop. Bjarni has
now met my friends and family in England, and my parents and
grandmother who still live in Kenya. I have shown him where I
grew up, and where I made the film whose screening brought me
to the Westfjords to start with. Neither of us currently has a home
or a job. The time has come to choose where we might make a
home together. Iceland? Where? England? Where? The stakes are
high when you start from scratch. Or, there are no stakes at all. It
depends on how you look at it. We've seen that we do adventures

well, but we're not quite sure how to do normal life, or indeed what that is supposed to be. For the time being, Bjarni is happy to remain near his family. He has travelled more with me in six months than he has in the rest of his life. I also long to be still; to be in a situation where I can craft a life. But this is not my habitat.

I watch the family chatting in Icelandic, frustrated that I cannot participate. I attempt to grasp at fragments of their conversation. Certain words I know but that is not of much use when I don't know how they relate to others. For now, I must bear with the paradox of being simultaneously present and absent. All of them except Bjarni's father *can* speak English, but I am the minority, and it breaks the flow to switch from their own language. Nor would I learn that way. For now, I must fathom relationships through actions and cadence. I have an urge to understand this place Bjarni comes from, the better to understand him.

As someone without intact roots, and with parents and a grandmother who live thousands of miles away, my considerations about where to be are surprisingly black and white. Many people tend to move for a job, or for someone they love. But when both people in a couple are open to being anywhere, and much of the world is in financial collapse, a different set of concerns floats to the surface of that muddy river. The prospect of a career job is something I might have to relinquish for a while. And besides, selling fish to tourists in the highlands thrilled me more than being a research assistant and filmmaker for a national gallery. I did that work to spend time in that place. That is reward enough.

I am interested in what kind of life would be most resilient during the crisis. That involves stripping things back to identify our basic needs and where they can best be met. Thoughts echo around my head, pros and cons silently crashing into each other. Here, besides a landscape that blows my mind, we have the support that the extended family offers. It is a big draw, having been self-sufficient for so long. The basics would be taken care of: no shortage of free fish and lamb, cheapish rent, cheap electricity, hot springs, good woollens knitted by the family, a mechanic and joiner on hand in the form of Bjarni's father. There is a network with whom I could exchange labour, and my savings could stretch further here if I needed to use them.

These things are appealing to my overqualified self when I think of friends with PhDs who are on the dole, unable to do anything except send off more CVs and worry about not making the rent. It would also be a huge change for me, and a challenging one. Eight hours' drive from Reykjavík, it is undoubtedly remote. I have no concept of what I might do here, or what my identity would be. I sense I would need to learn this new and difficult language quite well in order to figure any of that out. It would be, at the very least, an adventure. But I cannot move just yet. Soon I will leave, back to the UK for the summer to shoot a film commission I have lined up. Bjarni will stay here and go shrimping on a small trawler to get some money together for the next phase, whatever that will look like.

Bjarni's father, Haukur, reclines with outstretched legs on the black leather sofa, covered in a woollen blanket. This is his default position. Between work, eating and chores, this is where you will invariably find him in different stages of wakefulness, in front of a TV that is almost always on, sometimes simultaneously with the radio. Bjarni and I curl up, as new lovers do, on the other sofa. Bjarni's mother Gyða is sitting in an armchair with a sated smile. She is knitting socks with four short needles at right angles, taking up a coil of *lopi* wool from the floor, while barely ever taking her eyes off the screen. Her sister, Sjöfn, is perched on the arm of Haukur's sofa, excitable and, as always, ready for action. Salvar, their brother, sinks into another armchair, and his dear Natalía sits on the floor resting her back on his legs. Salvar is consistently in awe of his landscape, and tonight is no exception. We are all enrapt and the light flickers on our wide eyes.

This evening, the television is a worthy focal point. The evening news is mostly about one thing: a recently erupted volcano on Fimmvörðuháls. Curtains of orange light spray up from inside two newly forming craters. The vents hiss and hack like a giant who has been holding his breath for millennia, breathing once again. Molten lava flows away from the centre of the eruption. The new craters are to be named Magni and Móði, after the sons of Þórr (Thor, the god of thunder) – as the eruption is taking place near to the spectacular glacial valley of Þórsmörk ('the forest of Thor'). Where it cools, the lava clinks off in large flakes, and volcano tourists video it with their phones and digital cameras. The flow is gentle enough that onlookers feel safe getting close, despite warnings of noxious gases.

This is my fifth trip to Ísafjörður in one and a half years. I arrived here from Reykjavík this morning, with fire in my eyes. I had landed in Iceland only yesterday evening, and yet in that short window between one flight touching down and the other taking off, through serendipity I had witnessed one of the most impressive acts of nature I am ever likely to see. Less than twenty-four hours ago, I was standing watching this volcano in the dark with a man I barely knew.

Back in the UK, I had been staying with my volcanologist friend Hugh. At his house, I was privy to regular updates on the seismic activity at Fimmvörðuháls and read all the news articles, swept up in his excitement. The weather conditions had been bad for the first few days of the eruption, so it had not been possible for the media to get a true sense of it beyond seismographs. Yesterday, as I landed in Reykjavík, the weather cleared. The eruption was in the south of the country, just over two hours' drive from the capital. I knew I needed to get there.

I remembered a man I had met while running the shop in the mountains. He was a friend of Salvar and Natalía's – an outdoor photography enthusiast and mountain rescue volunteer. He'd likely be up for the adventure. I scrolled my mobile phonebook for 'Eiríkur'. I had him logged as 'Eiríkur Rescue', obviously thinking that a direct line could be useful one day.

He answered his phone straight away, pleasantly surprised to hear from me. It turned out he had been at the volcano for a few hours already, taking photos. It was the first good weather window since the eruption had begun and the lava was active. I assumed this meant my options were closing. But then he offered to come back to Reykjavík to pick me up.

'I could do with a break,' he said. 'Anyway, I'm quite sure it'll be totally different once it gets dark.'

I was blown away by Eiríkur's generosity, but from my experience so far this seemed to be the kind of thing Icelanders do without thinking much of it. They appear to enjoy showing people their country, and are always happy to have some fresh energy in their island days blown in by a non-judgemental outlander. As a small nation on the edge of Europe, which has had independence for only a century, approval from long-established, powerful nations seems to be important to them. Their reputation has been unfairly damaged by the financial crisis, and it is a double blow. The country's bankruptcy, for which the population may be paying the price for many decades to come, was the responsibility of a small elite of bankers.

The people are nonetheless being tainted by this poor reputation. The UK government's imposition of anti-terrorism laws to recoup money owed to depositors by Landsbanki, one of the failed banks, was an especially sore point. Many UK councils, universities and citizens had deposited in Landsbanki's high-interest online savings account, Icesave. I had considered doing so myself, but Bjarni had warned me against it. The UK used these laws to freeze the bank's UK assets when it appeared that the Icelandic government, who seized control of Landsbanki, would not be able to compensate its savers. For a mostly gentle, low-crime nation without its own military, to be effectively branded a terrorist was an affront. Icelandic citizens too had been ravaged by the fall of the banks and resented being tarred with the same brush as the reckless bankers.

Kindness is an act of resistance. As is humour.

When these powers were being thrown around in late 2008, just after we had met, Bjarni sent me an email saying only 'I made a video', with a link. I'm not sure what I expected, but it was not this: a spoof hostage video made with his flatmates, entitled *Icelanders are NOT terrorists*. In frame were three Icelanders wearing Icelandic jumpers, their heads cropped for anonymity, surrounding an Englishman on his knees, his arms tied behind his back and a Bónus supermarket bag on his head. One Icelander pulls the bag off to reveal the Englishman, sobbing. Another holds a piece of paper in front of him.

'Read the paper. Read the fokking paper.'

'I'm not doing it,' pleads the Englishman.

'Oh yes you are, or she will give you more Icelandic food.' A saucepan is pushed towards his nose and he throws his face to one side.

Eventually, he reads the words on the paper.

'Mr Brown... Icelanders are NOT terrorists.'

I was on the floor laughing with that one.

Around nine o'clock, as the light dimmed, Eiríkur pulled up in his jeep outside my guesthouse, happy to be giving an English woman a ride to a volcano.

Night in the south of Iceland, in spring as in autumn, is an actual and profound darkness. Light pollution quickly evaporates as you leave the city streetlights behind. In those shoulder months, by about five minutes day by day, the darkness increases or decreases incrementally, caused by a rapidly disappearing sun in autumn, and a keenly returning sun in spring. In those months, there is no snow on the ground to reflect the moonlight. Until you reach the fertile farming country of the southern lowlands, Salvar's 'flatlands', the ground is mostly dark jagged lava, which wicks any glimmers of light there may be into its suspended geology, held for now in solid form, but for who knows how long? As we descended towards the flatlands, the night was set ablaze by tunnels of orange light: geothermal greenhouses incubating tomatoes, cucumbers and peppers for the whole country. These were a brief intrusion into the darkness before we returned to the only light being the pools of headlights on the road and the glow of Eiríkur's satnav on our faces – a square of pixels meant to represent the unknown miles ahead.

Eventually we turned off Route 1. The road was tarmacked for a while, then became a dirt track – flying gravel ringing on the jeep's underside. We could see the glow from a long way off, an orange furnace suspended in the black. We got as close as we could and stopped beside a raging river. As I climbed out of the jeep, I could hear the water's force and extent but not see it. Eiríkur told me it was called the Markarfljót: *markar*, a form of *mörk*, meaning 'forest', and *fljót*, a 'broad river'.

Up above us, across the river, the silhouette of a ridge was backlit by a cloud of orange steam. The glow from the burning magma lit the steam clouds from underneath. Fountains of magma and rocks spurted from the fissure, high into the night. Hugh had told me about the tremors that led to this, their magnitudes, what caused them, which rock type was being spat out. But none of it compared to the immensity of standing under a dark-bright night, the half-moon now faintly lighting the glacier, and in the middle of it all the Earth rent open, revealing its inner workings. Black and orange. Light, steam and rock. That was all there was. And beyond the rushing of the meltwater river, the faint sound of these shifting from one form into another; the sound of transformation.

I wrote in my diary this morning:

I was struck by a realization of how we actually live on a ball of molten magma, a ball of so much light and the dark matte crust is very thin indeed. And then we cover it with all sorts of stuff which we convince ourselves is some sort of reality. But it is only a reality and, as always, the Earth just has to split, or shift, and all that can come crumbling to the ground. It's important to remember that.

'You were soooooo lucky, Sarah,' Salvar exclaims with a disbelieving smile, taking his eyes momentarily off the television to look at me, and pressing his hands together in front of his chest, as if to represent the right time and the right place converging. None of the family have seen an eruption in the flesh. I have been blessed with good fortune, they tell me.

From here, 850 kilometres northwest of the activity, for the next week or so the family will revel in the footage being transmitted daily. They will admire it with a fondness, as if the volcano itself were a family member – perhaps a newborn – making a spectacular achievement. That television set will be a hearth, even more so than usual: a window onto the quintessential fire.

Over the next few days, the television will show us the crowds of tourists arriving, the nation's delight in something happening here to offset the bad press surrounding Iceland's part in the financial crisis. I will learn some new words: I will hear of the chocolate bar called *Hraun* ('lava') and all the fizzy drinks, also referred to as *gos* ('eruption'), being discounted nationwide in celebration. We will hear of some Icelandic teenagers attempting to walk on the lava and being surprised when their soles melted – blaming the quality of the shoes rather than their own stupidity.

*   *   *

Three weeks later, on 14 April, the eruption on Fimmvörðuháls petered out. I found out in the departure terminal of Keflavík International Airport. I was buying some duty-free Icelandic music, about to leave for England. By then I was used to asking anyone and everyone the latest on Fimmvörðuháls, in the way that both the British and the Icelanders talk about the weather – though it was implicit that this was *much* more interesting.

'Any news with Fimmvörðuháls?' I asked the shop assistant, handing over the last of my króna.

'Oh, it went out this morning. Do you have your boarding pass?'

'This morning? Amazing. It's been erupting for almost the exact length of my stay.'

'OK. But now there's another one starting. Receipt?'

'No thanks. *Another* one?'

'Yup. Looks like Fimmvörðuháls triggered this one. They say it could be *much* bigger. You might see it from the plane. There's an ash cloud rising.'

He handed me back my boarding pass. 'You're going to Britain? Sit on the left if you can.'

This other one was Eyjafjallajökull, the volcano that closed the skies and that nobody could pronounce. It was named in parodies, descending eventually to E16: a word of sixteen letters beginning with E. It is the volcano that everyone remembers because with it came the realization that a natural event could bring the life that we take for granted to a screeching halt, and that nobody could ultimately be blamed. It is the volcano that allowed us to see what the sky might once have looked like before it too became busy; the loom of global air transport out of order for a while, the threads of contrails left unwoven. If they had known to break it down into its parts: *eyja – fjalla – jökull* ('island – mountain – glacier') they might not have found it so incomprehensible.

As I landed back in Manchester and switched on my phone at the luggage carousel, a text message came in from Bjarni:

14.04.10 13:13

Eyjafjallajökull is erupting.
2km long crack and the glacier
is melting. 4km high smoke cloud.
All my love to you xxxxxxxx

It turned out mine had been among the last international flights allowed to leave or land in Iceland for some time. Back in England the news reports featured passengers stranded at airports and departure display boards growing progressively redder with cancelled flights. People grew increasingly frustrated that their plans could be forced to change in such a way. The BBC reported that, *'For the first time in British aviation history, all flights into and out of the UK have been cancelled.'* Meanwhile, Bjarni sent me links to the Icelandic media which had responded with characteristic measure to the potential emergency situation. Before the eruption had even become visible, the Department of Civil Protection and Emergency Management had evacuated all areas in the immediate vicinity and Red Cross Mass Care Centres had been set up across the region. Most excitingly of all, once the eruption was in full flow, video footage of shockwaves rippling through the ash cloud had been captured for the first time and Bjarni shared them with me shortly after they were broadcast. I imagined him and his family sitting around the television, watching this in collective delight. There would be no talk in Iceland of all the things one could not do. All there was to do was minimize the damage and pull together. I was sure then who I wanted to live among. When this film was done, I would move to Iceland.

Flytja – To Move

October 2010

Autumn is well under way. It is almost winter.

During our Easter visit, we had spent a little time looking into options for houses to rent, with no luck – but we had time. I would not be able to move until the autumn anyway. Bjarni had stayed on in Iceland, but he could stay with his parents in the interim. My summer was spent in England shooting footage for a film commission. He called me one May day and said, 'I've bought a house.' This is not how I expected to become a homeowner. Surely there are years of saving, some missed opportunities, *much* discussion, I thought. Not in this family. It was called Bogguhús – Bogga's house – after the former inhabitant. Bjarni's mother was going to buy it 'as a project' because her nickname was Bogga and she liked the serendipity. She had planned to rent it to us, but Bjarni decided we could do more with it if we owned it ourselves. It went to auction. His mother withdrew her offer. Bjarni's ridiculously low offer was the only other.

Now my commitments in England are wrapped up, my belongings are on a ship headed north, and I am here ahead of them. Iceland:

home for the foreseeable. Me, here, now, to be with Bjarni, *is* my only commitment.

I have timed my arrival into Keflavík airport to coincide with a road trip south that Bjarni and his parents are currently embarked upon. Joining them, I can wend my way north to the house that is to become our home slowly, feeling into every bend and incline. By the time we arrive, I want to feel as if I have journeyed, transitioned; somehow earned this life.

It is good to see them all, and beyond exciting to think I am doing this thing called Life with Bjarni. I embrace him, long and deep; bury myself in the smell of his neck. The shape of our connection is unfolding with such grace, and I feel as if the craft of our life together is gliding across a still sea. What is the likelihood of us, two people from such different backgrounds, resonating so deeply that we fully trust this sea to carry us? It feels as if our story is already written, and all we must do is travel it. Should I perhaps feel more cautious? Still, it is a gift to have a wide-open heart, and an even greater gift to have two, open to each other. A heart reaches far beyond itself. People around us are drawn to the purity of our love. 'I want a love like yours,' Bjarni's sister confided at a friend's party last Christmas, as I painted Bjarni's fingernails gold.

I see Gyða and Haukur over his shoulder, standing at a discreet distance, letting us encounter one another again after two months apart, and smile. I feel part of a clan; part of a family who are woven into the land they stand on, and who can trace their ancestors back to the time of settlement. I know this land is not my own – I do not even really know what that means – but it is an inspiration to witness their seamlessness with it. It is something I long for, but which will always evade me by virtue of my rootlessness, my international upbringing. But I can observe and participate in *their* belonging, learn from it and reinvent its gestures when creating the shape of my own life.

Before we head north we shall go southeast. Bjarni and his parents are en route to Gíslholt in the flatlands, the birthplace of Bjarni's mother. They scoop me up at the airport in their red campervan Kroppinbakkur – The Hunchback – so named because of the domed skylight Haukur has added, 'acquired', as most of his materials are, from somewhere or other, in exchange for something or other. Hitched onto the back, there is a toolkit inside an old milk churn, painted by Salvar with a scene of a highland tarn. In the car park of the modern glass and steel airport, we make a colourful counterpoint to the flashy four-wheel drives in shades of black and silver. We are clearly not Reykvíkingar – people from Reykjavík.

I slide my suitcase under the double bed in the back and Bjarni and I stow away in the bed, tucked under a woollen blanket Gyða has knitted. I am glad of the opportunity to be horizontal: packing up to start a new life is exhausting. We have a lot of cuddling to catch up on too, and this feels like a lovely way to do it – half-asleep, carried through the landscape, entangled, and free. Haukur drives and Gyða knits, and knits, and knits, as if the world's becoming depends on it. My hands rediscover the undulations of Bjarni's body, which still feel new to me after each time apart. Meanwhile, the wheels of the van turn under us, remembering the mounds and curves of this journey they have made many, many times.

At Gíslholt, since my visit last summer, Gyða's brother, Sveinn, and their mother, Amma Sigga, have been doing what they always do. Sveinn attending to the annual cycle of his flock of sheep: gathering, slaughtering, tupping, lambing, grazing, making hay, gathering and slaughtering. And in between that, tinkering with the Fjallafang bus fleet, readying them for their summer in the mountains; running his lake fishing operation there; then bringing the buses home for the winter. Amma has been collecting clothes for the Women's Institute, saving things others are throwing out for a time her family will surely need them, knitting, making earrings, entertaining her 'boyfriend' and being matriarch. We are here to help Sveinn with the butchering of his slaughtered sheep: readying the meat that will fill his chest freezer and his family's bellies.

After sticking our heads into Amma's kitchen to greet her, we walk straight to the outbuilding where the butchering team will be, past the hens peering at us through the window of their henhouse, into the room with the mink tails hung up on a line. Sveinn is there with his sons, Einar and Jóhann, and his sister, Helga, and her husband and children. Finally, I meet Bjarni's cousin Hekla, named after the volcano we can see from here. With us, it makes a team of eleven, and this is only a small fraction of Amma's genetic empire.

Everyone is wearing aprons, smeared with blood: there is a production line in full swing. Some are preparing lamb shoulder, leg of lamb and lamb chops; others work the smaller strips of flesh into diced meat, or *hakk* ('mince'). The mincing machines are clamped to the work surface: small strips of meat are fed in from the top, a handle is turned, and pink worms of mutton extrude from the bottom into a tub, from which handfuls are scooped into food bags, ready for freezing. The efforts of this gathering will keep an extended family in sheep meat for a year. Over the cleavers and chopping boards, the siblings and the cousins exchange news and stories, and I try to make a good impression.

We break for dinner. Sveinn has a leg of lamb roasting in the oven, fresh from this year's slaughter. Amma invites me in to rummage through the bags of donated clothes for the Women's Institute, and the rest of the team make their way to Sveinn's house next door. When I join them, the television is on and loud. Einar and Jóhann punch each other on the sofa and don't really watch it. Everyone else is in the kitchen with Sveinn, except Bjarni. I hear him laugh and find him in the conservatory in a reclining chair, reading an enormous book.

'Hey, Bjarni. What are you doing?' I ask, clutching a newly acquired coat and felted woollen bag from Amma.

'Reading the phone book.'

This is a first. 'Er… why?'

'There's a *great* cartoon in it.'

He shows me, and sure enough in the corner of each page of the Icelandic phonebook, which contains the names of nearly all of the 320,000 inhabitants, there is a frame of a comic strip which runs through its entirety. Bjarni tells me it is by Hugleikur

Dagsson, an artist loved for his twisted and subversive takes on contemporary society.

'He was commissioned by the phone company,' Bjarni continues.

I wish I could understand the cartoon. It's clearly hilarious. I am excited that two years since the country's bankruptcy it can still afford to make life fun, while other places go for austerity. This cartoon's presence in such a ubiquitous and democratic object as a phonebook not only makes it look as if Icelandic companies support artists, but that they acknowledge and validate their raison d'être. I am already proud to call myself a resident of this country.

Almost every household in Iceland will have one of these tomes. And almost every person is listed – by region, in alphabetical order of their first name rather than their surname because family names do not exist. You are the son or daughter of your mother or father. Most people use their father's name, but others choose to use their mother's, or both. My Bjarni, son of Haukur and Gyða, could have been Bjarni Hauksson or Gyðuson, and his sister, Súla Hauksdóttir or Gyðudóttir. As it was, they were both the children of their father. There is naturally some repetition in the phonebook, and where it occurs within the same region, professions are listed to help with identification. I would later read about this gateway to the populace:

The first phone book was printed in Iceland in 1905. It was 13 pages long, and contained 165 phone numbers in all.

Now in 2010, 320,000 listed phone owners might share in the same joke. One day I might even be one of them.

We are called to the kitchen for dinner and tuck into a feast of the most delicious roast lamb. I am glad to be able to understand some of the conversation at dinner, two years since meeting Bjarni. He has been a good teacher. I cannot contribute much but I can participate; fragments of sentences catching onto me like burrs to a woollen jumper. I hope that, now I have committed to this place, the words in me will slot into place; that I can find a way to be myself, here, in this language. Finally, sated and tired, we head to bed. There are enough rooms and corners and pillows to accommodate all of us, of course.

We continue the butchering until Sunday afternoon, and are 'paid' for our help with various iterations of meat to take with us. The process all feels quite normal to me now but it doesn't get any less thrilling, this deal: walking away with food that has been overseen from inception to completion by the people standing around me; becoming part of this web by lending my inexperienced hands. Every time we sit down to eat it, a storyline will be traced back to this moment, and back, and back, just as it was when I first helped with the slaughter up north on Bjarni's aunty's farm.

It is time to leave; time to go and meet this new home of mine, to begin my new beginning. Amma gives us a piece of ancient but still-functional machinery she has been keeping in her basement. 'It's an electric heater for the water in our new house,' Bjarni says, loading it into Kroppinbakkur with his father. 'Pabbi will install it in our bathroom.' With these people everything is provided for, and money is never part of the conversation. I shall be sent off from Bjarni's extended family with food they have reared and something that will keep me warm, driven by his parents to a house they have readied for us to live in.

We shall not see Amma again until Christmas, when she will come north. Sveinn tends not to take holidays, or to travel much outside of his empire: the region around this farm (sheep) and the nearby highlands (fish). He has not been north in a long while, apparently, despite having four siblings up there. A few years ago, he drove around the whole country in twenty-four hours. It was a sponsored non-stop journey to raise funds for the construction of a swimming pool at his sons' local school. He and a friend alternated driving, sleeping, eating a huge tub of *skyr* and pissing in a bucket without ever stopping the car. 'Well, only once, to take a shit,' Sveinn corrected himself. The pool is now built, but Sveinn has not taken a long car journey since. Bjarni and I will probably not see him for a while. We pile the meat and ourselves into Kroppinbakkur, Bjarni and I stowing away into the bed again.

Now, on this, the last day of October, we retrace our tracks to Reykjavík, then north, and north, and north, headed for our new home. I think back to the first time I made this journey, just before Christmas in 2008 – totally in the dark, in every sense. As we journey, I realize the route is becoming familiar. I am able to gauge the journey's progression by certain landmarks which are exactly that: marks in the land. A perfectly straight ravine. A conspicuous campus of concrete buildings in the middle of nowhere called Bifröst, after the Norse mythological rainbow bridge that stretches between Midgarð (middle realm, our Earth) and Ásgarður (realm of the gods, who were known collectively as the Æsir). 'A training ground for capitalists' – as Bjarni calls the postgraduate university specializing in law, politics, business management and entrepreneurship. The stench of seawater trapped behind the causeway at Gilsfjörður – built without due consideration for the tide's breathing – which penetrates the campervan. Tungustapi – a hill said to be an elf church; and finally up and over Steingrímsfjarðarheiði – a pass which is the portal into the Westfjords, Haukur's territory. Occasionally, Gyða and Haukur call out over the engine noise to draw our attention to something: aunty Yrsa's farm, the summerhouse, the seals at the headland. Finally we spy the bright lights of Ísafjörður. It is late.

'You can just stay with us tonight if you like,' Gyða calls to us in the back. 'There's not much at your house... just a mattress, some pans, couple of chairs... like this.'

'Also breakfast materials in the fridge,' Bjarni reassures me from the pillow, blinking his eyes in his endearing way, like a cat, pleased with himself for having thought this far ahead. We prop ourselves up on our elbows now, not wanting to miss this moment – the prelude to homecoming.

I don't care that the house is almost empty. It is our home now and we have everything we need. Bjarni and I agree we want to sleep in it tonight; to arrive. So Haukur continues along the road in the darkening evening, left into the village, left up our drive and stops at the bottom of the front steps. The engine hushes at last.

The back doors of Kroppinbakkur open onto a world made of blue, and we are delivered. I can hardly believe this is where I live. A cobalt fjord held by indigo mountains: my new neighbours; my new view. Bjarni wraps me in the blanket from the campervan and carries my suitcase up the concrete steps to the blood-red front door. Before me, I see these new walls of mine up close for the first time: the corrugated-iron cladding facing off the salt evening air, its white paint peeling in the breeze. The decorative red window trims, which hint at the craftsmanship in this house, staring wide-eyed onto the fjord as they have done since 1902.

Krummi – Raven
(familiar name)

Late October 2010

I am in my kitchen. My first breakfast in this, my own, house: bacon and fried eggs. '*Beikon*', '*Egg*', it says on their packets. Learning Icelandic should be a doddle. Outside the sky is brooding. The snow has not yet come to stay, not enough to settle and reflect, so the shortening daylight is absorbed into the dying grasses. All the images that my eyes have drunk to get here, all the miles that my body has felt under it, and the fact of being in my love's arms at last: sleep came deep. This morning I am waking up to a new life. I haven't quite caught up with what that means.

Tap tap tap.

There is a tapping sound on the roof. It is one of various sounds the house makes. It is like a chatter of it getting to know me, as I make my acquaintance with it. I will come to know these sounds well. Perhaps they will collaborate to create a soundscape that describes Home.

I cut the deep yellow yolk. It spills out onto my toast. I observe the changing light; imagine what colour the walls would like to be.

They do not wish to be grey-white gloss anymore, or perhaps that is *my* wish. Soon everything outside the window will be grey-white. I know this, and I know that it will swallow me whole if I do not keep it out of my interior.

Tap tap tap.

I run my finger along the wallpaper beside my chair. I feel ridges underneath. Old houses like this were panelled in wood. I'm excited that this is likely what my finger detects. A wooden house in a place with no trees. A flat pack house from Norway, erected in 1902. Is there a heavy scent of pine that has been waiting for decades to breathe, trapped under the layers of wallpaper?

The radio burbles – the newsreader sounds refreshingly unperturbed. Not light-hearted, not overly serious, but matter of fact. I wonder if she is secure in a belief that most of what she is reading out will not directly affect her, or us. We are at the edge of the world. Or at the centre of everything, depending on who is speaking.

Tap tap tap. And a scratch of claws on the corrugated-iron roof. I wonder what creature it is.

Bogguhús: 'Bogga's house'. Bogga died a few years ago, in her nineties, after spending her final years in a care home. Before that she lived in this house for *seventy* years. For someone who has never lived longer than two years in any one place, this fact is so profound that I cannot imagine the house ever taking on a new name. She is part of it all. She is it and it is her. Up in the loft I have discovered an indoor washing line with her wooden pegs still on it. I imagine her, well into her eighties, climbing up the steep ladder on a rainy day, a basket of damp laundry resting on her hip, when she was told she could not do this anymore.

Bogga had spent her whole married life, and beyond, climbing up and down that ladder, moving across these floors, turning these door handles. It was her husband's father who had erected this house, fresh off the ship from Norway. As a married couple, they lived in it together with him and had only one daughter – unusual in this prolific nation of settlers. Bogga outlived all of them.

The primrose-yellow kitchen units and faux-marble formica tops are sturdy and have been well looked after since their installation in the 1950s. In England, this might be a highly desirable 'vintage' kitchen. Here, it is just unchanged. I imagine the preparation of family meals, the arrival of Bogga's baby, the young school-age girl running out of the door to the local primary school, which is now closed. I dare to imagine having my own children here, though I feel I must find a way for this place and this house to also become 'mine', on my own terms, before it can become 'ours'. I think I will keep the yellow. It sings of Bogga.

Tap tap tap.

I finish breakfast and go to the room which will be my study. It is at the front of the house, adjacent to the kitchen and looks out onto the fjord and mountains beyond. Every so often a bright red fishing boat courses slowly across the blue-grey vista. Just in front of the window, an old man walks past, as if it is his own garden. He is broad and tall, and stooped slightly forward as if towards his destiny. He wears a grey anorak, and polyester trousers with a crease down the front. The skin on his face is almost translucent under his flat cap.

'Errr... Bjarni,' I call. 'There's an old man in our garden.'

The man makes his way over to a rock by the perimeter fence and tips something onto it. Bjarni comes to look.

'Ah that's Ólafur. He's our neighbour. We have a lot to thank him for, actually.'

'Oh yes. How come?'

'He looked after this house for the eight years it sat empty. Kept the elements from getting the better of it. He was Bogga's son-in-law.'

'Aha.'

Bjarni has been working on the house for a few months getting it ready to live in and has got to know a potted version of the house's history in the process. I begin to sense how interconnected this community is, and how much people are rooted in it. If Ólafur is our neighbour, and was married to Bogga's daughter, that would mean the daughter did not move more than 50 metres in her whole life.

'Would you like to meet him?' Bjarni asks, swinging open the door to catch him on his way back. '*Sæll og blessaður. Hvað segir þú?* This is my girlfriend, Sarah.'

'*Blessuð og sæl,*' he greets both of us, raising one enormous hand. 'All moved in?'

'Getting there. Sarah's waiting for her boxes to arrive.'

After the obviously deducible first bit, I have no idea what they are saying and stand there, impotent. Bjarni does not translate while he speaks, and I have begun to understand why. It breaks the flow of an already subtle dance of words and silences.

Ólafur says something and points to the rock by the fence.

'What is he saying?' I ask Bjarni.

'He says he has left some food for Krummi.'

'Who's Krummi?'

'The raven… Well, it's a sort of nickname for *all* ravens. Like a fond name. Apparently Bogga used to feed him every day.'

A 'fond name'. This makes me smile. What little I know of ravens is my own cultural programming that associates them with death and bad omens. This suddenly seems lazy; lacking in curiosity about a more complex story. I've never been in a situation to spend time with them, to have my own feelings about them. The idea that a whole people could be fond of these birds, enough to have a nickname held in common, is inspiring.

Ólafur interjects, waving a finger in warm warning.

Bjarni translates: 'He says, if you forget, Krummi will come and tap on the roof to remind you.'

Ólafur laughs and curls his index finger. '*Tap tap tap.*'

I feel privileged that Krummi will be a neighbour who comes for a meal every day; that I will get to spend more time with this winged mystery.

After a long and comfortable silence between them, Ólafur turns to face the other direction and begins speaking again, gesturing towards the flagpole we have at the front of the house, as do many other households. I have never been a flag-flyer and I am slightly embarrassed that he has decided to raise ours. Is it in fact 'ours'? It is then that I notice it is at half-mast.

The raven *krunks* and flies down from the roof, his dark glossy sheen catching the light like an oil patch across the breadth of his nearly 1-metre wingspan. His primary feathers are dark splayed fingers playing the sky like a piano. His wings squeak the air as he alights on the rock, where Ólafur has left a pile of meaty bones. He is huge. His thick black bill rifles through the spoils, tugs sideways at sinews. This is the first time I have ever been close enough to a raven to watch the breeze tousle the tiny feathers where the bill joins his head, one black eye on us: kind, curious, irreverent.

'Somebody's died,' Bjarni says.

'Anyone you know?' I ask.

'Not sure. Ólafur says it's a couple. Apparently, they were on holiday in Turkey with their baby and had a car crash. Only the baby survived.'

I am sobered by this news. The untimely end of a new life as three. A child who will grow up never knowing their parents. Bjarni and Ólafur stand in silence, looking out to sea. There is no rush to find out who it is. The news will arrive.

It arrives the following day through Bjarni's mother. Surprisingly, I find out that *I* know the couple. Guðrún, a nature warden who worked with us during our summer in the mountains, and her man Jón. We met up with them a few months ago in Newcastle where she was studying, heavily pregnant, and she told me she was planning to move back up to Ísafjörður. When I had unpacked my boxes, I was going to call her for coffee.

I think of this poor infant, who I had stood beside as it floated in the sea of Guðrún's womb, now out in the world but suddenly bereft of the smells and sounds of its mother and father; gone so soon I did not even get the chance to be introduced, or to find out if this new life was a girl or a boy. It is brutal. They seemed such an invincible pair. Selfishly, I think of them already as two friends I won't have here.

And yet, standing here looking at this sea and these mountains, it is all so unbelievable. My sense of suspended grief is acute because, this same week, I have heard that a friend in England has taken his life. I cannot seem to process this news at all from here. I am not, as our circle of friends are, seeing those familiar rooms and streets without him in them, or hearing the absence of his infectious laugh at the pub. I almost believe that if I went back to England he would also appear. I cannot decide whether I am glad I'm not there, or whether I'd like to be with our friends, sobbing. I am not yet thirty and my friends are dying.

For now, the jagged shape of my grief feels coated and smoothed by this beauty like a pearl: very much present, given space, but held within a substance made of eons.

Krummi hops from foot to foot, pulling meat off the bones in a perfect black silhouette.

Bogguhús

Late October 2010

I remember the texts I received from Bjarni throughout the summer,
informing me of the progress he and his parents were making on the
house; snapshots of this place in another light.

> **30.07.10 18:54**
>
> Lying on top of Bogguhús phase one
> of chimney repair done. Lovely weather,
> lovely view, love you.

And here I am, seeing it for the first time as our home, made habitable
by their efforts. It is exciting to be with a man who knows how to
fix a house, or at least has parents who know. The chimney has been
mended and cleared so we can use the wood burner – a rarity in this
treeless land. We will have an endless supply of offcuts from Haukur's
joinery workshop to fuel the fire. New drainage has been put in around
the foundations. The ancient electrics have been made functional.

The front of the house faces the sea and mountains beyond. It
looks towards Snæfjallaströnd ('beach of the snow mountains'),

and beyond that to Iceland's northernmost uninhabited wilderness, Hornstrandir. Bjarni and I stand on the front step. The view from the front door is the one my mind conjured at the utterance of the words *The North*, before I found myself in it: a blue light, an expanse of sea caressed by rock, an openness, a clarity of air that brings distances closer and makes everything outside of this North dissolve.

Better still, Bjarni tells me, this new view of ours is protected. As a wooden kit-house imported from Norway and erected at the turn of the twentieth century, it counts as old, and the house has been assigned a minor grade of 'listed'. One stipulation is that nothing should be built in front of it. A dirt driveway unfolds from the flight of concrete steps at the front, through the grass and beyond the fence to the main street. But my attention is drawn back again and again to the sea and the mountains beyond; to the changing light; to this view that is too enormous to be called 'a view'. It is my new reality.

The front door is double. The inner one is more decorative, although sturdy and tight-fitting, with two panes of triple-glazed glass. The outer one is thicker and more functional. It is currently hooked to the stair rail of the front steps, so it isn't ripped off should a gust of strong wind come. In a few weeks I am sure we shall have to keep it mostly closed as the weather sets in. I come down the steps to ground level to explore the immediate nearby. The house stands alone in a field, encircled at the front and on one side by a low fence, and on another side by a small street at the top of a grassy bank. Ours is one of a cluster of about fifty houses which make up the village of Hnífsdalur, the oldest houses like ours lining the main street.

Though the house is rectangular and has four walls, only two sides have windows: front and back. I wonder if this is to do with prevailing winds or insulation. The windows are large at least – triple-glazed on the upper floor and single-glazed below. The basement is concrete, like the front steps.

By the back porch there is a large rock with a rope tied to it, which my eyes follow up to the new corrugated-iron roof, glinting under a white sky. It appears to be holding the roof down. It makes me wonder how strong the winds will get. The walls of the upper floor are clad in corrugated iron, old and quite rusty, except for the back façade, which is concrete scribbled with a tracery of cracks.

'That'll need replacing at some point,' Bjarni comments, unfazed. 'It's from the time when concrete houses suddenly became the thing to have.' He casts a glance over to the concrete bungalows that make up much of the village – the subsequent additions behind the main street. 'Bogga's family tried a "conversion" – smeared concrete *over* the iron.' He shakes his head, laughing.

Out the back, beyond the rusting washing line, a field of dying grass carpets the way to a wooden sheephouse with a corrugated-iron roof. Sheep have not lived here for many years. This field is not ours and it is not protected, but it is my view from the kitchen, bedroom and bathroom. I will have two views: one 'wild' and one 'pastoral/bungalow'. The field is about an acre. Bjarni tells me the word 'acre' comes from the Old Norse *akur* which means 'field'. Before the financial crisis, the town council planned to build four houses on this patch of land, which would have cut off our house from the sheephouse that once belonged to it, like a mother from its child. I am glad of the stalling of plans.

Behind the sheephouse, the miscellany of other house styles and colours that make up this village extends back into the glacial valley. But what I notice most are the valley's steep sides, as if the houses are toys that have slid to the bottom of a sack; and the huge boulder up there that looks as if it could topple at any moment and plough into our house. Bjarni tells me it is Hádegisteinn ('midday-stone'), said to be a cork on an eternal supply of mythical ale trapped inside the mountain, accessible to the one who manages to move the rock. Somehow that makes it easier to live with.

*   *   *

It takes a week for my boxes to arrive because of an administrative hitch in Reykjavík. One morning, I look out of the living room window to see an Eimskip lorry reversing carefully up the drive. A short man with a boyish face and glasses jumps out of the cab.

'Ah, it's my cousin,' Bjarni smiles, heading for the door.

'Who *isn't* his cousin?' I think to myself.

Cousin Pétur is invited in for coffee and chat. I marvel at what constitutes 'work' in this place. *This guy is on duty!* says the voice in my head, excited and bemused. Being a cousin, he also helps unload all the boxes – not officially part of the service but part of being family. I suppose there would be no Icelandic boss that argued with that principle. We stack the boxes into one room: layered, labelled cubes of black. In England, I wrapped them carefully in bin liners, naively imagining that they would be at sea for days, licked with spray, or left at ferry ports. These things are precious to me: the collected contents of a home I have not had until now. A lifetime of living and travelling in different countries and my appreciation for handmade objects has generated an ecology of storied stuff. It has spent years secreted in various homes, attics and garages across England, while I lived in house-shares too small for it all. This is the first time I have ever had all of my possessions in one place. This fact hits me like a wave.

There is a lot to unpack. It is not furniture, but things: a Mexican hand-painted ceramic sink bought from a centenarian's yard sale in Taos when I went to be the ring bearer at a friend's wedding; an Ethiopian talismanic scroll from when I did some research there after finishing university. All things of beauty associated with cherished journeys and dear people, which feel more important to hold onto with each passing year, as the world becomes homogenized and the vernacular is displaced by the mass-produced. As I've grown older, with more miles under my feet and more objects in my collection, each move has become more burdensome. I am relieved that this may be my last; delighted to arrange these things, to let them find their places.

This house just below the Arctic Circle makes a surprisingly fitting *Wunderkammer* for ornaments, utensils, hangings and rugs from India, Kenya, Morocco; from flea markets and car boots in Toulouse and London. In this place, with these objects out of storage, all my journeys are allowed to speak again – to me and to each other. They are reference points, now visible to me at once.

When we visited his birthplace last Christmas, Bjarni's father told me – Bjarni patiently translating – that, in the *gamla daga* ('old days'), farmers, who were also fishermen, had names for prominent features in the landscape, down to individual outcrops of rock. They knew their terrain intimately. This way they could, and still can, communicate the exact location of their sheep – especially useful during gathering time as they walk along the steep cliffs and over heaths. When at sea as fishermen, they would triangulate these features to make a mental map of good fishing grounds, often working them into a poem, the better to learn and remember them. These fishing grounds are called *mið*.

Mið can also be the sight on a rifle. *Taka mið af einhverju* ('to take the "*mið*" of something') is to use something as a frame of reference. And the related verb, *miða*, is found in *að miða eitthvað við eitthvað*, to compare something to something. Or *miða að einhverju*, to aim for something.

With my things and this house, in this craft of our love, I feel as if I may be able to triangulate myself at last, to help me navigate this next stretch: Where am I? What is here? Where might I be heading? I am locating my own *mið*, to thrive on this unknown sea. But my reference points are so many more than three. This may take a long time.

The Frozen Bell

4 April 2011

I awake to the feeling that something is different. My waking has more energy to it: it does not feel like swimming upstream in treacle as it has done. After months of darkness and dim, my eyes open onto a golden light washing into my interior world, generous beyond measure. The pine-panelled walls are honey, the cane chair is freshly cut straw. The paintings on my walls sing, and the shadows have been chased out of the room. I prop myself up on my elbow in awe of the spectacle that is my backlit white curtain, the ornaments on the windowsill forming an impromptu shadow puppet theatre. I look at my clock: 8 a.m. In my former life – in England or Kenya – this would have been a perfectly normal, even leisurely, time to wake up. But today it feels early, epic, right. Finally, the planet and the sun have aligned with my idea of 'normal'. The sun has moved to the east, around the mountain. I get up and look at the valley's new palette from the kitchen window. Every red and yellow thing embraces the light as if reunited with a soulmate. My dazzling red wool socks on the washing line are outrageously beautiful and full of hope. I pad around all the upstairs rooms in this new light – living room, studio,

127

bedroom and kitchen – and photograph them like a child who I know will grow up all too quickly.

I remember the morning in mid-February when my body had told me a similar, subtler message that woke me at about 10 a.m. It was not as obvious at first. Going to make a cup of tea, I quickly noticed that the faded red windowsill of my first-floor kitchen glowed with a yellow light. I gasped. Craning my neck over the worktop, I saw that one side of the back porch was also glowing. All around these two locations – these pinpricks of possibility – the landscape clung to the greyscale fug that had characterized the previous few months. Sure enough, a tentative finger of sunlight, following a very particular path and angle, was shining into my steep-sided valley for the first time since late December. Today, the whole hand has reached into the front of the house and grasped me.

In the nearby town of Ísafjörður, sprawling as it does across a spit in a wide fjord, the sun touched the residents again in late January after an absence of only a month or so. There is a street on the west side of the fjord called Sólgata – Sun Street. As well as being the way into town from my village, it acts as a geographical sundial. When the sun casts its first rays upon it, following its annual absence, the town's households celebrate *sólarkaffi* ('sun coffee') by eating pancakes filled with whipped cream and blueberry jam, with coffee. There seems to be a jam-maker in each household whose early September days are filled with preparing and storing the bucket-loads of blueberries, bilberries and crowberries they and their families have gathered from the surrounding mountainsides, which at that time were steeped red and yellow by the bushes' dying leaves. The berries themselves are intense: sweet, blue-black embodiments of the summer's light, which have kept us in vitamins and vitality through the winter. Boiled, strained and sweetened into cordial, boiled for longer, with sugar, into jam, and frozen whole to be eaten with *skyr* and cream.

Bjarni's parents live in Ísafjörður. Gyða invited us round for pancakes the day the sun returned to them, and I wondered how long it would be before we were making our own. Hnífsdalur, the name both of the valley where our village lies, and of the village itself, means 'Valley of the Knife'. Although it is only 4 kilometres away from Ísafjörður, it is the other side of the 'Knife': a steep mountain topped by a sharp-edged arête. In this northern fortress of the Westfjords which, in the winter at least, seems to keep the world and everything I have taken for granted at bay, this mountain feels like the final line of defence. Our house faces northeast and we are cupped in this valley by the mountains to the south, north and west. Our neighbour Ólafur has lived here for sixty years – a hefty share of winters. In January, after Gyða's pancakes, I'd asked Ólafur when the sun would return to us. 'April.' I thought he was teasing me. It turns out he was not. But here we are. At last, Hnífsdalur has been sliced like butter from the darkness.

When I first conceived of moving here, I had believed there would be a brief period of midwinter where the sun wouldn't shine at all, where it would be pitch-black day and night. I was curious about what that would feel like or what it would do to me. Arctic winter was a concept the nature of which I did not yet understand. But when I first conceived of moving here, I had thought of it as an experiment, an adventure. Maybe I'd stay for a year, then see how I felt about this place, and about Bjarni.

Bjarni's impulsive decision to buy us a house had changed all that. Or perhaps it wasn't impulsive, just sensible. The house cost less than a year of rent would have done, even if we could have found somewhere to rent. And the house was available. I am moved by the collective momentum for our togetherness. I am also learning that Bjarni does what appears to be the most straightforward thing at the time. He does not necessarily think through the implications. Perhaps when one operates like that there are no implications; one is dealing only with a continuum of present needs. Admittedly, I have craved a home to call my own for as long as I can remember. So, while my rational mind was shocked and subsequently enthralled to become a homeowner in such a way, my body filled out into the space almost as soon as I arrived. I wanted to get to know its textures and surfaces to see what we might make together. It would be my world and my work, so I threw myself into it. I cannot see a home in which I can do whatever I wish as a temporary arrangement. It is a gift that has come in strange and beautiful packaging.

This house I stand in has involuntarily shifted my perspective on how long this particular adventure may last, and how I approach its daily phenomena. With every challenge – the absence of light being the most significant – I find myself experiencing it not as an abstract point of interest but as something I will have to live with, to make a life among. I cannot observe and retreat to a familiar elsewhere. I have not come here under the auspices of research. I have come for love – for a landscape, and for a man and his family. And now, growing each day, love for a house. This has become my life.

My experience of the light's absence has been less intense, but more protracted, than the total darkness I anticipated. I wish I had it in me to keep a record of the times of sunrise and sunset; there is poetry in such accuracy. But this being my life, I feel it as a whole reality, not a set of data to be recorded and analysed. I know that when I first arrived in October the days were tangibly short, and that up until the winter solstice, every few days they shortened to a degree that in England would have signalled a seasonal shift. I have felt as if I am constantly running to adapt to a new reality. Each day, the darkness has nibbled further into what I consider possible. Underneath all of this, like shifting magma, I am adapting to a new reality of a magnitude much greater than the changing light; a reconfiguration of so many things I thought I knew.

A snow-blanketed worldview has been a constant from early October. Occasionally, it has been warm enough on several consecutive days for the whiteness to recede in patches and reveal the flattened, deadening grass underneath. Soon enough the snow falls again, until it is too deep to concede to earth. In those first few months of winter, as the days shortened quickly, the snow was blinding. Sunglasses were essential for driving. As the sun hit the snow directly from an ever-decreasing angle, the ground glittered. The ice crystals reflected the light in all directions.

They reflected the heat too. One morning I came into my kitchen, like today, to make tea. Some windows were open: the Icelandic way is to have the heating on and the windows open a touch, to keep the air circulating. The roof was thick with snow and the light bounced from the ground through our tall windows into the kitchen. I was hot in my pyjamas. I turned off the heating. I was still too hot. I stripped. I could not comprehend how thick snow could make me so warm, but it is both an insulator and a reflector – one of many paradoxes that are becoming my reality.

One of the first things I did was to paint the walls of the living room and bedroom a shade of ivory white, covering the grey white that they had been. I have not seen enough of the light's behaviour to choose a colour that might have an ongoing conversation with it, in all weathers. So I stuck to a white that had warmth in it. Each daub of new paint drank up any light there was, glowed with it, and threw the layer beneath into shadow. I have noticed Bjarni is reluctant – almost shy – to make changes to the house until I begin. It is striking because he has seemed so at ease in most other contexts: happy to improvise and create from what is around him. But when I think about it, his work to make the house liveable, even the purchase of the house itself, was in fact set in motion by his parents.

This became a problem for me when we were without hot water for several weeks. His reluctance extended to avoiding calling an electrician to fix our thermostat, and he would not let me call him either. 'He doesn't speak English anyway,' was his rationale. I tried to understand why this was so complicated, but he gave me so little to go on. Confusion became frustration and we had our first proper argument. Beneath his taciturnity, Bjarni was like roiling magma. He struggled to access the words which might diffuse the heat.

'This is all new for me too, you know,' he finally confided when we had calmed down. 'You think it's just a big change for you, but it is for me also.'

It's true I had not considered that. Moving from London to a tiny fishing village in the almost-Arctic where I didn't speak the language, the change for me was so massive that anything else paled in comparison. I had considered anything here *his context*. Our house was exactly between the village where he spent his childhood and the town where he spent his adolescence, in spitting distance of both. We saw his parents at least three times a week and he had aunts and uncles all around, one of them 100 metres away. And yet, he considered this a big change. I suppose it was, sharing a new house with me, a girlfriend, who wanted to change things even more. Change was apparently not his strong point. I found it hard to comprehend just how much it was affecting him, as he had seemed so adaptable when we travelled, and when we ran the mountain bus shop together. Not calling the electrician turned out to be a perverse way for him to regain some control. Although I could never get my head around the process, I tried to empathize with the impulse.

As the light began to dwindle, I was eager to quickly obliterate any shades of grey, of which there were many. At the point of last decorating, Bogga must have acquired a large vat of grey ship's paint – thick, gloss and impenetrable – which made it onto every skirting board and halfway up the bathroom wall. Its dullness breathed into every room, and I have retaliated with my colourful possessions.

From early December, the direct light became a rarity. Any light there was, was hosted by the snow; the meagre offering received graciously and shared. On clear days, the sky could still be blue or pink or both; the angle of light was lowering but transcendental. The last smudges of yellow and pink light began to evaporate from the white canvas of my terrain – first in the nearby and then from the distant mountains too. In the bowl of the glacial valley in which our house sits, the shadow slowly crept up the mountainside like a pair of dark diaphanous trousers being lifted to the waist. For a short time, the light still kissed the mountaintops daily and we could remember what it looked like.

My French friend Sophie came to visit in early December. She had just finished her PhD and was curious about how the Arctic winter might overwhelm her over-exercised rational mind. She brought five novels to read in a week, thinking we would be largely housebound, and there would be both the time and motivation for such literary indulgence. One day, in the brief window of daylight, we drove to the supermarket at the bottom of the fjord. Some light still shone on the distant mountains, but we were bathed in shadow. There the seawater mixes with fresh water flowing in from a stream. We saw that the fjord had frozen over at that point, less saline. Dark basalt rocks poked up through the leathery ice layer, which had peeled back from around them, like the eggs of a large boreal bird hatching. The brackish water had frozen quickly in layered stages. It was solid but not thick. We stepped out onto it and broke panes of ice over our heads because it was fun. We skimmed ice fragments across the glassy surface, which continued unhindered for 200 metres and halted in the white distance like full stops on an empty page. Then we turned our gaze downward to the ice layer itself. There, growing either side of cracks in the surface, were delicate bristles of white ice crystals, fine as a toothbrush; bubbles of air trapped within the ice on their way up, each moment flattened and separated into stacks of coins. We were there an hour, maybe two. Sophie did not read five novels that week.

When the sun finally dropped below the horizon, I had no precedent for such a disappearance. I did not feel as much in that moment of knowing as I did in the gradual dawning of the fact that it would not return for a long time. At about the same time that the natural light disappeared, it was replaced by the illumination of Christmas lights around every profile upon which it was possible to hang them – the squares and rectangles of house windows, the masts of boats in the harbour, the wheels and cabs of tractors parked at farms, and the crosses in the graveyards.

'Shall we go see the graveyard?' Bjarni and his sister had suggested, in the run-up to Christmas. I had thought it a strange idea, but was infected by their excitement, and was open to going along with strange ideas. They took me to the Ísafjörður cemetery, the largest in the Westfjords. It could have been 4 p.m. or 10 p.m., one as dark as the other. But as we rounded the top of the fjord, a sea of cross-shaped, flashing, multi-coloured lights unfolded in front of me. The graveyard felt alive and festive; more like a Las Vegas graveyard theme park than an actual place of rest. I was touched at how the dead seemed to be not just remembered but involved in the festivities. It was like nothing I had ever seen. It seemed uncharacteristically bawdy, but I could not explain why.

One Saturday, in the brief window of daylight, Haukur, Gyða, Bjarni and I drove into the *djúp* – in and out of the fjords, past the seals, past the summerhouse, beyond Haukur's birthplace, collecting Aunt Yrsa en route – and on to Mjóifjörður. In the valley, there is an adolescent patch of pine plantation and, for years, the farmer has let Bjarni's family gather Christmas trees from this slope above his farmhouse. This far north, young saplings are planted close together, to shelter one another from the wind. When the trees are more established, they need to be thinned out. These trees in Mjóifjörður had exceeded human height and formed a 'forest'. Wearing fleece-lined overalls, we waded into this dense green world to choose our trees, a Christmas scent unleashed by our bodies brushing past their branches.

Haukur and Gyða sawed down a lush and full-bodied tree and loaded it into the trailer hooked onto their trusty red Iveco. They added a few more for the extended family, Yrsa's, and another straggly one for good measure. Fortuitously, Bjarni and I found one whose branches had grown mostly on one side. A corner-shaped tree for our small living room: perfect.

Next stop was the farmer's smokehouse beside the dirt road. As the day dimmed he met us there with a torch and we entered into a tar darkness. My eyes adjusted slowly and the afternoon blue fjord glowed through the open doorway. The white beam of his headtorch brushed over dozens of blackened joints of lamb hanging from the rafters, leg to leg, shoulder to shoulder. *Hangikjöt* – 'hanging meat': a Christmas speciality. Just as they had chosen their trees, by some combination of aesthetics and feeling, they now chose their lamb legs from the ceiling.

'What does he smoke them with?' I asked Bjarni, as we headed back outside.

'It's meant to be birch, but I think he also uses dodgy things, like fenceposts.'

On the way home, as we rounded the bend into Haukur's home fjord, a road sign signalled a viewpoint with a picnic table. Royal-blue border around a white square containing a stylized black table and pine tree. Haukur pulled in, stopped the van and jumped out. Beside the picnic table he began to dig a narrow hole. By this point, I had stopped asking as many questions as I once had. Suddenly, he was at the back of the trailer, dragging off the straggly tree and dancing it into the slot.

He climbed back into the driver's seat, smirking. 'Always bothered me it didn't look like the sign,' he said.

On New Year's Eve, every village has an enormous bonfire, and fireworks are set off with abandon. In the weeks running up to it, Hnífsdalur village hall was transformed into a firework supermarket, complete with shopping trolleys and cashiers. The fireworks are sold by the Björgunarsveit – the volunteer-led mountain rescue service –

to raise the majority of their funds for the year. In charitable spirit, people support them by spending hundreds of pounds per household on fireworks. Some of the fireworks are named after heroes and villains from the sagas. This winter, two years since the financial crisis exploded, I noticed a few boxes had been rebranded: no longer named Njáll or Eiríkur but 'The Bankers', a sticky label placed over the old name.

By January, that kiss of pink on the mountaintops had disappeared too. I ceased to have a shadow. Everywhere *was* a shadow. And quite unexpectedly, Bjarni went to sea. Although it was cheap, Bjarni had borrowed money to buy the house from his parents, and he is averse to being in debt. When we set up home in October, he had started a 10–5 job as the manager of a friend's magic shop. It suited him: his rotund and bearded figure presided over the jars of herbs and crystals like a wizard, and he was known in the town for his knowledge and courtesy towards customers. Best of all, he was home by 5.10 p.m., which I didn't realize at the time was a luxury. His friend, the shop owner, wanted to keep the shop running through Christmas and the sales, but then close it down. It was one project too many in her catalogue of life projects, and somebody in the east had offered to buy all the stock.

Come January, Bjarni was out of work. I was occupied editing the documentary I had shot in England during the summer, and could support myself, and us, for a while off the proceeds. He went to buy milk one evening and a trawler captain had been standing next to him in the queue at the supermarket. He knew Bjarni was from a good family. In the Westfjords, this is enough of a basis for offering someone work, it seems, regardless of experience or qualifications.

'Have you got a job, Bjarni?'

'No.' Bjarni always answers questions directly, and literally.

'Are you looking for one?'

'Yes.'

Although I tried to temper my objections with an open mind, the anthropologist in me saying, 'This is part of Icelandic life. Stay curious,' dread loomed beside my heart. This is not what I came for. I came to live with him, not without him.

Since joining the trawler crew, Bjarni has been allowed to come home irregularly, for a few days – or a few hours – at a time, mostly when the weather is too bad to fish. When he is home, I feel I have to pack all of life into those moments – getting him to help with things I could not manage, sharing stories I have not been able to tell – then grow increasingly anxious that he is about to leave again. My memories of those moments feel more intense than the long unravelling hours of the winter that I have faced daily. They are like looking at holiday photos weeks after returning to normal life. But being mostly alone with this winter has allowed me to face this place as I might have faced him, had he been here. To encounter the joys and struggles of a new relationship with unfamiliar terrain. I have found love in unexpected places.

During the hardest period in January and February, the dawn starts at 11 a.m. and the day is over by 3 p.m. In between, the world is washed over by a diffuse grey light, like an underexposed black and white photograph. That time and that colour has merged into the present moment, with infinitesimal increases in energy drip-feeding into me. Mostly, I am sluggish and feel abandoned by civilization. I am just surviving. In this time of shadowed sub-zero, there has been nothing to do but turn inwards. At least it is dry and often still, as if we are suspended in the long moment between the year's inhale and exhale. On these still days, people hang laundry outside on the line. I follow suit and bring in jeans and shirts that are flat and stiff as a cardboard cut-out.

What I know is that it has felt like a thick fog through which I have waded. Some days it has been hard to climb the stairs, or to remember what my ideas were. I have clung to a surety that I do have some ideas dwelling still, inert, inside of me. The feeling of winter has been so physical. I have found my mind to be a muscle that I need to manage my expectations of, given the conditions. I have been attending a yoga class since January – which has saved me – rationalizing that a physical imposition can be balanced out by a physical response. In doing so, I have learned that the words for 'spirit' (*andi*) and 'to breathe' (*anda*) have the same root in Icelandic. *Beygja* – bend. *Djúpt* – deeply. *Halda* – hold.

Each day, in the narrow window of diffuse daylight, I walk the valley in all weathers except gales. I hope that by doing this it may slowly start to feel 'mine'; that the valley and I may begin a dialogue of belonging. It has not started yet, but nobody has seemed to be very talkative in winter. The mountains, too, keep their secrets close under their snow blankets. This physical activity has at least kept my mind supple enough to have patience for the unlocking that the return of the light must surely bring.

The disappearance of direct light makes me look not to the horizon, but to the ground beneath my feet. Ice forms fat fingers around blades of grass. Streams freeze, are covered in snow, and occasionally gurgle invisibly underneath it all. The basalt mountains are invaded by ice which prises its fingers deep into their fissures and encrusts their cliffs with icicles sometimes a metre tall.

But it is the minutiae of the ice's artistry that captivates me. On cold days Bjarni's workshop window, single-glazed, is a canvas for a most delicate patterning of ice which Icelanders call *frostrósir* – 'ice-roses'. Crystals form into quills and replicate themselves across the windowpane like a translucent feather bed. In England, I have occasionally seen this on car windscreens. But I have never experienced the wonder of being able to stand with my eyes close to it, the crystals like a glass engraving backlit by a blue that only the Arctic knows.

When the weather is not still, it is fearsome. All garden furniture and trampolines were tied down at the beginning of winter as a matter of course. Our wheelie bin blew into the sea when the bin men neglected to chain it back to the fence. The wood of the house creaks and groans in these storms. I keep telling myself it is a good thing if its wooden structure dances and adapts. *Beygja* – bend. *Djúpt* – deeply. *Halda* – hold. It has been here long enough to know what life may throw at it, though I cannot abate the fear that a large object may blow in through the window. On nights like these, I lie awake, clutching the hem of my duvet and hoping. On days like these, I feel like a trapped animal. I do not even want to venture into the garden, let alone attempt a conversation with the valley. I wonder if I am weak of spirit when, from my window, I see a man walking backwards in a blizzard, his back braced against the wind. But yes, I have found love in unexpected places.

I have witnessed the majesty of *glitský* – nacreous clouds: pearlescent wisps the colour of an illuminated oil patch and the weight of a passing idea, they appear just before sunrise or after sunset. Their height in the lower stratosphere means that they dazzle in the low-angled light, backdropped by the surrounding dim.

At night, a different energy takes hold of me. I am energized by the darkness: it is not heavy. It crackles, and the sky feels infinitely high. On clear nights, when the moon is full, it has seemed as if it is brighter than the day. One night, I sat out on the front step reading by moonlight, just because I could. Often, I am reading a book or working on my film until 2 a.m., knowing I need to ride a wave of energy whenever it comes, all previous schedules abandoned. I will look out of the window or stand at the threshold before bed, breathing the night in. On some nights, the faint green glow of the aurora borealis begins to bloom out of the darkness, pulsing and growing until the only thing to do is put on my coat and boots and head out into the valley. Its curling mantle redefines dimensions of space: smudges out the line between the real and the mythic. To walk alone in the middle of the night with the hushed crunch of my footsteps in a green-lit bowl of snow: that is what I came for. That is what living is for.

There is no growth of vegetation by which to measure the year's progress. The only change that occurred across those long weeks in shadow was that the sun's light, golden, eventually kissed the distant mountains, bringing at last some colour again. But with the light *reaching* me now, the difference between yesterday and today is like the difference between night and day itself. The light has returned to the Westfjords, to the far mountains, to my valley, to my house and to me; and with it, life will begin to awake.

Bjarni will be home today. As always, I do not know for how long. I do not know why he is still going to sea on a trawler when he knows how much I loathe his absence, and when it's not financially necessary, at least for now, to do this job. There must be something to it for him that outweighs its impact on me – something I cannot understand. Today, the weather is still and bright at the same moment that we shall be together. It is a rare constellation of phenology and circumstance, and I am delighted. I can show him what I have been doing with the house, in this new light. We can go for a walk together in the sun; to explore our nearby, to linger. I will see if the mountains have anything to say when he is with me.

*   *   *

We head not up the valley, as I most often do, but towards the shore. That is where the sun is, and where Bjarni enjoys poking around in rock pools. Bjarni decides to take his bicycle and circles around me, chatting happily as I amble from our track onto the street. As soon as I set foot onto the untouched white snow layer of the pavement I see my shadow for the first time in months. I had forgotten that a shadow could exist as a distinct entity. As I walk along the street, I watch it, bemused at this companion who moves like I do, who now seems like a version of me that existed until today – not fully here, but stretched out and deep blue. Finally, it peels away, and I come back into my body.

The cemetery is on the way down to the shore: four turquoise concrete walls enclosing the deceased in right angles. We are stopped in our tracks. At the gate to the cemetery hangs a brass bell, rung when a burial is taking place. The gate is called the *sáluhlið* – the gate of the soul – and the bell tolls from the moment the coffin enters the graveyard until it touches the bottom of the grave. A little way off to the right of the gate is a standpipe for visitors to use, to tend to plants in summer. At a moment that nobody witnessed, this standpipe began to leak. The water leaked through a crack so tiny that a jet was forced in an arc across the gate and landed on the bell. It continued to arc and land and arc and land as the temperature fluctuated around zero. Over days and nights, this arc has frozen and dripped. Now the bell is draped in a jagged skirt of icicles, unmoving and un-chimeable. And an arc that should be a motion, a moment, is held still as a solid object. We stand in silence, awed.

A frozen bell. Like living without your partner, or snow that makes you hot. Something which shouldn't be and yet is. It seems not to fulfil its purpose, but becomes instead something beautiful and unexpected, which only a peculiar constellation of circumstances could have created. This frozen bell is a constellation less anticipated even than our being here, together, as the sun returns.

A Floating House

It is a most unlikely house move. One that only people like you and Haukur would think to do. It is an image of caution thrown to the wind and dreams indulged; what happens next makes a story that will be told for many years to come. I still tell it now, although the orange digits in the bottom right-hand corner of the photograph read 26.7.94.

In the centre, looming large, is a juxtaposition I have never seen, and may never see again: a pitched-roofed corrugated-iron-clad house, flanked on one side by empty red and yellow oil barrels, sitting in the shallows of a bay. Behind it, across the water, a mountain slopes straight up from the sea. Patches of green vegetation cling to the sandy-coloured rock: the slope looks worn like threadbare corduroys. At its top, the mountain becomes a dark-grey basalt terrace, still streaked with the white of last winter's snow. There it meets the grey-white of the clouds overhead, which float across a deep turquoise sky, casting spots of sunlight to dance on the mountain.

In the foreground you walk across the frame, clad in orange overalls, your thick brown hair scraped back in a ponytail ready for action. You are removing a work glove to take up your camera. You smile fully at someone out of frame – perhaps one of the many friends and family who have gathered to participate in this adventure. It is a smile that reveals both your shyness and your pride. You know this is a special moment indeed, and that days like these make you glad to be alive. The sun is shining, and the water is still; so still that the house is reflected perfectly in it, until the mirror fragments into a dark seaweedy shore. You could not have asked for more, and everybody knows it. It is a perfect Arctic summer's day.

At the back corner of the house, black welly-booted and calf-deep in the water, Haukur is clad in matching overalls and is bent over fastening one of the floating oil barrels to the house. Another man, your sister's husband, in blue trousers and a chequered shirt, saunters through the water just behind him, his hands in his pockets as if out for a stroll. His gaze is cast on the back of the house. Perhaps he is judging how many barrels you will need on that side.

Peering out of the decorative upstairs window at the gable end is your twelve-year-old daughter, Súla, squinting into the bright sun with her toothy grin – her head framed by the top window and her body by the bottom. Right beside her, similarly dissected by the window frame, stands her closely aged cousin, Funi, who has already mastered his nonplussed expression so young. Their heads rest on their fingertips, which pinch the window in a gesture of uncertainty and excitement. The top two panes of glass are missing, allowing them to feel the play of the sun's warmth and the cool of the glacial breeze on their faces; to smell the salty sea. They look to the photographer seeking reassurance. Who could it be?

The white corrugated-iron roof is peeling off on the left side, like birch bark, and slightly rusting. At the top of the roof, a ladder emerges out of a hole, on which your niece is standing, confident and carefree, resting her elbow on the ridge. Behind her, sitting at the highest point and looking down towards the sea, is your teenage son. The boy Bjarni who will become a man who will become my husband. He is red-faced and focused. He is torn between enjoying this moment and letting his fear of still water get the better of him. He is as far from it as he can get. He does not know in this moment how much that drowning incident at summer camp will affect him in the future, dunked by his peers until he could barely breathe.

Your children are happy entertaining themselves, and what you are about to do is one of the most inspiring and formative acts of parenting you could hope to offer: to show them, not tell them, that imagination can make the unthinkable happen.

Behind you and behind the fluorescent digits in the bottom right-hand corner, bathed in sunlight yet concealed somehow by shadow, is a boy. He holds his arms behind his back and looks up at the other children. He wants to join them, but he is shy. He is not as close as your children and your sister's children are, born within months of each other. All the children understand that floating a house is a particularly special and fun thing to do. But they do not yet realize how rare in this world is the inspiration and courage required to pull it off.

Soon, when all the barrels are attached, you will all sit on the shore and wait for the tide to rise, to lift the house from the ground so that you may tow it with Arngeir's boat, to the place two fjords from here where your Haukur was born, to the patch of land he has inherited. There, you and your kin will work hard to make it a liveable and beautiful summerhouse. You shall spend many happy summers there, avoiding the world – no, *meeting* the world – listening to the eiders and hiking to the top of the mountain. Tending to your vegetable garden by day and knitting by bright night. Haukur will repair an ever-growing collection of rowing boats, and occasionally chase seals in one of them. In the evening, he will read the old Icelandic stories out loud to whoever will listen. Your extended family will descend from all around the country at the end of August each year to pick the thousands of bilberries, blueberries and crowberries that thrive on that land, which will carry you all through the winter.

One day your son will bring me there, and I will fall in love with him, with this house, this tale and this land, like I have no other. One day over dinner I will ask you, 'Did you never worry it would sink?' You will reply, 'Yes, but wouldn't it also look beautiful at the bottom of the sea?'

Trúlofun – Engagement (*trú* – faith, faithfulness; *lofun* – a vow, a promise)

30 April 2011

My grandmother turns ninety at the end of May.

'I don't want to be ninety,' she told Bjarni and me when we visited her in Kenya a couple of years ago. 'It's too much.'

But life has other plans, and soon it is time to start travelling south, and south, and south, to be with her for her birthday party. This is the first time since moving up here that I will connect present life with past, in one journey. Arctic to Equator: lines of latitude inscribed on a globe, to which storylines pay no heed. Poised at the edge of departure, it feels like an epic journey. My home up here is an unlikely trajectory for my life to have taken. I am sure my parents felt the same when they moved from England to Kenya when I was a child. But they chose that path. I feel like mine chose me.

It feels strange to leave *now*, crossing paths with birds migrating northwards. Bjarni's winter fishing tours are over so he will be home much more, which I have longed for. The light has recently returned and I feel creative, generative – like my ideas have started to thaw and

I need to catch their drips into some container before they evaporate or seep underground. As tough as the winter was, it bedded me in, and made Elsewhere dissolve. I want to be around to witness this birth of life. I have vegetable seedlings germinating. Bjarni has built shelves into the windows in the bathroom, pantry, bedroom and kitchen so we can make use of all the light there is. I have never had a garden before, let alone a garden in the Arctic. Gyða has given me armfuls of yoghurt pots from the canteen at the school where she works, to use as plant pots. I have no idea how many seedlings is too many, so I just fill the window shelves. As I prepare to leave, I watch each day for the circle of deep brown compost to break into green.

Bjarni wants to drive with me as far as Reykjavík. He will not be coming to Kenya this time. We spent three months with my grandmother that first trip, and they made friends and made peace with the fact that they may not meet again. Bjarni wants to use his land-based time to see to the house: the roof needs changing for a start, and we need to take advantage of the short window of summer. I feel bad leaving him to it, but his parents will help. It is an eight-hour drive to the capital if you go directly via the coastal route. But we decide to make a holiday of the road trip south and take the mountain and ferry route across the bay of Breiðafjörður; spend a couple of days over it and visit the island of Flatey – the only inhabited island in the archipelago.

'You're going to love Flatey,' Bjarni beams. 'It's really special.'

Apparently, it is about 2 kilometres long by 1 kilometre wide. It's a haven for those birds travelling northwards. There are no cars and only two families live on it all year round. Many more turn up in June to occupy their summerhouses and it buzzes with the kind of life that belongs to another era – slow-paced and convivial. We'll be there a few weeks before the summer mode begins: just us, the two families and the arriving birds. One of the families operates their home as a guesthouse and we make a booking; it's still too cold for camping.

'That's nice. We have the day to travel there slowly,' Bjarni says. 'The ferry's not 'til evening. It'll be beautiful through the mountains. Forecast's good.'

'It'd be fun to have a fire down on the beach when we get there.'

'Good plan. Let's take some wood.'

We always travel with firewood – a small bag of offcuts from Haukur's joinery workshop. There just aren't any mature trees. Once upon a time this was a forested island, but the settlers did a thorough job of cutting down almost all of the trees: to make charcoal for smelting, for tool handles, for boats, and to clear the land for livestock grazing. Afforestation schemes are under way here and there, but gathering firewood from the small patches of woodland that do exist would feel sacrilegious: the 'forests' are so embryonic. No visitor to Iceland will escape the joke: 'What should you do if you get lost in an Icelandic forest? Stand up.' I notice the absence of leaves rustling particularly now that spring is here. In winter, the silence was more expected. Now I anticipate the sound of vegetation, but the trees and shrubs are small and low, silent, hunkering down out of the wind.

I have tried to persuade Bjarni that we should plant trees around the house as a wind-break, to create a micro climate for other things to grow.

'It'll spoil the view,' was his response.

'The trees *are* the view.'

We are clearly not going to agree on this. I've noticed that a feeling of spaciousness and an ability to see far into the distance seems to be considered almost a citizen's right: to see weather coming, or visitors coming; to be able to respond spontaneously, to feel free. Many people seem under the impression – bodily if not intellectually – that the way they see a landscape is the way it has always been. No Icelander on this island has lived through a time where vertical entities, be they human or tree, stood close together as a norm rather than an exception. Nor is such a time part of a cultural memory: no stories I have heard are mossed and wooded. A long view in the landscape does not necessarily equate to a long view in approach to life. But perhaps this is an effect of rapidly changing weathers, and the fact that the ground we stand on is moving, forming, eroding. Too much planning is futile.

'I'll go and get some beers too,' I say, heading out of the door.

I go to the tiny Vínbuðin – the 'wine shop' – a state-owned alcohol franchise. It is the only shop that can legally sell alcohol and there are three of them in the whole of the Westfjords. Three for 7,238 inhabitants, and the tourists. It's still early so I miss the rush, thank goodness. Hordes usually descend just before it closes at 6 p.m. When Icelanders have to navigate small spaces their spatial cultural legacy does not appear to serve them well; a morass of bodies trying at once to be free and not to impinge on others. I arrive to find that for the first time the Vínbuðin has real cider. Previously, it only stocked sickly sweet Swedish ciders. But here it is: dry Somerset cider – my favourite tipple from England. Knowing I will soon be able to taste this makes my longing for mature trees more acute: trees hanging in fruit, orchards, the smell of woods and the incremental measure of time by the leaves' unfurling, browning and falling.

Making a life here these past months, I have enjoyed the way that the general lack of choice of food and drink up north has made me more resourceful, and more grateful for things when they come. It reminds me of when I moved to Kenya aged eleven, and I believed I had to accept that I would never see a jam doughnut again, although Mum would get Marmite sent out. Instead, I got to discover things like *mkate wa tambi* – a Swahili spaghetti cake, baked with coconut milk and cardamom. When we do go to Reykjavík and have the opportunity to stock up on almost anything, I have no desire for it. I have come to appreciate what is here.

Thanks to my adopted family, I have discovered all the things you can prepare with a sheep, from the delicious *hangikjöt* (smoked lamb), through the perfectly palatable *kæfa* (a fatty mutton pâté) to the more challenging *pungur* (singed, boiled ram's testicles) and the shocking to look at but surprisingly edible *svið* (singed, boiled half sheep's head – the 'best' ones with the eye still in the socket). And Bjarni has come home from every fishing tour with a bin liner of fish: monkfish, cod, halibut, coley. Once, he came back holding a ten-litre bucket of lumpfish caviar that was going to be thrown overboard as the lumpfish was not part of the fishing quota. We went around the whole village door to door offering it to neighbours as it doesn't keep for long.

But I have missed cider. As strange as it may sound, I am convinced that its availability here will significantly improve my quality of life: I can drink my trees, even if I cannot grow them quickly. I buy two crates in case this is the last delivery for a while. The manager insists I can make an order for more if it's not on the shelves, but I am beginning to learn what promises mean here. They are intentions, implicitly tempered by a host of variables which remain beyond the control of the intender.

* * *

We wake early to a pink-skied morning – the first day of May. We are approaching the time of year when the sun does not set. The sea is still, and we are excited to be spending a few days together, going somewhere new. It is warm by Icelandic standards: ten degrees perhaps, and is due to get warmer later. My bag for the two-day Iceland leg of the trip is much bigger than my three weeks of Kenya luggage. Iceland bag: Icelandic jumper, thermal leggings, hat, gloves, wellies, cider, firewood. Plus another waterproof kit bag with a load of filmmaking gear: I am learning that you just never know what is going to happen, or when, so better to always have it with me, even if I'm not sure what film I am making yet. Kenya bag: vest tops x3, skirt, birthday present, swimming costume, sarong, flip flops, passport, vaccination logbook. I sling them onto the campervan bed and we climb into Maríubjalla – Ladybird – our red and black Toyota HiAce. We have not done this since our road trip around the country in 2009, and we are both at our most content on journeys like this – free, continually improvising. But it is hard to leave my home, and my plant pots in the windows, and the roof that needs fixing.

We wend our way on empty roads towards the blue mountains, and after forty minutes the tarmac ends and we reach gravel track. It snakes steeply uphill to a pass where suddenly we are driving alongside a bank of compacted snow 5 metres high. The road-clearing trucks have carved right into it like a knife through thick icing on a cake. This snow never completely melts: the depth just lessens over the summer. From the top we can see that the weather ahead is glorious and there are blue skies all around. The russet track curls all the way down the green valley like a snipped ribbon. The skin of the mountains is streaked with the vertical scars left by falling rocks. The road has no barrier and its edge is a sheer drop many metres below.

'Want to drive?' Bjarni says, apparently not ironically.

'Not now, thanks. Another time.' I can barely look out of the window as a passenger, though I suspect being the driver helps with feeling in control. I am just not ready for so much newness in one day.

We descend the other side of the pass into Arnarfjörður – Eagle Fjord. When we reach the bottom and drive alongside the shore, the water sparkles like hammered silver. A majestic waterfall cascades down the head of the fjord in strands, like layers of long white hair.

'Remember the name of that one?' Bjarni tests me.

'Dynjandi.'

'Good. Meaning?'

'Making a din.'

'Correct! *Well done*, my love.'

As we approach with open windows we hear Dynjandi's thundering grow louder. We turn off the road to the small car park at the bottom, where dandelions are starting to bloom in a meadow – the first flower of summer scattering yellow into the greening skygrass like daytime constellations. The thundering fills the air, the sound taking on a tangible form. It is insistent but not imposing: it simply insists that words are unnecessary. I recall the name Rjúkandi, another waterfall near Bjarni's parents' summerhouse. I remember it means 'smoking' because of the vapour it sends up, visible from far away. I make the connection that the ending *-andi* makes the word a verb, a process. The waterfalls I have met in other parts of Iceland have always been called something *-foss*, with *foss* meaning waterfall. Dettifoss – 'falling waterfall', reputed to be the most powerful in Europe; Goðafoss – 'waterfall of the gods', into which, so goes a nineteenth-century myth, the Lawspeaker Þorgeir Ljósvetningagoði threw his statues of the Norse gods as he instigated Iceland's conversion to Christianity in the year 1000; Skógarfoss – 'waterfall of the forest', proving that there was forest when these falls were named. I wonder if it is a characteristic particular to the Westfjordians that their waterfalls are verbs, named for the witnessed outcome of their natures, rather than for their place in topography or history.

Up close, I see that Dynjandi descends in terraces, and that the white strands of falling water come from a narrow and very powerful river, spreading over a wide cliff. All the snowmelt from the tops descends here, it seems. The mountaintops in the Westfjords are flat, ground to a horizontal by the pressure and movement of millennia of glaciers. I think of the 5-metre-high section of snow we passed earlier, how that is a minuscule fragment of the snow that has gathered on these mountains all winter, and which is now being drawn towards the sea. We scramble up to its different levels – each with a distinct personality – and feel the morning sun on our backs, blooming through our woollen jumpers. We sit leaning against one another; leaning into this life of ours. It feels like the beginning of the year, and the beginning of time itself; the beginning of life. We do not need to talk much, Bjarni and I. This says everything for us. We come down and drink tea in silence sitting at the door of the campervan, a snipe drumming in the air above.

I have longed for this. Our stories have led us here. No matter how disparate our origins, our union feels like a given, as if we were waiting to meet all these years. This is a story neither of us have written, and this story is a verb. We are simply listening.

Our reverie is broken by remembering we are on a schedule. We climb back into Maríubjalla, me behind the steering wheel this time. I feel confident to drive now: no sheer drops, just mountain desert plateau. We bounce up the track beside Dynjandi until we are above it, cross the river from which it issues and look down on Arnarfjörður. The sea surface dazzles light and a boat draws a dark line of wake across it. The profiles of the mountains separating us from home recede in flat layers of ever-deepening blue. Up on top the snow glows brightly, its crystals sparkling in the sun. Where there is no snow, the plateau is gravelly and sodden: the ground is saturated and there is little vegetation to drink it in. Small pockets of meltwater glint beside the road as we pass them.

A little further on, we spy the blue curve of Breiðafjörður – Wide Fjord – opening out beneath us, down on the other side of the plateau. It is scattered with thousands of tiny islands glowing a yellow green, like an Earth before landmasses collided. One of those islands is where we are heading. Flatey – 'Flat Island'. There are no buildings at all in this landscape, and no trees tall enough to interrupt the view, all the way from here to Stykkishólmur – the ferry terminus on the other side of the bay. Space takes on a temporal dimension. We can make out the lone ferry that we shall soon board: a speck making its way towards us, still far away. I feel if I looked hard enough, I could see us sitting on Flatey tonight, a fire lit on the beach, thinking and looking back to now.

We descend along a gently rolling gorge, which becomes dense with willow and birch, and we are birthed onto the coast road as the ferry grows larger on the horizon. There is still time for a soak in the hot spring – one of my favourites, right next to the sea. The small gravel car park has one vehicle in it. On our way down to the shore we meet the farmer who owns the land, and the spring. He has just cleaned it out ready for the summer season, but today we have it to ourselves. We slide into the clear, hot water, which trickles in from a small cascade down the cliff. The pool is made of a circle of rocks loosely damming this flow, and is deep enough to submerge our shoulders when sitting. Water splashes over the stone wall onto the stone beach, and eider ducks cruise calmly in the nearby shallows. We know by looking at the sea when we will need to move: we can keep watch on the ferry's approach from the hot spring.

At 5.30 p.m., we pull up at the wooden cabin at Brjánslækur, which serves as a ticket office and café, and explain our journey: Brjánslækur–Flatey today; Flatey–Stykkishólmur tomorrow. We board the ferry leaving Maríubjalla on deck and head up to the viewing lounge. Before we climb the stairs, a crew member corners Bjarni and says:

'Keys?'

Bjarni hands them over, then a smile of recognition spreads over both of their faces. '*Nei há.*'

'Davíð, this is Sarah, my dearest. Sarah: Davíð. We used to work together.'

I love that the Icelandic word for girlfriend is 'dearest': *kærasta*. While I long to be able to express my own identity, I am happy with this as a label. It beats *tengdadóttir Hauks Kálfs*: 'daughter-in-law of Haukur of Kálfavík', which is what took hold while Bjarni was at sea. They chat briefly in Icelandic, catching up on the past few years as Davíð directs cars onto the deck. Then Bjarni takes my hand and we continue upstairs.

'How come you gave him the van keys?' I ask.

'There's no cars on Flatey.'

'But, so… how does it work then?'

'Davíð will park it for us at Stykkishólmur and we'll get the keys back tomorrow.'

'Do they explain that to anyone else when they ask for their keys?'

'I guess… if they ask.'

'But our stuff's still in the van.'

'Oh shit, yeah.' He runs back towards the car deck. 'What do you need?'

'The bigger bag. And the firewood.'

'OK.'

'And the *cider*.'

I go out onto the viewing deck and sit on the hard, white plastic benches. It is sunny and bright, but the breeze has a real chill now we are on the water. Snæfellsjökull glacier is a near neighbour, standing tall to the south. I go to the railings as the ferry pulls out of the harbour and Bjarni reappears with my filmmaking kit bag slung over his shoulder.

'Thought you'd want this too. The rest's in the luggage racks.'

'Ah, thank you!'

The kit bag is so integral to my sense of self that I forgot to mention it. I don't see my filmmaking gear as luggage: it has always been an extension of my eyes and ears. Increasingly though, it seems my eyes and ears are distracted from the idea of capturing footage. I want to simply be in the midst of what is unfolding around me, relating with it, experiencing it with my whole body, not through a viewfinder. Not trying to pin down what I do not, and may never, fully understand. 'Capture'. What a strange word that is: to take into one's possession by control or force. Or: to record accurately in words or pictures. How can the same word define such different impulses? What could recording without possessing look like?

The world around us is a cold pearlescent blue. I snuggle into Bjarni's bear-like side and pull my hat down over my ears. Now we are on the sea I feel suspended inside the time and space that kept switching places up on the plateau. This place is like nothing I have ever seen: thousands of tiny islands and skerries appear to float and are mirrored in the calm water. Puffins criss-cross comedically between them, the bright orange triangles of their webbed feet dragging behind their frantically flapping wings. Fulmars dance with the ferry's wake, diving for churned-up quarry. The sky is blue. The Westfjordian mountains to the north are deep blue and table-like. Snæfell mountain to the south is cone-shaped; liquid and solid at once, ridged and riveted with snow.

Peckish, we descend to the canteen in the underbelly of the boat to order a burger. It smells of frying fat, the spiced salt that is sprinkled on chips with abandon, and diesel. Behind the counter I notice boxes of chocolate bars called *Prince Polo*, *PrWstur* and a third, wooden box that is marked *Lyklar*. I know this means 'keys'. So *that* is the system. We eat our greasy burgers in the dingy canteen. It hits a spot but I'm glad to return to the deck.

It could be an hour, or a day, that passes before the engine begins to hum at a lower frequency and I notice a flat island with a scattering of shapes and bright colours that signals human habitation. As we draw closer, I see that most of them are the old style, like our house, clad in corrugated iron with decorative window surrounds. There are no trees. Faded fluorescent buoys are scattered along the shoreline, and the wrecked hull of a wooden boat lies beached askew on the south shore.

There is a small gathering of people at the harbour. One catches my eye in particular: an old man with a white beard and a sparkle in his eye visible from some distance. He wears a sailor's cap on his head and a red neckerchief tied in a knot at the collar of his oversized anorak. Beside him is a wheelbarrow. The ferry docks and only we walk down the gangway. This man reaches out his arm to greet us.

'Hafliði. *Velkomin.*'

This is our host, and the wheelbarrow is our luggage transport. We follow him, delighted, up the only track to the former doctor's house – a carved wooden sign above the door reading 'Læknishúsið' telling us so: now Hafliði's home, and our bed for the night.

He passes us our luggage and notices my video camera.

'*Nú.* Are you making a film?'

'I think so, but I am not sure what it's about yet,' I smile apologetically. The look he gives back suggests he understands how this can be so.

Once we have stepped into his warm house, we realize that the early start and the cold sea air has taken it out of us. We have a nap. Everything I have seen today needs time in a crucible of dreams. When we wake, the view out of the window is more ethereal than a dream. The light is lower now and the cold blue everything is gilded with orange. I cannot wait to be sitting down on the beach, with the eiders and the cider.

We wrap up warm and grab the bag of firewood. Haflíði's wife Ólöf runs into us at the door.

'Got everything you need?'

'Yes, thanks.'

'What's that?' she asks, pointing to our bag.

'We'd like to have a little fire down on the beach. Such a beautiful evening.'

'Well, you needn't have brought any wood. There's a great pile of it down by the shore. We collect it all year for our New Year's bonfire. Help yourself.'

As we approach the pile, it makes our small bag seem laughable. It is driftwood, offcuts of structural timber, old furniture, all piled high – and it is only May. At the very top of the pile, as if placed there for this precise moment, are two beautiful antique armchairs, upholstered in olive-green velour. We fish them off the top and place them both facing the sea behind a strandline of dulse.

Bjarni builds a small fire and I crack open the brown glass bottles. We sink into the armchairs and watch a nursery of eiders float by. I remember back to the time I first met his grandmother and she placed us in chairs facing each other, because our relationship was new. 'We now face the world, together,' she had said. We are warm, we are comfortable, and we are in one of the most beautiful places on Earth. We feel truly blessed. This is perfection: my cider, Bjarni's view, armchairs and a fire gifted by providence. It turns out you don't need trees to have a fire. You can have abundance without growth. Or can you? The trees that made this timber had to grow somewhere.

'When shall we get married then?' Bjarni asks, without any ceremony whatsoever. The only discussion we have had about marriage was about how we already felt united, and how a party would be fun, to celebrate that fact.

'Twenty-third of June. I don't care which year, but I like that date,' I respond, surprised by my calm reaction to what is happening.

'You know that's Jónsmessunótt – Midsummer's Night...?'

'I didn't, no. I just like the number twenty-three. And June seems like the best month for the weather. But... even better.'

'... When the seals remove their skins and reveal their human forms? And the cows speak?'

'Done.'

'*Skál.*' We clink our bottles together and take a swig of England; drink in this bright Icelandic night.

Selur – Seal

2 May 2011

I don't know how many hours we spent sitting in our armchairs on the beach. We were not measuring time, just witnessing the steady approach of the water's edge; inhabiting our togetherness. The difference between high tide and low tide on Flatey can be up to 6 metres, greater than elsewhere in Iceland. As the water inched up towards our seaweed frontier, I remember trying to persuade Bjarni that we should ask his friend Davíð from the ferry to get those armchairs back to Brjánslækur so we could pick them up later. It's the kind of thing that feels entirely possible around here.

'And then?'

'You could pick them up in the van on your way back home.'

'No, I couldn't. They're too big for our van. And I won't be coming back the same route.'

'Your dad will be working over this way soon, won't he?'

'He's got the same sized van as us. And it's full of tools.'

'But they're so beautiful. I can't believe antique armchairs are just going to get burned.'

Bjarni shrugged. When it comes to our life together, Bjarni and

I seem to have been allocated shared quotas of both dreaming and pragmatism. But we rarely make use of either of these qualities at the same time as each other. It is a dance. But the outcome always seems to be resourcefulness and abundance – and, very occasionally, frustration.

As the fire flickered and glowed at our feet, we watched the sun descend slowly in the sky; the seaweed sigh and plop in the lapping waves; pairs of oystercatchers commuting, their sturdy orange beaks almost glowing in the low-angled light; a curious fulmar in its slow repeated fly-by, meeting our gaze each time in a sideways glance: a long poem which the Earth itself was writing.

There was a phase in the evening in which the sea and the air stilled; completely stilled. Every single blade of grass was in sharp focus, each one with its own height, shape, shadow and character. At a barely perceptible moment, droplets of dew the colour of clarity formed on these blades, suddenly, like an implicit agreement coming to fruition. A golden world of sea and islands, pebbles and seaweed, dandelions and lambs, tractors and brightly coloured houses, was instantly contained within each crystal globe, curved into a new reality.

The day had been full, rich. A chill came with the stillness even if darkness didn't, and we finally turned in.

We slept deeply in this Doctor's House, in our room which has something of a teenager's bedroom about it, circa 1984: grey curtains with diagonal blue and red stripes, matching bedding, and a red plastic-coated bed head. This is the first Icelandic guesthouse I have stayed in; we have always stayed with family or friends, or in the van.

I now realize it is an Icelandic thing, rather than a Bjarni's family thing, to have two single duvets on a double bed.

'It's not always a couple sharing a bed,' Bjarni explained. 'Could be friends; family members. Anyway, this way couples don't spend the night wrestling for the duvet.'

I found it lacking in intimacy at first, but soon began to appreciate the genius of the idea. You can sleep alone, together.

* * *

Feeling refreshed and looking forward to the day we have ahead of us to explore the island, we make our way down to the kitchen. Ólöf has prepared a breakfast spread of Gouda, bread, cucumbers, sliced red peppers, rhubarb jam, pancakes and whipped cream, and a huge thermos of coffee. She is a round woman in her seventies who seems always to be grinning. Her apron is smeared with finger-streaks of flour.

'Please, sit down. Help yourselves.' Ólöf lifts her head slightly when she speaks to us so that she can look through her glasses, which live halfway down the bridge of her nose. 'Good fire?'

'Very good,' Bjarni smiles, pulling out a chair. 'You're right. Plenty of firewood.'

'Yes. We've even decided to get married,' I add, slightly surprised that these words have fallen out of my mouth at all, but also to a complete stranger before anyone else. The reality of it seems to belong to this island in a way I cannot quite explain.

'Congratulations!' Ólöf beams. 'When?'

'Jónsmessunótt.'

'*Perfect.* Egg?'

'Yes please,' Bjarni grins. 'Fried.'

He loves a spread. I know there will be little left when he's done. We look into the back garden and see their hens jabbing at the bright green grass.

'Ah, your own eggs. Great. Fried for me too, please.'

'Just started laying again recently.'

'We're going to get hens, aren't we, Bjarni?'

'Yep.' He is loading a slice of bread with rhubarb jam and cheese – a combination I have been converted to.

I establish that this has been Ólöf and Hafliði's family home for many years, that the children have moved out but one of them lives next door with his wife. He's out fishing – good weather for it. I wonder if that's his old bedroom we've been sleeping in. The Doctor's House guesthouse is officially Ólöf's business and she is also the postmistress of the island, and makes jam and handicrafts to sell to tourists when they start arriving, which is soon.

Bjarni does not ask questions, I've noticed. My curiosity, when juxtaposed with his way of simply being, sometimes makes me feel like I am interrogating, rather than just being interested.

Bjarni stirs whipped cream into his coffee.

'Can I see your handicrafts later?' I ask Ólöf.

'Of course.'

Hafliði glides into the kitchen with the smell of outside on him – salt tang, sweet grass, ice on the wind from Snæfellsjökull – and a

rifle slung over his shoulder. He hangs it on the back of a chair and pours himself some coffee.

'The birds are arriving. Beautiful this time of year, before it gets busy.'

He pulls a photo album from a shelf and sits down beside me, starts flicking through it. I speak a little Icelandic to him and he speaks a little English to me and whenever we can't understand one another we turn to Bjarni. Hafliði points at a photo of a man holding a boom microphone with a fluffy cover, clearly taken just outside this house.

'Like you. Know Chris Watson? Englishman.'

'Is that Chris Watson? Actually, I have met him once.' He is a sound artist who did many of the recordings for David Attenborough's documentaries, and he was a guest lecturer on my Ethnographic Documentary MA.

'He was here. Stayed in Doctor's House.'

'No way!'

'Recorded birds. I listened through his headphones.' He lets a long slow whistle escape through his teeth. 'Flatey went into him.'

'I can believe it. Same here.'

I flick through the photos and see how little Flatey has changed. It is a place apart, where time stretches and then curves to fit inside drops of dew at midnight.

Hafliði asks us our plan for the day, and Bjarni tells him we'll just wander the island until it's time for the afternoon ferry. This is a paradise. Why would we do anything else? He insists we see the church, for its beautiful mural, and gets up from the table.

'I go to help my son now. He sent message they caught a seal.'

'Can we come with you?'

'*Já.*'

'Bjarni?'

'I'm still eating breakfast.'

There's no time to wait: Hafliði is already at the door, so I follow alone. I grab my stills camera and nothing else. We stroll the 100 metres down to the harbour, where Hafliði's son's small boxy white fishing boat is mooring. As the large ferry also has to dock here, the harbour wall is high and towers above this boat. The catch has to be lifted out by a crane and winch. Gulls circle above and dive at the water as the guts are swept overboard. A beige plastic tub full of cod is lifted up, then across, then down onto the jetty – fishy water squirting out of the drainage holes in the corners.

The crane hums back down and a woman in bright orange rubber dungarees hooks at something in the bottom of the boat. The cable is winched up again and, like a soul leaving a body, a horizontal dark mass peels into the air and rises vertically, snout down, tail up, spinning on an invisible point. The crane's arm reaches across to position the seal over Hafliði's wheelbarrow parked on the jetty. The seal sways now, and turns, in a trance-like dance, round and round like a dervish. My imagination puts music with this motion. It is dead, but it is animate; I am entranced. I wonder how I can have *not* brought my video camera for this fluid moment. I try to just watch it; take it in.

The seal lands gently but inelegantly in Hafliði's wheelbarrow. With bent legs he hoists it up and heads towards the gutting shed. I run to open the door for him.

'I will skin this later, if you want to film that?'

'Can I?'

'Sure.'

I walk back to the Doctor's House to see how Bjarni is getting on with breakfast, and to look at Ólöf's handicrafts. Bjarni has alleviated the need for much washing up, wiping the plates clean with a salivated index finger. He actually licks the plates at home, and I wondered how far he'd go in a guesthouse. He eats with an Arctic mentality: as if you must take advantage of abundance when it exists, as there may be times of dearth. In his father's generation this was a real concern, but now the dearth never seems to come. He is larger than his father.

Ólöf's handicrafts are displayed on a bookshelf in her living room. She has some beautiful hand-knitted mittens in the old style, with angular points in the hands, and a snowflake pattern. There are woollen socks, a few Icelandic jumpers, lava bead necklaces that I see everywhere and now know the lava they are made from is not Icelandic. The rhubarb jam has just been made, rhubarb being the first fruit of summer, pressing pink and urgent out of the wakening ground. Rhubarb, too, being the beginning of my story with this place, the reason I am in Iceland: that crumble I made for Natalía and Salvar having inadvertently landed me the job co-managing Fjallafang. I see a pile of skins in a box: furry, white and flecked with grey spots.

'What's this?'

'Seal skin,' she responds nonchalantly.

I haven't ever seen a dry seal and am surprised at how pale and fluffy it is. They look so dark and slick when they're wet.

'*So many*. So... do you *hunt* seal?'

'We don't go out looking for them, but if my son sees one when he's fishing, he shoots it – if it doesn't have a pup.'

'So Hafliði will be adding to this pile, and your family will eat the meat?'

'*Já*. Seal meat is special.'

'Isn't it?' I respond, an internal jolt prompting me to reflect on how living here has changed my attitude. I recall the naivety of my resistance to the radio's noise when I saw the seals that first Christmastime, and then my shock at the idea of them being hunted for food. Some visitors once asked Bjarni how he stayed warm in winter. 'By eating things that are good at staying warm in winter... like seal,' was his characteristically witty, and slightly exaggerated, reply. Seal is not an everyday food.

I have tried *selspik* a couple of times: seal blubber. Haukur and Aunt Yrsa always seem to have a small supply, and bring it out on special occasions. I like it. It feels like eating solid light. It is true that my diet eating frequently with Bjarni's family – most often fish and potatoes, lamb and potatoes, and occasionally seal – has added a thin and effective layer of fat to my body. And it does not feel like the kind of fat that results from excess. It feels healthy and supple, and it keeps the cold from me. I have never been present when a seal was shot, though I once joined Haukur when he saw one from the summerhouse window, which lingered for a while close to shore looking at him. A moment came where he got up, slung a rifle over his shoulder and strode out to his wooden boat. We cruised down the fjord to where he'd seen it last submerge, but it did not reappear, and Haukur quickly accepted it. Hunting in this way, where the prey comes to the hunter, or in Hafliði's case through lucky happenstance, involves such long odds that, upon success, the food is savoured and eked out, every part of the animal used. It has made me feel differently about it. I'm not *for* it, but it's no longer unconscionable to me.

Bjarni is ready now to be my sound guy. I am not sure if I am ready to be a camerawoman. I have so many questions that I don't know how I will manage to film without asking them. I am trained in observational documentary – a style in which events are allowed to unfold and the protagonists tell their own story through their actions, in order to present an 'authentic' representation of reality. There is no voiceover, no presenter and no interviews. The filmmaker is usually the invisible or unobtrusive observer, the fly on the wall. But it does not feel particularly authentic to me to make out that I am invisible, when I am present and implicated in entanglements that shall be ongoing, and not only for the camera's interest. When I was at university the current scholarship talked about self-reflexivity: acknowledging and unpacking the presence of the anthropologist filmmaker, their impact on the scene, and the baggage and preconceptions they brought to 'the field'. But films in which the filmmaker did this effectively on camera, or through the structuring of the film, remained uncommon.

Although the depth of my curiosity borders on the ethnographic, I am not an anthropologist here. I am Sarah trying to understand this place because I am in love with it, and in love with a man who is so deeply *of* it. If I wish to know something of someone, or they wish to know something of me, who am I to stay silent, or invisible? We are all trying to make a life on this island. I decide to head out the door with my video camera and see what happens.

We only get as far as the picket fence at the front of the Doctor's House before something intrigues me. I press the record button. A dead raven is flopped over the fence, wedged between two uprights: it has been placed there. I zoom in on the bluish sheen on its wing feathers, the diffused reflection of overcast sky in its solid black bill. Flies begin to land around its eyes.

'It was bothering my lambs.'

Suddenly Hafliði is behind us, his gun slung over his shoulder again. I swing round slowly and point the camera at him. He doesn't mind a bit. He is just slightly unsure whether to look at me or the camera, which is at chest height.

'Hopefully the other ravens will heed the warning,' he continues.

Bjarni starts talking to him. While I don't understand every word they are saying, I can tell that it's interesting. But there's not much point having footage that has two voices but not two faces. Bjarni is both 'Icelander' and 'sound guy'. What to do? Both of these labels are crude. I frame them both – Bjarni wearing headphones and holding my shotgun microphone. I hear and understand Hafliði say he doesn't like ravens. I have come to respect them a lot. I cannot help but interject; jump to the ravens' defence – in Icelandic. Hafliði not only understands me but responds in Icelandic. This is a first. Up until this moment, when I have tried to speak a whole sentence in Icelandic, people have turned to Bjarni and asked '*Hvað er hun að segja?*' ('What is she saying?'). Now we are all having a conversation – Hafliði, Bjarni and Sarah – and the record light is still flashing. It is messy, but it is truthful. Nobody is subject or object.

Bjarni and Hafliði begin to walk down to the gutting shed, where the seal is, and I follow, running alongside like an idiot trying to film them walking towards me, then walking away from me. What is this for? When we get to the shed it is easier: a contained space with a man who has a task – to skin a seal. Hafliði asks Bjarni to help him lift the seal onto the metal work surface. Bjarni puts down the boom mic and strides towards the seal. I call him back as he is still connected to me via the headphone cable, umbilical. I decide it's best if I wear the headphones; I'll signal to Bjarni if there's a sound problem. It seems likely that he will be occupying multiple roles.

They lay the seal on its back. It is a lighter colour than when it was fresh out of the water, but still nothing like the white furry skins in Ólöf's living room. Once the seal is laid out on the work surface and Bjarni has the mic in position, we all seem to drop into a silent groove, our roles both clear and natural. It is captivating to watch, to listen to and – judging from Hafliði's focused expression – captivating to perform. He has clearly done this many times. I get the sense that Bjarni is taking this in as something he wishes to learn how to do, so he is not losing out by not having the headphones. But the sound of the sharp knife slicing through the skin is so extraordinary and crisp, that when I shift positions with the camera I pass the headphones back to him to let him share in it. His eyes widen, and he gives me the thumbs up. His experience has just been heightened.

Like an emperor dividing up territories, Hafliði scores lines around the flippers, the tail and the neck. In one steady, dextrous sweep he scores from the neckline to the tail-line. The grey continent is now intersected with white borders. The knife is turned horizontal and slipped under the skin where the neckline meets this meridian, and tugged along it loosening the skin from the blubber. Hafliði moves the knife up and down this meridian a few times, travelling further from the line each time. Then he does the same on the other side. Quick and steady: alternating one side then the other. Soon, the skin lifts off; a skin that will join the pile in Ólöf's living room. Where a seal lay moments ago is now a mound of ivory-white blubber with grey flippers, grey head and grey tail. My world is inverted once again.

One might think that only so much can happen in twenty-four hours on an island less than 2 square kilometres large, with a permanent population of five. But it is exactly this fathomability of scale, and this absence of distraction, that opens my body to take in what is there, and dive ever deeper. I am no longer having to filter out noise – visual or aural. I am present and curious, and life crackles through me as it does through everything else. So much has already happened this morning – a potent lifetime of images – but it's still well before noon. We have the day to explore this tiny island before the ferry comes for us, to complete the final leg of the route we began yesterday. This pause has been a cleft into a layer beneath the one we usually inhabit. Iceland is allowing me to tumble down these clefts with a frequency I have not experienced before. This one on Flatey is particularly deep and I have no urgent desire to climb out.

We wander back up the track from the harbour towards the handful of houses that make up the village: past a redshank piping on a fencepost, one leg bent beside the straight one like a luminescent rune; past the one red tractor; circled by the island's only dog. We get to the highest point of this Flat Island – the site of the church that Haflíði has recommended we see.

I remember watching a film on TV a few years ago with my 'in-laws' called *White Night Wedding* by Icelandic director Baltasar Kormákur. It was set on Flatey and one scene happened in this church. Part of the plot involved the groom's flashbacks to a former relationship with an artist, who strewed seaweed in beautiful patterns throughout their house, across the bed and down the stairs, to express what she was feeling. I remember being struck then by the idea of taking what you have to hand – your shared world of matter – to convey, to challenge or to construct concepts that seem unnameable; to give them something familiar to be hooked onto.

We step inside the church. Haflíði is right. All across the vaulted ceiling and above the altar is a vivid, dynamic mural. It is not only beautiful but resonant. It weaves the rocks, the sea, seals, lambs, birds and the people of this place into fragments of many stories, both from the Bible and from here. It was painted by Catalan artist Baltasar Samper and his wife Kristjana in the 1960s in exchange for food and board on Flatey. In typical Icelandic connectedness, they are the parents of Baltasar Kormákur, the film director. I read that all the faces – Jesus and his disciples included – are based on people who lived here, or still do. Each time they came to church they could recognize themselves. There are fishermen in boats, a man scraping clean a seal skin, a woman doing laundry on a washboard, priests praying, laymen reading, a man catching puffins with a net and pole. Through a textured white wake at the top of the arch, created where the sea of one scene meets the sky of another, a white-tailed eagle courses towards Jesus, above the altar. The Messiah is not robed in white, staring at the heavens. He is a bearded, broad-shouldered fisherman dressed in an Icelandic jumper, looking out at us. Kneeling at his feet I see a man with the face of Hafliði – white bearded, stoic and calm. Hafliði: husband, father, grandfather, sheep farmer, bird lover, lore keeper, raven killer, seal skinner, host.

Like a dew drop forming, this arched ceiling and these artists have met to curve a lived moment into something eternal. Here there are many stories, nested together, stretching across time and space.

Þakið – Roof

20 May 2011

I arrive in Nairobi to find that my grandmother, Nan, has been rushed to hospital, ten days before her ninetieth birthday. Her Parkinson's is advanced, and she cannot swallow. I manage to tell her that I am engaged, and about my house, and my first full winter in the Arctic, but she has tubes down her throat and her wrists are tied to the bed to stop her from pulling them out.

'Bjarni sends his love,' I tell her.

Her eyes beam in recognition from behind an oxygen mask.

A few days later, she dies. 'Nan never wanted to be ninety, remember?' I console Mum. 'She said it was too much.'

Even though there have been a couple of scares before, Mum – her only child – does not seem to be prepared for this moment. It is strange to hear her making phone calls now about how best to dispose of a body. It will be a cremation, so that her ashes can be taken back to England when my parents return. Nairobi was never Nan's 'home': she was moved out here aged seventy-three when it became clear my parents were not returning to England anytime soon. But she grew into it well. She enjoyed the weather and the birds. And she liked her friends at the nursing home where the residents live in bungalows with support staff and an on-call nurse, albeit bungalows with bars on the windows, like my parents' house and every house we know – one of this city's defences between the 'haves' and the 'have-nots'.

Several phone calls throw up two options: the municipal crematorium or the Hindu crematorium. This would have been an easy choice for my Christian mother had she not just been told by a friend that the municipal crematorium's furnace is known to malfunction. Sometimes they wrap coffins in cardboard and douse them in petrol to help them burn, she was told.

Mum deems it preferable for Nan's body to be under the watchful eyes of Brahma, Vishnu and Shiva. She speaks loudly and slowly down a crackly phone line to the Hindu crematorium, trying to understand, and to be understood: how it will work; how we will get the body from the hospital to the funeral parlour and from the funeral parlour to the Hindu crematorium.

'They're offering cremation on a pyre or in an oven,' she reports to me and Dad, covering the mouthpiece with her hand. 'I'm thinking the pyre.' Her face is making an expression I am familiar with from growing up here. It happens when she is using all of her resources to convince herself, and others, that everything is under control when it is quite clearly not.

'Are you sure? You realize you'd be able to see her body parts burning, Mum?'

She is taken aback by the plainness of my truth-telling. She clearly doesn't like either option, but concedes I have a point.

'Oven please, then,' she hammers, her voice cracking.

The hospital, the funeral parlour and the Hindu crematorium are on completely different sides of Nairobi, a heavily congested city at the best of times. Much of the next few days is spent in traffic. It is a far cry from Ísafjörður – that faraway now-hometown of mine, where kindergarten, school, nursing home, hospital and cemetery are all built along a short stretch of road. There, there is no crematorium, and burial dates are determined by when the ground is thawed enough to dig a grave.

We make the decision to go ahead with Nan's birthday party at my parents' house, reinventing it as a memorial. Catering has already been arranged, a marquee hired, and Nan's friends are coming, so we might as well seize the opportunity.

A few days before this, the time comes for her 'funeral': the only time that all three services involved in her death and disposal could coordinate. There are just a few of us: me, Mum, Dad, a family friend, her nurse, the nursing home manager, and the priest. The body has been transported to the funeral parlour by the hospital.

Mum opts to see Nan's body one last time, but I decline. I prefer to have the memories of the three months Bjarni and I spent dropping in for tea, watching the birds together, telling her all about Iceland. Mum comes over, looking disturbed.

'*Her wedding ring isn't on her finger, and it's not in the bag of stuff they gave me from the hospital,*' she strains in a whisper.

Wow. Stealing a ring from a corpse. We will never know whether it was someone at the hospital, or someone at the funeral parlour, and there is no hope of getting it back. It is the way it is. I am surprised but also not.

The last rites are read at the funeral parlour and Nan's coffin is loaded into a hearse: a black Toyota HiAce van, like our campervan back in Iceland, and also like all the *matatus* – the public transport minibuses that swarm Nairobi. I decide to ride in the hearse so as not to leave Nan alone should the driver get lost. As I climb in, I notice there is a coloured light on the roof, like on a police car. We slip into the gridlock of traffic – Mum and Dad a few cars ahead.

'What's the light for on the roof?' I ask the driver once we're on the move.

'It is a siren. In the bush when there is a funeral, maybe the body is being carried from the city, back to the home place. So, when we drive back to the home place with it, we can put on the light and the siren and inform people that in the area there will be a funeral. Jungle telegraph,' he laughs heartily. 'Shall I put it on now for you?'

'No. No, thanks.' I cannot help but allow a laugh to escape.

I have not been present at many funerals. This is the weirdest so far and I doubt it will be out-weirded: I am part of a fragmented cavalcade through city and slum in a black *matatu* with a siren, headed for a crematorium belonging to a religion completely alien to my nan – who is behind me in a coffin – and to my family. I like the idea of a body being returned home though. I look out on the seething mass of movement that is Nairobi and think about how many people die displaced.

'Where is your home?' the driver asks me.

'Iceland.'

'Ice...?'

'Iceland.'

'Me I don't know it.'

'OK, you know England. Then north of there is Scotland...'

'Manchester United!'

'Yup, north of Manchester is Scotland...'

'I know Scotland.'

'And then more north, really far up... that's Iceland.'

'More north than Scotland? Eh! So... it's north of the world.'

'North of the world.' I nod in admiration at how he has nailed the feeling of that place.

We proceed through car horns and smog, street vendors and disfigured beggars, to the Hindu crematorium. There, my grandmother's coffin is lifted out of the minibus hearse onto a rusty trolley. There is an open-sided, covered area organized into rectangular piles of logs: the pyre cremation zone. A dog trots around them, snout down, in a never-ending search for something. Together, we wheel the squeaking trolley into a spartan marble-floored room, white and grey. One wall is mostly occupied by the oven door: dark glass in which we can see ourselves. Along the other three walls, statues of Hindu gods about a foot high rise from the floor. I see bright colours, gestures, eyes: Brahma the creator, Vishnu the preserver, Shiva the destroyer.

I imagine my nan in this wooden box; think how this is the last thing she would have expected for herself, but also how she would have accepted it with a smile and a shrug. This is absurd, and so circumstantial. How does a life story end here, when it began as a girl who was 'dirty white' – as her half-sister bullied her, referring to a multiracial ancestry that they did not share – in a diamond mining town in South Africa? A dislocated end and a challenging beginning, via fifty years in suburban Southeast England.

A Hindu man enters and stands in a corner of the room with his head slightly bowed. His dark hair is oiled and parted at the side. His white shirt is spotless and well ironed, and the sharp creases down the front of his trousers divide the cloth into darkness and light. As we step back, he pushes the trolley towards the open oven door, his body bent forward. There is no curtain, no pretending. I notice he has bare feet, dark hairs protruding from each toe. The coffin is unloaded, the trolley removed, and the door clicked shut. He approaches my mother, his head cocked to the side.

'You want to press the button, madam?'

As if on auto-pilot, she walks over and presses a round red button. The roar of inferno fills the room. We watch the flames engulf the coffin. The dog continues to circle outside.

Later, I call Bjarni and try to relate what has happened. I think I just want to hear about somewhere else, something else. Anything else.

'What are you up to?'

'I'm putting my cock into a bag.'

'I beg your pardon!' I explode with laughter and it is needed.

'I killed it earlier and now I'm cutting it up to put in the freezer.'

A few queries reveal that his aunt, Yrsa, donated her hens to us straight after he returned from dropping me at the airport. An Arctic fox had got into their coop at her farm: one had died, and the others were traumatized. She had also given us her cockerel. But it being summer the cockerel did not know when to crow, and so it crowed all day and all bright night. A neighbour complained, Bjarni killed it, and he is preparing it for future eating as we speak. I realize he is totally aware of the *double entendre*. I wonder what the word is for *double entendre* in Icelandic.

'Anything else?' I smirk.

'A polar bear washed up, probably from East Greenland.'

'Alive?'

'Not anymore. Police shot it.'

'What? They're an endangered species.'

'Yup. As usual, Iceland doesn't have a policy for what to do, or money to do much else than shoot, apparently. It didn't use to happen much. But this is the fourth one in three years... young one. Before that, there hadn't been one for about twenty years I think. They say it was a threat to humans... which is bullshit because it landed in Hælavík, in Hornstrandir – super remote. Some tourists were camping there apparently. Anyway, what about survival of the fittest?'

'Shit.'

'Exactly.'

Polar bears are native to neighbouring Greenland, but not to Iceland. They thrive in coastal regions where the sea is nutrient-rich

185

and currents prevent ice from becoming too thick; where drift ice merges together to become pack ice then disintegrates again – the annual cycles of surface extent integral to the cycles of marine life. They feed primarily on seals, travelling long distances to hunt. To catch their prey, they are often found at sea on floating platforms of drift ice. Their southernmost range is defined by how far the ice reaches in winter. The climate is changing faster than they can: rapidly melting pack ice in Greenland is leaving the bears adrift, forcing them to swim further. Sometimes Iceland is the closest place to make landfall. It seems that the places they have landed are sparsely populated, if at all, but if there is any risk to any humans – be they residents or hikers – the bear loses.

This is yet another detail that is making me re-evaluate Iceland's, or Icelanders', environmental credentials – at least those I projected onto them. The 'pristine nature' here, as inspiring as it is, as cherished as it is, may provide a false sense of security and dearth of accountability. 'We are so few' was often the answer, if I asked, for example, why people drive everywhere, guzzle fuel like it's the 1950s, and leave their car engines running – summer or winter – while they go and do something else.

'And the house?' I continue down a crackly phone line.

'Oh *já*. The weather was so good when I came home, I decided to just start with the roof, not wait 'til June. Bit too hot for my liking though. I took the old roof sheets off – that was a quick job. But then the other night I was woken up by water dripping on my toes. Coming from around the ceiling light – bit scary.'

'Could say that. What happened?'

'The snow had started again. I had to get Mamma, Pabbi and Salvar up on the roof in the middle of the night and we nailed on anything we could find – a sail, plastic sheeting, stuff like that. I shovelled the snow out of the attic, but it got a bit wet, so now I'm trying to stop the mould from growing there, with vinegar.'

I can picture the scene: four family members up on a roof in the middle of a bright night, hammering in May snow to save a house. Knowing them, they were probably laughing. For the first time since leaving I am relieved not to be there, but sad to have missed it. I'm not sure how I would feel in a home without a roof: it seems to be antithetical to what a home is supposed to provide. At this oblique angle in which I find myself at this moment, though, I can see how similar these two places I have called home are: how everyone is trying to respond creatively to problems as they arise, with limited resources; how nothing is a given; how encountering these spontaneous ways of doing things is both undermining my reality and expanding it; how everything is a dance between creation, preservation and destruction – Brahma, Vishnu and Shiva. Who knew that Kenya could be a training ground for a life in Iceland?

A Walk in My Valley

Late June 2011

By the time I return, the new roof is on – a dazzling crinkle of galvanized steel reflecting the never-ending light. Its newness throws the weathered, ageing surface of the house's four walls into sharp relief. We shall have to re-clad the whole thing at some point, before the elements start making themselves at home.

Bjarni has been busy while I've been away. He has built a hen coop and partitioned part of the shed as sleeping and laying quarters for our new flock of five Icelandic hens. Creation. Just outside the hen bedroom, in the corner of the shed, I notice there is a fish hanging from the ceiling, about a foot long, with a scooped incision in its side. Beneath its dull grey skin, the flesh is a deep terracotta, dry-looking.

'Erm, Bjarni?' I say, pointing at it.

'*Rauðmagi*, from my father.'

'*Rauð... magi*. What's that again?'

'The male lumpfish. Means "red belly". See?' He points at its underside.

'And it's smoked or what?'

'Let's say "cured".'

'So… basically, hung up?'

'Yep. If we keep it out of the sun it will be good for a long time.'

There are barely any flies here, and even in summer the air is cool and dry out of the sun. The wind travels from glaciers and snow-topped mountains. Now, the difference in temperature on each side of the house is enormous: at the back, out of the wind and in the sun, I can feel hot wearing only a vest top. Around the side, out of the wind but in the shade, it is cool and I need long sleeves, even a wool jumper. Where there is wind and shade, it is only a few degrees above freezing. The weather forecast differentiates between 'actual' temperatures and 'feels like' temperatures, and now I understand why. I remember when we worked in the mountains we stored our personal supply of perishable food for weeks under the awning on the front step of our bus-home, in only a polystyrene box. It never perished. Here, we are significantly further north. Our shed, it seems, is a lightly ventilated fridge and, judging by the absence in its side, this lumpfish is Bjarni's snack whenever he comes to feed the hens. Preservation.

The ravens have gone further from the vicinity of the house for now, higher in the sky. I still put out food for Krummi sometimes, but in summer other sources will be easier to come by. He returns occasionally to tease the neighbour's dog, sit on the fence, see what's happening in the village. Winter is his time for intimacy; his time to excite over the bones and animal scraps I leave on the rock at the front. Now, the hens have taken over as waste managers. Our scraps – vegetable, fish and meat – go to them.

Sometimes they get a treat. Every so often, at closing time at the Old Bakery in Ísafjörður, we acquire a bin bag full of bread and pastries from the owner, Mæja, who also happens to be Gyða's neighbour. She is always trying to find things to give us for our home and our life together. She says it is 'special'. The hens go wild for the *snúður* – a dense doughy cinnamon spiral coated with chocolate. Their chests inflate with delight when it thuds into their coop, among the grain and crushed mussel shells collected from the shore to strengthen their own eggshells. Creation. They gather round the *snúður*, trumpeting, stabbing staccato with their beaks. Destruction. Anything the hens don't like goes on the compost pile, which is recently begun. There was no point starting one before now, and I wonder if there is any point at all: for nine months of the year, it will be a pile of freeze-dried scraps.

But, for now, we are all beginning to relax into this new life, and life courses into us. The fundamentals are taken care of. Each morning when we open the hens' gate, they leave the coop and peck around in the wildflower meadow at the back of the house. The verdant grasses are now taller than them and grow ever upwards towards the sun. Everything is colour: the world is no longer blue or grey or white. It has the sound of summer, even the sound of the sun – *sól* – in it: yellow *brennisóley* ('meadow buttercup') glowing under our chins; *melasól* – pale yellow Arctic poppies which track the sun's path. There are the deep pink flames of *hundasúra* ('sheep's sorrel'), the leaves citrus in our mouths; and the pale pink confetti of *hrafnaklukka* – 'raven's clock' – cuckoo flower in English. This

190

time of year when the ravens have cruised up to the cliffs and crags to tend their young is the same time I would hear a cuckoo call in England. The Icelandic name signals the retreat of a bird; the English an arrival. Among all this, the bright red of the hens' combs emerges now and then from the grasses. Every evening at exactly seven – any change in light indistinguishable to me – the hens return through the open gate of the coop, process up the ramp and through the small opening into the shed, made small enough that an Arctic fox cannot follow them. Preservation.

Bjarni has dug a vegetable patch at the front, some distance from the house so as not to be damaged when we do come to replace the cladding. A hitchhiking tourist, who was after an 'authentic' experience, came and helped him for a day. The soil was full of rocks and they used them to build a low stone wall, to create shelter from the cool wind.

'I thought it was like a labour camp,' Bjarni told me. 'But he seemed to enjoy himself. Mamma fed him haddock after.'

He has planted potatoes. Now I will plant my seedlings; see what survives. It is good to be home and tending to it. Much more than cultivating vegetables, I am cultivating a life: a way of belonging that is a constant improvisation. One that allows me to be part of a web of relationships and one in which I have agency. This life is my loom. There is uncertainty and abundance. This is where I get to be Sarah, and Bjarni's 'dearest'.

Before I left for Kenya, I was told that the local tour company urgently needed French speakers to guide cruise ship tourists for the summer months. I went to their office, and told them I speak French. And English, obviously. They asked if I was happy to do both.

'Sure.'

'OK. We'll contact you whenever we know the bookings from the ship, like, the day before. Here's a docking schedule for the summer so you have an idea. Most shifts it will be one tour, maybe two.'

I couldn't believe that was it: no interview, no CV required. No one on their staff could speak French to check that I could speak French: my word was enough. Why did Bjarni and Gyða let me spend so long making an Icelandic CV when I arrived? Why did *they* spend so much time helping me translate it? I have never used it. Or at least I have tried to hand it in on my job searches, but I have been met with blank stares. Through doing it I learned some words at least, each word appearing to be made up of many:

Ferilskrá – CV (*ferill* – track/career; *skrá* – written record)

Sjónrænn mannfræðingur – visual anthropologist (*sjónrænn* – visual; *mann* – human; *fræðingur* – expert)

Tungumál – language (*tunga* – tongue; *mál* – affairs/business)

Tvítyngdur – bilingual (literally 'double-tongued')

Kvikmyndagerðarmaður – filmmaker (*kvikmynd* – film (literally 'motion picture'); *gerðar* – maker; *maður* – human)

Framleiðandi – producer (*fram* – forward; *leiðandi* – leading)

And now I am about to be a *leiðsögumaður* – (*leið* – way; *sögu* – story; *maður* – human). Looking at the pieces of this beautiful word, I realize it seems to describe my temperament. It holds less assumed authority than 'guide', less suggestion that there is a fixed destination of knowledge to which I would, or should, know the way. Rather, we will travel together discovering as we go. Of course, there will be geographical destinations, but the stories I tell about them, and on the way to them, can be my own: what is it like to live here as a foreigner and as part of an Icelandic family, to be insider and outsider? What is it teaching me? Though I have not yet managed to land upon the voice I need to make a film, or to pin this place down in some way, I can tell stories, uncertain stories; stories in which the mountains, the silence and the past get to speak.

According to the schedule, there are thirty-three ships coming this summer, and thirteen of them will contain passengers I might guide. The guiding job is freelance, a reflection of the variables in this trade: like any Arctic boom, tourism is fickle. The company clearly doesn't want to deal with permanent staff on its books. Theoretically, this flexibility means I can do the shifts I want, although I am aware that I might have to seize the opportunity the next two months present to make the majority of the year's income. Until I am fluent in Icelandic only menial jobs will be available to me in winter: that has become clear. I would consider working in the fish factory below our house, were it not for the fact that I would learn very little Icelandic in the process: Poles and Filipinos pick the worms out of fish fillets here – each an island as they listen to music through their earphones to alleviate the boredom.

The house is secured against the winter to come, the hens are happy and laying, a guiding job is in hand, the cod and haddock move further and deeper in summer, some of the trawlers stop fishing. This means Bjarni and I are both home, and the sun is shining. Finally, I feel safe to just be: to work some days and venture out into the valley, and further afield, in my time off. In the absence yet of any compost to enrich the new vegetable patch, Bjarni and I take a spade and a wheelbarrow on an evening walk up the valley, where there are horses. We cross the cattle grid to find them there, chewing contentedly on the lush carpet of growth. It is a perfect U-shaped glacial valley. A river snakes the valley bottom, peaty dark and glinting in the sun. Hay meadows flank the river, which is eternally replenished by snowmelt from the mountains soaring above.

'Good evening, you fine, fine horses,' Bjarni coos at them. 'May we take some of your shit?'

It beguiles me how he talks to animals, children and older people alike: those are the beings with whom he is most comfortable, to whom he relates. The mares gather around us, curious. They sniff, and flick their manes, their chest muscles twitching. I feel the warm air from one horse's nostrils on my open palm, beneficent in the cool of evening. The green bowl of the valley is curved into each of their liquid black eyes. Tentatively, we begin to scoop some of the snow-flattened manure out of the grass, and they do not object. I don't know how much it is rotted but at least we know it is from last summer.

'You were lucky to be away in May. You missed the worst season,' Bjarni tells me. 'As the snow melts, before the new grass comes, all last winter's dog turds, vomit and fireworks are uncovered, layer by layer. It *stinks*.'

He is likely exaggerating about the concentration of rubbish and excrement, as he exaggerates about many things, in order to make a better story. But when there is so little detritus, any that does exist stands out. Bjarni's family, more than some, is offended by it, and sees it as the slippery slope that it is. I suppose that a mentality of 320,000 people living in an area about the size of England might not result in a culture of accountability for clearing up, although I, too, wish it would. This landscape elicits a reverence in me. For others, it may be an empty space waiting for humans to make their mark: to procreate, to build, to cultivate, to dispose. Briefly, the 'pristine nature' is shown to be an illusion.

We pile the manure high and wheel the barrow back home.

'Know what this is called?' Bjarni asks, pointing at the wheelbarrow.

'*Skítahjól*?' I suggest.

Bjarni bends over laughing. 'A "shit wheel"! Nice one, my love. I like your thinking.'

Bjarni, his mother and her siblings love word games. They are greatly amused when I invent new words for things I have not yet learned. Sometimes they adopt my word as a family in-joke. I enjoy that: it makes me feel accepted; allowed into their language on my own terms. They know that I am making my own map. Mine is no different from their ancestors' process of creating a vocabulary for new inventions and concepts from pre-existing words and imaginaries. Like wellies: *stígvél* – 'stepping machines'; or computer: *tölva* – 'number oracle'; or dongle: *pungur* – 'scrotum' or 'sac'.

'It's *hjólbörur*,' Bjarni corrects me. '*Hjól... börur* same as wheel... barrow. But I like "shit wheel" better.'

Broken down, I see how so many of these words are the same as my own, or, they follow the shape of how I might name something if I was left to describe the world in my own way. Words say much about the way we think, so learning a language is also learning a way to think. This way, this Icelandic way, stirs something old in me. It returns me to a place before, a place of beginning again, which is more like 'home' than anything else I have felt. When I notice the sound of a known word in an unknown word, I can make camp in that familiar place and explore new routes from there; get to know what it is hitched to this time. Little by little I make my world anew: I point, I ask, I am told, and I begin to see how it relates – to my language, to its function, to other parts of its world, and to a history we share.

Learning some words, I journey back to a beginning that is elemental; the very relationships that created the thing crackle into life in the utterance of it. The word for 'electricity' blew my mind when Bjarni explained it: *rafmagn*: 'amber power'. Static electricity was discovered many centuries ago when amber was rubbed with animal fur, he told me, creating a spark. I looked into it further: those sparks were created and documented by the ancient Greek philosophers. Amber's light-inducing properties led them to name it: *ēlektron* (meaning 'formed by the sun'), from which the English word 'electricity' was eventually derived many centuries later. In the late nineteenth century, as news of electricity's technological applications washed up on these shores – not least the life-changing possibility of electric light – Icelanders soon found a way to create it for themselves from falling water, and later from geothermal steam. But they honoured its origins in the naming. And it turns out, so did I, every time I used the word 'electricity'.

Before electricity arrived, and before even kerosene lamps began to be imported in the mid-1800s, there had always been a space for words and stories to be shared and created, even in deepest darkness and poverty – especially then. It was those stories that could push back against the encroaching darkness of winter and bring conviviality to the necessity of working through it. On turf-roofed farms in the winter evenings, once the work of the autumn's sheep-gathering and slaughter was complete, the household would gather in the *baðstofa*, a shared attic living-room-cum-bedroom, to do the wool work essential to clothe themselves. After dinner, a single lamp would be lit, of animal fat, fish liver oil, whale or seal blubber, the wick made of bog cotton. In its glow, the head of the household – or whoever could read – would read aloud from a book: the sagas, folktales, the Bible. While listening, the others – men, women and children alike – would card and spin wool, knit, darn or weave, using the shared light to do this necessary work of making and repair.

And before there were books there were oral stories and poems. In these ways, even when resources were scarce, everyone could share in a story, could learn those stories, could use words to remember the past and imagine the future, could learn how a good story is told. This was the tradition of *kvöldvaka* ('evening wake'). This shared history has no doubt nurtured the nation's love of books and a way of speaking and relating the events of the day which sounded to me like a story long before I learned the meaning of the words.

The *kvöldvaka* tradition dwindled at the beginning of the twentieth century, as electric light arrived and spread, and eventually the television replaced lamp and reader all at once: the capacity of electricity to extinguish, as well as activate. But traces of it persist. Whenever we join Bjarni's parents at their summerhouse, the house which they floated on the sea, Haukur gladly assumes the mantle of reader to the household. The house is off-grid, equipped only with kerosene lamps which are barely ever needed in the endless light of summer. In its small wood-panelled living room decorated with old horsehair rope, antiquated farm tools, and a shelf full of well-thumbed books, Haukur reclines on the sofa as he does at home, legs outstretched, reading aloud from the almanacs and the folk stories, maintaining his family's connection with their past. Gyða sits opposite him in her armchair, knitting without cease. And we listen. It is the quality of this listening that I love, even if I cannot fully understand the stories.

I enjoy Haukur's role as reader of the household, because it amuses me to watch everyone give this man, who is usually such a joker, their full, almost reverent, attention. But I wonder how he came to earn the role. When he reads there is no drama, no affect; the tone almost unchanging. It is not monotonous in the sense that it is boring, but it is as if he was not reading it with any feeling; as if he saw his role as only to bring the words into the world of sound, not music. Perhaps what I perceive to be the sound of feeling is different from what he does.

Once, I chose a book.

'Can you read this, please?' I asked, passing it to him.

From his horizontal position on the couch he reached out for the book, and read the title over his glasses. He opened it and remained silent. I watched his eyeballs scan the words and wondered if he was looking for a good bit. He turned the page. Gyða continued knitting. Bjarni cleaned his teeth with a toothpick. The silence continued.

'Can you read it?' I repeated.

'I am reading it.'

'No, I mean *to us*!'

'Read it *out*?! Well, that's not what you asked for.'

It was not enough for him that I am learning to speak such a complex language, and will be for years to come. I asked him to *lesa* not *lesa úpphátt* and that is what I got. He knew what he was doing and probably found it hilarious. Part of me did too. He was tough on me, but I admit these antics galvanize me to learn quickly so I might meet him on my own terms.

Electricity has eventually changed everything here, as it has the world over. Changed the age-old rhythm of the seasons, made work possible at all times and in all places, made tomatoes grow in Iceland. And it is Iceland's capacity to generate so much of its own cheap 'green' electricity that makes it attractive to the aluminium-smelting companies, which may change everything once again. Part of me admires Haukur's stubbornness to keep a little corner of this earth without it, and to keep alive the practices that don't depend on it. There is resilience in that. On this, we are very much aligned.

* * *

The first words I learned were the names of wildflowers and herbs, as Bjarni and I made our first road trip in Maríubjalla in June 2009, at a time of year when the flowers sing loudly for two weeks and the leaves are most potent. I painted some on the inside of the van door, with their names – *geldingahnappur, klóelfting, holurt* – so they would be the last thing I saw when I fell asleep and the first when I woke up. Gyða has always given me Icelandic herb tea at Christmas – a mix of leaves she has picked that sprout from the hillsides in early summer. She has shown me the plants and told me their names. This year, I want to gather my own herbs, in my valley, and give some back to her. I call Gyða.

'Hæ, hæ. I'm wondering if it's still OK to gather the herbs for tea?'

'It's better in early June, before they've begun to flower. The taste is strong in the leaves then, but... just try it. You remember what you're picking?'

I don't think of the plants in English: I got to know them here. What I see in my mind's eye when she asks the question is their shape, their colour and the sound of their name: *ljónslappi* – 'lion's feet'; *rjúpnalauf* – 'ptarmigan leaf'; *blóðberg* – 'blood of the rock'. Only later would these shapes and images become hitched onto alpine lady's mantle, mountain dryas, and wild thyme, when I had read about them in books.

'That's right. But Sarah...' she interrupts, unusually.

'Yes?'

'What's happened? Do you know you're speaking to me in Icelandic, in full sentences?'

An invisible moment has arrived in which these words I have been gathering like herbs, have infused. There are enough words in me now to improvise a world, to express, and to be understood. I have been speaking Icelandic, and so has she.

'Maybe it was being away. It allowed the words to settle.'

A mutual joy fills the distance down the telephone line and brings us closer. We can communicate.

I walk out the door with this new-found freedom and power, to gather herbs in my valley. Here, walking among the flowers and the fundamentals, I am allowed, and able, to have a relationship with this place. Through words, through imagination, through living and tending, I can go back to a beginning: not *the* beginning – there is no beginning and there is no end – but *a* beginning nonetheless. One in which my thoughts are not yet housed; one in which they make a home for themselves and take their cue from the place they are in.

Göng – Passage/Corridor/Tunnel

July 2011

We are in a tour coach ploughing along the 7-kilometre road tunnel that bores through the mountain between my village, Hnífsdalur, and Bolungarvík – the last village along this stretch of the Westfjords. When I use this tunnel day to day – to drop Bjarni at the trawler, to go to the pool – if I am silent I find that, as I move into and through the mountain, deeper, deeper, memories begin to surface on that grey concrete canvas. Some of them are mine. Others seem to belong to the mountain.

Visually, it is an uninteresting part of the tour and as a guide I often feel compelled to fill it with anecdote. Today, I resist the microphone.

'So, I heard Icelanders believe in elves and trolls.' A white-haired, be-fleeced American tourist leans forward and calls out above the engine noise to my seat at the front of the tour coach.

It is a statement that many tourists put to me, a little proud to have some 'insider knowledge' and apparently oblivious to the fact that it is the one Statement About Icelanders that almost every foreign visitor makes. It is framed as a sort of question, but really what they seem to want is for me to confirm it; to say that, from my observations, these Icelanders really *are* kooky, and to relate my own experiences here of the supernatural.

What can I say? Yes, there are legends and place names, hills and rocks and plants and astrological phenomena, Christmas traditions and natural events all associated with elves and trolls; all of which are still related, if the matter arises in conversation at home, or when moving through the landscape. There is *skessujurt* – 'troll woman's herb' (lovage) – growing in my garden. I pass Tungustapi, a hill referred to as an 'elf church' every time I drive between the Westfjords and Route 1. My mother-in-law has told me that the aurora borealis is the elves dancing, and that you will never see it on New Year's Eve as that is the night the elves come down from the sky to move house.

'I guess they're not moving this year?' I said to her last New Year's Eve when my parents were visiting, and to their delight, the aurora made an appearance after the village firework display.

'It's after midnight,' she responded, beaming.

The *gamla daga*, the 'old days' which Bjarni's family often speak of, are an amorphous 'once upon a time' spanning the period from the ninth-century settlement era to the teller's childhood years. It is at once imaginary and real; faraway and nearby; folkloric and practical. In the *gamla daga*, belief in the supernatural surely shaped behaviour. This belief was, and to an extent still is, a murmuring background to existence. It is a doorway through which one might step into a more reciprocal relationship with the land and sea. My surroundings here seem so vast, so volatile, so open; so transcendent and indifferent. I can imagine, in the time before we holed ourselves up in centrally heated houses around a television-hearth which flickered with Elsewhere, that there was a compulsion to break down the landscape and phenomena into narratives and characters that the limits of the human body could fathom, to which it could relate. Once upon a time, belief in the supernatural must have felt like a means to survive on this rock in the Atlantic, and to navigate uncharted moral territory: brought by the settlers in their wooden ships with the livestock and the Old Language; sown and grown and adapted to this new context.

Just above Ísafjörður, the port into which the cruise ships dock, there is a corrie – a steep-sided hollow – in the side of the mountain, nicknamed Tröllasætið – 'The Troll's Seat'. It looms large over us at the end of every bus tour as we round the fjord onto the spit on which the town is built, and pull into the harbour where the cruise ships tower over the buildings – three times the height of the tallest. Allegedly, in the fjord below this mountain, directly below the corrie, there is a depression in the seabed. There is one legend associated with this corrie, which I tell the tourists as we round the fjord, if only because it might open up a doorway to a more intimate relationship with this place, which they can then take home to their own places:

The Westfjords is a frilly appendage to the corpus of land
that makes up the rest of Iceland. They are joined together
by an isthmus, and Breiðafjörður, the bay to the west of this
isthmus, is scattered with an archipelago of more than 3,000

islands – some no larger than a house. It is said that in the
gamla daga – *the old days – two troll women wished the*
Westfjords to be separate, and independent, from the rest of
Iceland. Trolls being giants who turn to stone the moment
sunlight touches them, the troll women began digging
away furiously at the neck of land, so as to achieve their
goal before sunrise. In their fervour, rocks fell from their
shovels and landed in the bay of Breiðafjörður, becoming the
archipelago of islands that exists now. The isthmus narrowed
with every scoop of their shovels to the neck of land we see
today. One of the troll women wore herself out with all this
digging so she sat and rested with her aching feet in the
fjord. The corrie we see above us is the impression left by her
behind; and the deep harbour the impression left by her feet.

I have heard people talk of *álfasteinar* – elf stones – several times.
They are particular boulders that have a presence or a special beauty,
where elves are thought to dwell. Roads and buildings have been
built around these rocks, so as not to destroy them. I have heard
particularly of one road construction project near Reykjavík where a
mediator was brought in to communicate with the elves. The elves'
permission had not been sought before construction commenced.
This was thought to be the cause of a series of misfortunes that
beset the project, trucks and diggers breaking down with unlikely
frequency. I know an artist, Lisbet, who has an *álfasteinn* in the
basement of her postbox-red, early-twentieth-century house. The

basement was built around the stone. Lisbet regularly lights candles on it to honour the elves.

And *huldufólk* – the 'hidden people' – they have come up in conversation: a species of being, born from a reworking of the Christian creation story. The *huldufólk* were described to me as small people resembling humans, who are slightly dirty and raggedly clothed. The story goes that Adam and Eve, in fact, had many children, but when God came to check on them they showed him only two: Cain and Abel. So ashamed were Adam and Eve at how dirty and poorly dressed their other children were, that they hid them. So offended was God at their disbelief in his omniscience that he doomed their hidden children to remain hidden forever. A room can have people in it, but it may be twice as full of hidden people.

But none of these are my experiences, nor the experiences of the people I know well. One thing I can say with conviction, however, is that I have seen a ghost. It happened before I moved to Iceland, early on during the month-long road trip that Bjarni and I took in our campervan in September 2009. It has never happened to me before, and nor has it happened in the same way since: an instance where I was irrefutably looking at an apparition, and what I saw was reconfirmed by another. We were in the south of the country, in a region called Álftaver. Route 1, the only main road, was at that point some distance from the coast and we were looking for a spot by the sea to park up for the night. Our needs for a park-up were basic but important: flat; with clear running water that would not have been affected by sheep; absent of other people; hopefully with some sort of driftwood or old fence posts we could make a fire with and preferably beautiful – a quality that was available in spades.

We turned off Route 1 along a farm track and headed towards the sea. Either side of the track was coastal flatland with a skin of short cropped green grass and the occasional pink mound of moss campion. I imagined it was peaty underneath. At no point on our journey had we seen many people – this was Iceland in September after all, when the tourists have left. But something struck us individually as we bumped our way along this track, past a few farm buildings: *there was no life at all.* There was not a sound or a movement in the farmyard, no insects flitting across the windscreen, no sheep, no horses in the fields, no *birds.* There are *always* birds in Iceland. Although I noticed this fact, everything was new to me then. As much as it was an anomaly to my experience so far, it did not disturb me as it did Bjarni.

'I don't like this place,' he said. 'It's so… *lifeless.*'

'Let's just see where the track goes. Maybe it'll get better.'

We continued to the end of the track, and parked. There we saw that the flat ground was raised in geometric rows covered in turf, like the long-deserted ruins of a farm or small community.

'This is spooky,' Bjarni reiterated his discomfort. I was beginning to agree.

We saw, or imagined, doorways, hearths, the life that might once have crossed in and out of these overgrown rectangles.

We needed to fill our water bottles. Bjarni found what looked like a spring, pulsing like a large eye from the skin of grass. He recoiled. I walked over and looked into it. The flow of the clear water tousled a mane of deep green algae that clung to the bank. Intermittently, as it was lifted by the water, it revealed several bones cleaned of flesh and sinew. Sheep bones? Human bones? We did not know. But it was the final cue to leave. If we could not drink this water, we could not live here either, even for a night.

Bjarni started the engine and pulled away without hesitation. We bumped back along the dirt track, the dust barely settled since our inward journey. No insects, no birds, no people. We rounded a bend and the farmyard we had passed earlier came into view. The corrugated-iron barn emerged like an abstract painting, its flaking painted layers blown off to join with the wind.

'Ah look, there *is* someone,' I exclaimed, palpably relieved.

Bjarni was silent, and attentive to the farmyard. We were driving alongside the open space of the concreted yard now. Within this rectangle of space was a man on horseback riding towards us, but parallel with the road. I too fell silent as all my energy diverted towards fathoming what I was looking at. There was a man, on horseback. But he, and the horse, did not move like a man on horseback, or like a horse carrying a man. They glided across the yard without the slightest undulation. And as more details of the rider came into view, it got even stranger.

'Bjarni, tell me what you're seeing right now,' I implored, hoping at once that this was not real but wanting him to confirm that he could see it too, so I could know I was not delusional.

'There's a man, on horseback, but he's gliding across the yard... and he has this long, grey, straggly hair down to his chest, but it's… he has no face. The hair is all around.' He continued driving slowly.

'That's exactly what I'm seeing.' As we passed him, I turned in my seat to look at the side and back of his head. From every angle he was long, greasy, grey hair. I cannot speak of his features, for I did not see any. There was no face.

'Let's get out of here,' Bjarni said, as if we weren't already.

A few weeks later when we returned to Bjarni's parents' house in Ísafjörður, we regaled them with stories from our trip. Gyða listened attentively, while knitting, and Haukur lay outstretched on the sofa as usual, watching a loud television. This story was the first to be told. It needed telling: we were brimming with it.

Unusually, Haukur turned down the volume. '*Haaaa.* Tell me what this ghost looked like again?' He cleared his throat.

We repeated the details of the gliding, the long messy hair and the absence of a face.

'That's the ghost of Jón Steingrimsson. That's what he looks like, I've heard. He's well known down there.' Haukur stated this not just as a fact, but a fact that appeared to be of the most everyday kind. He turned the volume back up on the television and we continued our evening, my reality having shifted tectonically.

I moved to Iceland a year later, into the house that had been inhabited for seventy years by Bogga, now passed away. But the house's familiar name, Bogguhús, reminds us daily how she and it remain inseparable. I feel her presence as an immanence exuded by a home that has been cared for and loved, which has born witness to love and life in its various guises. Mine and Bjarni's is another story for those walls to cradle.

When my family came to visit last year for our first Christmas in this house, Bogga made an appearance of a different nature. For the first time in our co-habiting set-up, there was tension between Bjarni and me. He appeared to be, and admitted to, intentionally making life difficult for me. I knew there was something deeper going on, but he did not have the tools to articulate it at the time. Naturally, it expanded to become a tension between Bjarni and my family. It was all the more awkward as I wanted my parents to like him, but in this moment I did not much like him myself.

One night he was out late with friends when the rest of us had gone to bed. Bjarni and I were using the guest room on the ground floor so that my family could have the warmer upstairs rooms. At 2 a.m. I was woken by the loud noise of someone climbing the wooden staircase between floors, then moving the furniture around upstairs. I lay in bed trying to figure out if it could be my parents, or vermin, and being slightly afraid. I just wanted it to stop so I wouldn't have to see what it was. It stopped, and I went back to sleep. Soon, it happened again. Footsteps climbing the stairs; the scrape of chair legs on floorboards. Unable to take it anymore, I leaped up and went to the staircase, muttering: 'Why on *earth* are they moving furniture around?' At the top of the stairs, there was a trapdoor. I pushed it up and emerged from below, expecting movement, disruption, wakefulness. I found stillness, silence. My parents sleeping, breathing deeply, snoring. *Nothing* was happening. Confused, I returned to the guest-room bed.

It happened again. I texted Bjarni:

22.12.10   01:48

Where are you? Was that
you coming in? If not
either we have a very large rat
or there's a ghost xx

Bjarni finally returned and I desperately hoped it *would* happen again, just so he would hear it. His warm mound of a body lay next to mine, alert. After a few minutes, there it was: footsteps, moving furniture.

'It's likely Bogga,' he said quietly. 'She won't be happy with how things are between us.'

His explanation made a profound kind of sense to me. I could not claim that I did not believe in ghosts. I had seen one with my own eyes, and now I was living with one. Like the overgrown traces of the farmhouse walls in the south, Bogguhús was not simply a place where we would live *our* lives, but where the legacy of other lives still lived. We lived in a continuum with them. In so doing, we were in a living, breathing relationship with the walls of a house, as much as with the ground these lives were built upon: the earth and the pine panelling still held the echo of their passing. I was beginning to see what it might mean to dwell in a place.

* * *

'Some do believe, yes,' I say to the American tourist and turn to face the tunnel again, the arch of light at the other end quickly growing larger now. Today, I do not fill the silence. Today, we are passing through.

Að snúa – To Turn;
Snúið – Complicated

August 2011

The coach driver Trausti and I got along well. He liked a joke and was diligent, and he took an interest in the landscape we drove through on each tour. He was proud of it. Trausti was from Hnífsdalur – my village – and even though he now lived in an apartment block, 4 kilometres down the road, he would always be a Hnífsdælingur. We had done the full 'Life and Culture' tour with a coachload of English-speaking tourists. This one had been easy. I could be funny in my mother tongue, in a way that was not so fluent when I did the French tours. The English were always a bit stiff on the tours that started early in the morning, but they soon lightened up when they realized, with tangible relief, that they would be able to understand my accent because I *was* English. The mood was buoyant, and we were on our way back to their cruise ship. We had just been through the 7-kilometre road tunnel through the middle of the mountain.

'You *must* write a book,' so many of them urged.

'I will, I will,' I promised – them, and myself – though I wasn't convinced I had the capacity to put this experience into words in a way that did not compromise it somehow. They just want a good story. But I am invested in preserving its integrity. I knew it would involve a slow and patient metabolism of experience into words – words which could hold all its paradox and uncertainty; words which could trace my path as insider and outsider, criss-crossing, braiding.

We had just emerged from the darkness onto the coast road, when Trausti suddenly turned right, unannounced, into Hnífsdalur.

'What are you doing?'

'We should show them our village, shouldn't we?'

'I guess… OK, everyone, Trausti has decided you should see the village where he is from and I now live. My house is this one coming up on the right.'

Trausti slowed at the brow of the hill, where my rusting white corrugated-iron-clad house stood facing the sea, marooned in a meadow of wildflowers just behind the village bus stop. The decorative deep-red window frames were peeling, and I became aware of how strange the roof looked now that people I didn't know were looking at it. 'Corrugated-iron cladding is the best protection against the salt air here. The roof is silver because we have just replaced it and you must let it weather for two years before painting it,' I explained.

But they didn't care. They had spotted something else and were drawing their cameras up to the window. Trausti halted at the top of our drive. There, leaning on one elbow on the rickety gatepost, was Bjarni. He was dressed in grey corduroys and a tatty coat, chewing on a stem of grass and contemplating the sea. One green-welly-booted leg crossed the other and his face glowed pink behind his ginger beard. He was the perfect picture of a 'rural Icelander', and everyone on this coach thought so too. A battery of cameras bleep-clicked urgently. Tourists from the opposite side of the coach leaned over the others to capture the scene too.

I was troubled. In that moment, he was commodified into one dimension. People who had never spoken to him would be showing that image at dinner parties, putting it on Facebook. What did they know? I suddenly felt ambivalent about my role. I wanted to show people this place, tell them about the people. I wanted them to get a comprehensive impression, warts and all, while admitting it was only my perspective. But taking an image of my partner and reducing him to a stereotype seemed the very opposite of what I was trying to do. I waved at him apologetically through the glass. I realized I had crossed over irreversibly to the inside of this community. From the perspective of mass tourism, my home was a quaint, slightly decaying 'traditional' house. And my man was an 'authentic local'.

Like a true Icelander, Bjarni appeared unperturbed, and the coach continued on.

Innflytjandi – Importer/ Immigrant

October 2011

Life has quietened. Now that winter has come, Bjarni has returned to the trawler to catch cod and haddock, despite my reluctance for him to leave. No alternative job has presented itself over the summer, and he has done what is easiest.

A couple of weeks ago, the tourists vanished in a movement that was both incremental and sudden, like a puddle evaporating in strong sun. They have washed around the place, and many of our lives, all summer. Much energy has been diverted towards seeing to their needs. Plans have been made around dense shifts of tourism work. Only brief holidays could be taken, despite this being the only season in which domestic travel is really feasible. But with the tourists' arrival, work was created. We were reminded what the world outside of here is like, how members of an array of nationalities think and behave. Tables and chairs were placed outside the three bars and cafés in Ísafjörður, which bustled with life. Beautiful young Icelanders enjoyed pretending that they were on a Continental café terrace: exposed their skin, wore sunglasses, sipped frappés. Tourists climbed up beside waterfalls, hired kayaks, bought Icelandic jumpers, tasted rotten shark in the Maritime Museum.

By late August, the self-drive tourists in their rental cars and campervans had emptied out, back to their term-time lives in Europe and the USA. September saw a couple more cruise ships disgorge on a place that was perhaps closer to the passengers' fantasies: free from the other hundreds in brightly coloured anoraks looking for the same pristine solitude. The last tour I guided was on 22 September – several weeks after Icelandic children returned to school, the bureaucrats returned to their offices, and the Arctic terns took flight back to the Southern Hemisphere. Finally, the day came when *Boudicca*, the last passenger ship of the year, cruised slowly out across the fjord towards the open sea – right to left across my living room window – after ten hours in port: enough, apparently, for the 900 passengers to 'do' the Westfjords. It was a gargantuan block of white, like a contour-less iceberg seated on a dark, sharp-beaked hull. A floating façade, pierced with hundreds of tiny windows from which the passengers gazed at my valley, in which my house sits, in which I sat at my window, looking at them. *Boudicca* vanished into the blue distance and this quieter life returned.

This life has its own rhythm. Its pulse is regular and steady. But each day looks quite different, as the darkness returns like curtains drawing in on either side of the day.

I know I can do guiding work every summer now if I want to. It went well. The pay was relatively good. My tips were generous, and now fill a large jar on my windowsill which once contained Euro Shopper gherkins – dollars, pounds, euros; notes and coins jostling for space, ready for the next trip to Europe. The praise was high and the prompts to write a book about my experience of this place helped me feel my observations were valid. It was a boost to my morale to find something I could do here, but this kind of work does not feel real to me. It is a temporary period of frenzy, and I am wary of commodifying this place I love.

Time here has shaken off my ego. I accept I will not find any kind of work that is obviously linked to my qualifications. I must think more laterally. I have not lost sight of my long-term aim to make a film about this place. I think the film is about resilience, although at the moment I am preoccupied with learning to understand the edges of my own. But I have spent the summer observing that many visitors come and consume packages of 'Icelandicness'. These packages, repeated and shared, become the narrative as presented to the world, and narrative becomes cliché. Now, more than ever, I see how necessary it has been to get inside of this life, before attempting to speak about it.

I speak enough Icelandic now, I think, to have a go at a job that requires regular interaction with Icelanders. So the question becomes not 'What can I do?' but 'What will be most useful to the shape of our life now?' A staff discount at the hardware store would be useful while we are renovating the house – that is clear. I spend a lot of my time and money in there already.

I go to Húsasmiðjan, the hardware store, and ask the manager if there is any work available.

'Only in the florist department,' he says, apologetically.

'Even better,' I respond.

I leave with an application form. If I get this job, I will be arranging living things – colourful, *green* things – rather than screws, all the white-grey winter. *And* I would get the staff discount on hardware. This is as good as it will get out of tourist season, for now.

Bjarni is not here to help me fill out the form in Icelandic, so I go to the extension of him: his mother. I am beginning to grasp just how much my perception of Bjarni is influenced by what his parents and aunts and uncles do for me in his absence, and what they do for us when he is around. There is no line where they end, and he begins. With this team at his back, in and out of each other's houses on an almost daily basis, many aspects of our life feel taken care of, secure, even when he is not home. I associate him with this feeling of abundance – I never lack hand-knitted woollens, a mechanic, food, firewood – but ironically the thing that is not readily available is him. It couldn't be more different from my own family. Although I know we could depend on each other in times of need, we have lived on different continents since I was sixteen. My entire adult life has been one of independence.

The form is fairly straightforward and Gyða is patient: name, phone number, email, a small box for why I think I am suitable, and no CV requested. Before I leave, she feeds me pan-fried horsemeat in breadcrumbs from her brother in the south, and focuses on the positive in her chat: what will be in the future rather than what is now, which is that I don't have a job. She still seems to believe that I haven't really worked since arriving, by which she means a 9–5 with a salary where I am visible to the community. I wonder if self-employment, or tourism work, are in the same category as hobbies in her mind. I think it has bothered her more than me.

'*Þetta reddast*,' she says, for the umpteenth time – 'It will work itself out.'

When I return to the hardware store to hand in the form, I make sure I chat to Laufey, the head florist, so that she can get a sense of me, and hear that my Icelandic is sufficient. Being so basic, the form has reduced me to a few lines, and does not show who I am related to. For once, on the form I stand alone, as myself, but stripped of my professional experience and qualifications, to a foreign woman with 'an eye for colour and form'. For once, though, being able to say I am related to somebody she will know might be my preferred descriptor.

Laufey is friendly and warm and walks between the counter and the cabinet of fresh cut flowers, selecting stems as we talk. She arranges a bouquet of roses, hypericum and some kind of fir, slicing the ends off the stems, one by one, in deft diagonal strokes. She squints occasionally as she looks at me, as if to see beneath the surface of the slightly choppy flow of Icelandic conversation. I manage to drop in the names of my man and my father-in-law.

'Leave it with me. I'll let you know soon,' she says, wrapping the bouquet in cellophane and curling a ribbon bow with opened scissors.

I know I could do this job sufficiently well. I am fortunate to have an eye for arranging things and I feel the skills needed for creative endeavours pool into one another, even if apparently discrete. I doubt there will be many people applying who can actually arrange flowers, and so I feel confident, given that this seems to be the main part of the job.

Back at home, an email tells me I have been invited to a film festival in Belgrade for a screening and director Q&A of the film I was editing last winter. I decide to go: I don't have a job, I do have enough money and Bjarni is not home. I can still retain a strand of my identity, even if I cannot do it here. A parallel life off this island seems the only way to do it. When I tell Gyða I shall be away for a couple of weeks I get the sense that she does not know how to compute this dual self: an immigrant with basic language skills who will be lucky to get *any* job, and an apparently successful filmmaker who attends events internationally. She cannot put herself in either of my worlds and so she smiles and says, 'Great.' I wonder if she thinks her son is funding my existence, because the kind of work he is doing is visible by his absence, and by his tiredness when he returns.

Before leaving I go to get some Belgrade tips from my Serbian friend Svetlana, who lives above the bookshop in Ísafjörður. I tell her I've applied for a job in the flower shop. 'Congratulations. Ah, I hope you get it. That's a *nice* job.'

A couple of days later I take the domestic flight to Reykjavík to catch the international flight. When I land there is a text message from Svetlana.

07.10.11 12:09

Looks like flower lady gave job
to someone she knew. He's a
guy... Guðni. Doesn't know how
to arrange flowers. That's Iceland
darling! xx

I am devastated, and it shocks me that I am devastated. It is only an assistant florist position, but still, it is something I could imagine doing and enjoying. Suddenly the prospect of winter has become a long grey blank rather than Gyða's projections of what the future would be. I wonder if I should even return. What am I doing in Iceland if Bjarni is not home? Shouldn't I wait for him to get whatever it is out of his system that made him go to sea in spite of my resistance to it – feeling indebted to his parents; a kind but misguided intention to support me financially; or something else he has not yet unpicked – somewhere I can make a life that doesn't hinge so completely on him? But my heart is loyal and there is a wedding to plan.

Every time I leave the island to go elsewhere, I go via England to visit friends and family, pick up supplies, gorge on culture. This trip is an ocean of movement, colour and people. This time I am shopping for a wedding. I would like to find a wedding dress; one that has a story in its threads and is practical for an outdoor ceremony. I don't mind if it is old: stories are carried from person to person, place to place. In London, I pop in to a dealer of Afghan textiles I know. She takes me to her home to show me her special collection. In among the bright colours, tassels and trims, there is a black dress on the rail which calls to me. The long cotton skirt is heavy and full, and the bodice is hand-embroidered with tiny stitches in ochre, rust and duck egg blue. The shoulders are narrow like mine, and the sleeves are embroidered with delicate deep-red leaves. I slip it on and we both know: this is the one. Its story, whatever it is, fits my body exactly.

I enjoy the search for interesting objects – I encounter worlds I might not otherwise have known existed. During my week in Serbia I continue looking for accoutrements. The film festival staff get behind my quest and send me off with a couple of anthropology students to a place in the hills around Belgrade where replicas of regional folk dress are made. I come away with an appliqué felt waistcoat for Bjarni. Back at the film festival, a city newspaper interviews me about my film, and my search for a wedding outfit. I am sent the article later, but I have no idea what it says.

Just before I return to Iceland, laden with colour and other worlds to weave into that one, I see an email in my inbox from an address I do not recognize. It is Laufey from the flower shop. In broken English, she is telling me it didn't work out with someone else, and the job is mine if I want it. When can I start?

This is ideal. I am energized by my trip, confident that I am still a filmmaker even if I am not making one yet. I have the wherewithal – imaginal and material – to begin dreaming a wedding. And now I can begin a life that takes me further inside this small Icelandic village, through a job that I have acquired not by family connections, nor by ability, but by circumstance.

I start as soon as I return home. My shift begins in the *kaffistofa* – the 'coffee room'.

'He would come in here and hang his head in his hands like this,' Laufey explains when I ask what happened with the other guy. 'He had something going on. But he needed too many breaks.'

There is a thermos of sharp, stewed coffee on the table and a foot-long piece of Danish pastry for us to help ourselves to. I am given a name badge, a till card and a contract I do not really understand.

'Do you know how much the wage is?' I ask Laufey. I learned when looking for work that this is not a question one asks before being offered the job or, as it now seems, when accepting it. For work like this, a job is a job, and you are paid what you are given.

'I'm not sure. But it's definitely not much.' She does not meet my gaze.

I do not understand how people make ends meet here. Since the crisis in 2008 the króna has devalued massively – to almost half what it used to be. Whenever I make a conversion to pounds in my head, nothing adds up: life should not be possible. What I know is that the average hourly wage seems to be equal to or less than the cost of a hamburger. And yet the international press is always lauding Iceland as one of the wealthiest, most egalitarian nations, with the highest quality of life, happiness quotient, and books read per capita. These are not features that have struck me particularly, but I have not seen any poverty. Either the situation is being misrepresented or the state-sponsored baseline for 'wealth' and 'happiness' has shifted while I was unaware. In my experience though, the mutual support of extended families makes up for other lacks: it is a wealth of a different kind, but not one the governments measure. I have not yet had to buy fish, or lamb, and it is some of the finest I have ever eaten. But for this I sacrifice a co-habiting partner and must run around on a hill in the snow once a year, chasing after sheep.

'You get a 20% staff discount though,' she adds, smiling.

I remember that this is the reason I applied in the first place, and satisfy myself with the knowledge that everything I have to spend in this store will feel like money back. And I will get to improve my Icelandic in the process. Not only that, but this is the only flower shop in the whole of the Westfjords. I am well positioned, over time, to meet almost everyone who lives here and see how they express themselves with flowers. Finally, they will be able to place me in their world: *Sara Blómakona* – 'Sarah the flower lady'.

Laufey puts me to work immediately. There is no training as such, just learning by doing. I am to keep the refrigerated cabinet of flowers looking good by cleaning the vases and keeping on top of the blooms – trimming them, taking off dead heads and cleaning slime off the stems. If a stem wilts a little I should snake florist's wire up its length to support it. It has taken a lot of energy and care to get these flowers to the Westfjords intact, and their lives must be prolonged as much as possible. To my surprise, she tells me that most of them are grown in Iceland, in geothermal greenhouses in the south.

The hardest part of the job is learning to use the computerized till. The combination of new words and new technology taxes me and is doubly stressful when someone is waiting to be served.

A woman asks for a bouquet of white lilies, and Laufey nods at me giving silent permission to take it on. I make a perfectly acceptable arrangement, but I worry I am being too slow, and rush the diagonal slicing of stems at the end. I slice a finger and red blood pools from the cut. I try to continue and hope that nobody notices, but some blood drips onto a lily – colour on the blankness – and the customer looks uncomfortable.

'Go and get a plaster,' Laufey says, coming up beside me and seamlessly taking over. Nothing more is said except, 'Just remember to cut away from your body, with the knife.'

As I get more familiar with the tasks, I enjoy the opportunity to chat with people. They seem to know more about me than I do about them – or at least, that I am Bjarni's girlfriend and Haukur's 'daughter-in-law'.

The following day, day two of the job, Laufey asks me to start displaying the new Christmas stock in the homewares section. Meanwhile, she potters behind the counter preparing oasis rings for Christmas wreaths. At midday, folding up her green apron she says, 'OK, I'm going home.'

My shift ends at four.

'You're going to leave me alone to run the shop?' I ask in disbelief.

'You're going to make mistakes,' she responds, smiling kindly. 'Might as well get them over with.'

226

* * *

In November, I get a phone call from the local newspaper, *Bæjarins Besta* ('the best town'). Apparently, they like to publish features on new residents. One of their journalists, Huldar Breiðfjörð, has heard about me and would like to do an interview. I am intrigued: I have not done anything particularly newsworthy except be here – for a year already. And, judging by the apparent response of the community to my presence – barely a question asked of me *at all* for my first four months, and not many thereafter – I have no reason to believe that anybody would be particularly interested in my story. I agree to have him round, curious as to what has made me suddenly become visible.

'You haven't stayed two years yet,' a colleague at the hardware store told me. 'They want to see that you're staying before they make an effort to know you.'

Huldar arrives at the house one evening after I've just finished a shift in the flower shop. I welcome him into the living room, which I've temporarily transformed into a pop-up shop of jewellery I have made. I have decided to attempt a pre-Christmas 'open house' and invite the neighbours I do not know yet and those I do; put up a poster at the supermarket to expand the clientele. This article may even help drum up some trade. My jewellery-making started years ago as a hobby, then I began to sell pieces each year at Christmastime, for a little extra income. It has an African influence to it, and is mostly made from beads I collected in Kenya, which originated from across that continent. My necklaces are displayed on calabashes, graceful like the suggestion of a slender woman's neck. I can see from his expression that it is not a world Huldar was expecting to enter when he knocked on the door in this small hamlet. We take seats in opposite armchairs and a subtle smell of Kenya – preservative butter and wood smoke exuding from the calabashes – weaves around us.

Huldar is a writer and a traveller, who has decided to come and live in the Westfjords for a while, for the peace. 'Reykjavík was too intense,' he says. He is typically quiet and reserved – the space between his phrases much larger than the phrases themselves. He sips the tea I have given him and ponders each thing I say.

I find the long pauses both pleasant and slightly uncomfortable. It feels unexpected that the interview is happening in the first place. I was expecting a more standard dynamic of interviewer asks interviewee a lot of questions, but I find myself filling his silences unbidden.

The photographer arrives part way through the interview with a different energy altogether. I recognize him: he's the guy who runs the kayak hire place. He asks me to pose with the jewellery I have made. He clicks and zooms and plays with the lights. In the middle of it all, his mobile phone rings. A few words are exchanged with the caller, even fewer with Huldar. He says 'Bye' and runs out the door. Huldar is unfazed.

'Is everything alright?' I ask.

'There's a fire in town,' he says, looking up from his notes with no change in expression.

'And he's the "breaking news" photojournalist?'

'No. He knows how to scuba-dive, so they need him,' Huldar continues, as if that makes perfect sense.

'Sorry, I don't follow.'

'Scuba-divers are confident with breathing apparatus and moving through spaces with obscured vision. The fire service here is pretty small, so for larger fires they need volunteers. Fire and water – it's all the same.'

*   *   *

Laufey has shown me how to make Christmas wreaths with the rings of oasis she has prepared. We have had a big delivery of fir branches, from Norway I think, the long boxes now stacked on the floor beside the counter. I am preparing the wreaths for orders by laying small sprigs of fir horizontally into the oasis, slightly overlapping, working my way around the ring and holding them in place invisibly with wire. There is a box full of variously coloured decorations to pin onto them. We are going to need a lot of wreaths because, Laufey tells me, people take them to the graves of their loved ones at Christmastime. The longer I spend in this job the more fascinating I find it: I am preparing gifts for the ancestors.

An old man comes in to make an order for two of them.

'One with pink baubles and one with blue – for my sister and my brother.' I am tickled by this choice of colours, not only for two adults but two deceased adults. 'So you're from *Kenya*?' he adds.

'Not from there but I grew up there. How do you know?'

'I read the article in *Bæjarins Besta*.'

He says he will come for the wreaths later, when he's done his shopping, and turns for the door.

I remember back to the interview, and Huldar's comment about scuba-divers making good fire fighters, with their skill to act calmly with obscured vision. I am startled by the revelation to be found within that observation: that, with practice, it may be possible to move through life, sensing my way, even when I feel blind to the details. Trusting the process and the unfolding flow, even when I don't understand why things are a certain way, or what will happen next. To accept that often things are not what they seem. There is a difference between learning and discovery. I am beginning to learn – no, discover – that people *are* interested in me, in their own way. Asking a lot of questions is not the Icelandic way: that would be deemed an intrusion on my own personal right to silence. By being in a newspaper that almost everyone here reads, I have made a large stride on the journey from anonymity to intimacy, with neither asserting its shape on the other.

I take out a large branch of fir from the box and snip it down into small feather-like sprigs. A strong scent of Northern forests is released with each snip and my fingers become tacky with sap. A black beetle drops to the counter with one of the branches. I place it on my palm to look closer. It is motionless: dead or very cold from the journey. It is about an inch long; black with a hard carapace and thick antennae. I place it on the shelf beside the counter.

The radio seems to have been playing the same ten songs since I started working here a month ago, and it is driving me a bit mad.

Laufey brings me a coffee and places it on the counter. I didn't drink coffee before I came to Iceland and now I seem to have at least five cups a day. It's what you do to interact, even if in silence. The coffee is strong, and as soon as it wears off you need another.

She leans over my shoulder to check my work.

'What is *that*?' she asks.

'A beetle. It dropped out of one of these branches.'

'*Nú!* We have to call Náttúrustofa.'

'What's *that*?'

'The Nature… Office, or something like that. They do the researches. This little guy is *not* from Iceland.'

I feel foolish for not having thought more of it. Her reaction confirms my instinct: this beetle is an immigrant. It is too big and too bold to belong here. Everything Icelandic I know is diminutive, apart from the people and their jeeps. But I am not familiar enough with island life to know that an immigrant species is potentially a problem. I would probably have let it warm up and walk off into this world, if it isn't already dead. A position of caution seems to be the default. Laufey puts the beetle in a small box and goes to make the phone call to the Náttúrustofa.

By lunchtime all the hardware store staff have seen the beetle. They have been passing it round in the *kaffistofa* in their coffee breaks. They come to ask me where it was; how I found it. It amuses me how *this* seems to be what is newsworthy.

Later in the afternoon, Margrét, a stoic checkout assistant with spiked grey hair, walks briskly over to the florist section, clutching one hand over a telephone mouthpiece. She is quaking with excitement inside the red blouse of her Húsasmiðjan uniform.

'It's... *RÚV!*' she whispers emphatically, passing me the telephone, her sparkling blue eyes wide with delight and disbelief. RÚV is the national broadcaster – the Icelandic equivalent of the BBC, and the Ísafjörður branch of Húsasmiðjan is about to get its moment of fame. She lingers to see what happens.

I hold the phone to my ear. 'Good afternoon. May I help you?'

'Yes, I'd like to order a Christmas tree for the Ísafjörður branch.'

'One Christmas tree,' I repeat, glancing at Margrét. 'Would you like it delivered?'

Deflated, she returns to her post at the checkout.

The Strangest Silence

Last night the weather was wild. The sea wall below the house boomed as the breakers heaved their guts over its girth. Lying in bed, I could feel the impact like a distant explosion, over and over and over. The wind's howl was a mournful constant as it coursed ice crystals down the treeless valley past my house, and in a few places, squeezed itself through crumbling window putty in a high scream. Every so often, a gust would slap the air and the house would shudder, the wooden panelling creaking with the jolt. The ability of the house to dance with this wind, and the fact that it still stands after 108 winters, reassures me. It is the windows that I worry about, and the objects that, if not well secured, might be hurled through them.

Recently, when Bjarni was home from sea, we went to our neighbour Ólafur's for coffee and waffles. Ólafur showed us a framed photograph of the village in 1952, taken from an elevated position on the side of the mountain above us. It was summer in the photograph. The steep green sides of the valley, the cluster of red houses at the river mouth looking out onto a flat blue sea, had been hand-tinted with colour. He pointed to the old school, almost obscuring it with his

233

enormous finger. 'That winter,' he said tapping the glass, 'the school blew away. The children ran out from underneath it as it was riven from the ground by the wind.' Such extreme facts being delivered in such a casual tone is a habit it is taking me time to get used to. More recently, cars, and our own wheelie bin, have ended up in the sea during storms. Staying awake can do nothing to deter flying objects. But alert to changes in the wind's pitch, I can brace myself against the potential onslaught of a shattering bedroom window.

Sleep came fitfully as I attempted to achieve some semblance of protection with my thick down duvet; as I tried, and failed, not to imagine Bjarni out on that sea – his trawler a small metal box being tossed around on a seething infinity. 'Many women in Iceland live like this,' I told myself, repeating his mother's words, though they seem at odds with the kind of life I wish to be living.

The next time I woke, I lay there wondering how Bjarni's door-frame-shaped bruise was healing from the last storm at sea. He had not mentioned the incident until I asked, when he was back home this last time. He had been standing topless at the kitchen sink one morning when I noticed the straight purple lines that extended up both his sides and crossed his shoulder blades. He was doing the washing up with his legs spread wide and his forehead pressed against the cupboard – a stance he assumed to stabilize himself while working in the ship's kitchen, and which he could not shake on dry land.

'Oh, that. Yeah it still quite hurts,' he had said, reaching a sudsy hand round to his back.

'*What the hell happened?*' I had asked.

'Well, the boat was rocking – *a lot.* The only thing I could do was brace myself in the doorway below deck. But the boat jolted, suddenly, and two of my shipmates, Darri and Hákon… 100-something kilo guys… they hurled into me. I didn't fall but I did slam into the door frame.'

I placed my hands gently on his skin. It was cold. A layer of fat, from a lifetime of eating fish, lamb, seal and whale, kept his warmth in.

'Will you take a picture for me?' he had asked, smiling. 'It's probably kind of beautiful.'

With my camera I zoomed in on his shoulder blades. A horizon of deep purple seeped downwards into red, like the colours of the sun that doesn't rise but just gestures in midwinter. In its own way it was beautiful, and I might have found it so if it was not such a visible marker of the challenges we are facing in order to have a home together: the togetherness hardly ever comes. He is absent and in danger daily. To cope, I must try not to think about him and not get too attached when he is home.

'It's good money,' my 'in-laws' keep telling me. But at what cost? For reasons I cannot fathom, working on a fishing trawler seems to be considered one of the most desirable jobs to have in Iceland. It's true, it pays the best wage you will get in a rural area – which means most of the country outside of Reykjavík. You get as much free fish as you and your family can eat: a bin bag per tour is the unofficial standard. But you are on shift all the time. Even if you are 'off duty', when a catch comes in it's all hands on deck. I have visited his living quarters – brightly lit, sparse, linoleum covered. A TV in the corner of the kitchen-diner is the only link to the land world. Sleep is grabbed in fragments in a pungent narrow bunk in a tiny room for four. The shower barely works and, besides, there is not much time to have one. When I visited, a row of bright orange rubber dungarees were collapsed around the uprights of industrial white wellies, awaiting action at a moment's notice. Some of the fishermen have evolved for a life on the ocean. One of the older members of Bjarni's crew told me, 'If I ever took a holiday, I'd go on a cruise so I could still be at sea.'

Bjarni is the trawler's cook as well as a fisherman. Because of the resulting double shift, his time off to sleep falls during the only four hours of light that exist in these winter months. He will have a winter of barely seeing daylight. It is hard, dangerous work. The trawlers land for only three reasons: extremely bad weather, landing the catch, and mandated holidays. *Sjómannadagurinn* ('Seaman's Day') – the first Sunday in June – is the only day except Christmas and New Year when trawler crews are legally obliged to have shore leave. When bad weather comes, or the catch needs landing, they land at the nearest harbour, which does not necessarily mean home. Bjarni's time off is rare, and I will never know when, or for how long, he will be home.

Once, about a month ago, he landed for only three hours. I had to be satisfied with going down to the harbour to grab a kiss – him stinking of fish guts. That time I was lucky: I was allowed to join him on his supermarket spree to restock the ship's kitchen with supplies for the crew. We exchanged news and affection while he filled a shopping trolley. I will never be able to read a label for 'Icelandic cod' simply now, knowing the price – human and ecological – at which it ends up on our plates.

When I dropped him off this last time, we had managed to have a few days together, though he was tired and bruised and the weather was bad. I found those days hard to relax into, as I never knew when the text message would come from his captain – day or night – instructing the crew to return to the boat. Fortunately, it came in the afternoon, so I took him to the harbour. I drove back through the mountain tunnel to our home, to find I had twenty missed calls and a text message that read:

02.02.11   13:08

My wellies!!!!

When I called back they had already pulled out of port. In the boot of the car were his steel-toe-capped thermal wellies, emanating the putrid tang of his livelihood. I worried that he would be doing this tour in leather lace-ups, more vulnerable than usual – no grip, no support, no protection.

I cannot call him once he has left the fjord. All I can do is track the boat's movements on www.marinetraffic.com – a worldwide boat-tracking website which surprisingly provides some solace. Seeing that the boat is moving at a certain speed in a certain direction indicates at least that it has not sunk.

*   *   *

Bjarni is not here, and I, and our windows, have survived the night. Marine Traffic suggests he did too. Now, it is still and crystal clear. I sit inside my second February, just after midwinter. It has snowed since October and may continue to do so until May. Munching on some toast in the kitchen, I re-read the *Bæjarins Besta* article with my slightly increased Icelandic vocabulary. The headline translates as 'The Silence is the Strangest', a mysterious poetic counterpoint to the awkward close-up of my smiling face. I find it interesting that, of all the words that came out of my mouth in that interview, it is these that the journalist has chosen to summarize me with. Not words describing anything that I might expect people here to find noteworthy: my childhood in Kenya; my career as a visual anthropologist; the fact that I am an English filmmaker who has decided to up sticks and live in Iceland during the aftermath of the financial crisis. But an observation conveying my response to life here. Perhaps he recognized that this response was more revealing than anything else I mentioned.

I notice how differently I have come to feel about the silence in this short time. I realize that the radio is not on, as it used to be – almost constantly. I feel less need to drown out an absence of something, or distract myself, finding myself strong enough now to be curious about what *is* here. If I do switch on the radio, I do not reach straight for British podcasts to keep me anchored in my former identity, rather listening to the melodic burbling of Icelandic Rás 1, which has begun to make some sense to me now. There is little variation in tone in the presenter's voice between radio

documentaries, two-for-one leg of lamb offers and the obituaries
– all offered at a steady pace carrying listeners through the day
without sensationalism, ceasing just before midnight for some
hours of silence.

On 23 December, Þorláksmessa, the anchor, reads out Christmas
greetings sent in from well-wishers to loved ones around the country.
They read out all of them, taking the day over it. Soon, between
the middle and the end of March, as every year, there will be an
announcement that touches my heart: *Lóan er komin* ('the golden
plover has come'), marking the beginning of spring. Although spring
is a tumultuous time of fierce winds and schizophrenic weather, it
means we are on the home run to summer, and the return of life. I
have come to perceive the *plok* and *krunk* of the ravens, the purring
wings of a flock of snow bunting, the *diireee* of the golden plover, the
drumming of the snipe, and the cooing of eider as sound markers
and companions of the shifting seasons.

Icelandic is a difficult and beautiful language. But I have noticed,
as I utter my sentences incorrectly, that much of being understood
is about my finding an appropriate pace and cadence for my words;
leaving space in between them for other less tangible things to be
heard. There is much going on in that silence. I am understood better
when I do not rush to understand or express everything immediately,
as I once might have done. It feels to me that an Icelander, or a
Westfjordian at least, cannot thrive any better within a crowded
sentence than in a city. I have begun to change shape to see silence
not as an absence of words but as a presence of a different character.

I have begun to see, too, that this place is not at the edge of the world, but the centre. It is only remote if you are not standing here, as Bjarni's family has been and will continue to do, noticing when the snow comes later and thinner. Noticing the storms becoming more frequent. Noticing that the puffins are so few some years because there is little for them to eat. It is the nexus of so many relationships which hang in the balance: the flow of ocean currents, the regulation of the world's temperatures, the seasonal choreography of life, the making and unmaking of the world itself.

After breakfast, I go out to the front step and inhale the sea air. It is tight in my nostrils, freezing the moisture within them, and it parches the back of my throat. The sea before me is flat, as if the storm never happened. It is 11 a.m. and has only recently got light, up there in the sky above. The valley floor where I stand remains steeped in indigo; the colour of snow in shadow. Today, the yellow light of a still-hidden sun will only creep a little way down the vertiginous slopes of the mountains that surround me. But the most important thing for me is that it exists at all – a promise of things to come. The raven preens himself, perched on the lamp post at the end of our drive. He is ragged and all silhouette against the blue. He contorts to put himself back together after a rough night. I wonder where ravens go in storms like that. I smile but it hurts my teeth to keep them exposed for too long, so I lick them with my warm tongue and make a mental note to remember to smile inwardly.

The weather is too good to stay near the house, so I grab my oversized down coat, hat, gloves and thermal wellies to head out into the snow, into the valley. Everything is hushed. The soles of my boots creak their tread into the blankness and the sound is improbably loud for one woman's footsteps. Behind the house, I walk across the small meadow making the first trace of the day that will show the village my movements. I stop to look back and admire my sturdy house from behind. The rusting corrugated iron and some of the window frames will need seeing to, soon. We have said this many times. Its backdrop is a still blue theatre – the wide fjord from which Bjarni departed into absence. No cars on the road, no people out. They will have left hours ago for work, for school.

I hear a sound from the raven like a pebble being thrown down a well – a sound I had never heard before coming here, but it has become a constant to my days. It seems to be made by his beak, but I have never been able to get close enough to see exactly how before he lifts off the fence, his glossy wings beating a slow feathered ululation. *Plok... plok...* It is loud; the only sound I can make out above the gently sighing sea. It echoes in this stillness, the cliffs playing with it.

The raven is probably hungry. The rock out front where we leave him our lamb bones and fish skins will be covered in snow after last night. These ravens who pass into and around and through my days have anchored me. They have been companions all winter, calling from the lamp post, squeaking the air with their fly-bys, asking of me a ritual that ties me into this place as I share my food with them: flesh, bones and skin.

I have come to see their intelligence, their curiosity and playfulness. They come and go as they please, in pairs or solo – black

241

shuttles on winter's loom. I don't know exactly how many there are, or really which is which. They are all Krummi, all Raven – a diverse collective presence, rather than individuals. It is only at the bend in the road on the way into Ísafjörður that they gather in any number, at least where humans can see them. There, about twenty can often be found conferring with each other – a *hrafnaþing*: a 'council of ravens'. The same word can be used for a gathering of people. Raven: *hrafn* – the word sounds like the bird's call when it greets a friend.

According to the Bible, ravens have done their own thing since the Great Flood. Before he sent a dove, Noah sent a raven to see if there was dry land. But the raven did not return. He didn't need to. There would have been plenty of carrion in the floodwater: all those beings who had not been selected to be saved by the ark. Perhaps he was not interested in being part of a narrative of exclusivity, instead busying himself transfiguring destruction into creation; death into life.

From the kitchen window, I once watched one tease a dog who was availing himself of my garden's facilities. The raven waddled towards the dog and took a peck at his tail, jumping aside as his muzzle bared teeth and snapped. Staring this canine opponent in the eye, the raven waited until the very last moment to alight.

I have even seen them skiing. Driving carefully along the coast road, I noticed that the steep snow-covered slope beside me was scored with two sets of thin parallel lines running down from the top of the ridge. No sooner had I silently wondered to myself what had caused these lines, than a pair of ravens appeared on the ridge and slid deftly downhill. When they reached the road, they took off back to the top of the ridge to do it all over again.

At the bottom of the meadow out back there is a wooden sheep-house that once belonged to Bogguhús. It is now owned by the town council, but our neighbour Ólafur maintains it for them. In exchange, he uses it to store his tools. When I moved here it was painted yellow with a red roof, but one day last summer I saw Ólafur heading towards it with that bucket of grey ship paint that never seems to end, the same one Bogga – who was his mother-in-law – had used all over our ground floor. Or perhaps that was his handiwork.

As it is the view from my kitchen window, I could not bear the thought of losing even more colour, given how winter drains it from the landscape. I asked him if I could paint a mural on its large double doors. '*Bara ein blóm* – Just one flower,' he said. His sister-in-law had overheard from her neighbouring garden and told him to stop being so tight. I painted a large *trompe l'oeil* of the valley in summer, so that the village might always have a portal to that season, with the sheep sorrel and the dandelions, the rushing river and the melted snow. When I had finished, Krummi flew by in repeated loops, from his perch on the fence at the front, round to the back of the house and past this mural, over and over, until he finally landed in front of it, looking up, taking it in like a guest at an exhibition preview.

The more time I spend with the ravens, the more curious I become. I have read that they are as intelligent as primates. They remember faces; remember how humans behave, sometimes passing on that knowledge down the generations. If you are kind, they will reward you. If you are cruel, they will retaliate, or flee. And they mate for life. With a lifespan of more than forty years, this means they are no strangers to commitment. They are devoted and affectionate partners and prefer spending time in their pair bond rather than in groups. Their courtship rituals are beautiful and acrobatic, and they are also no strangers to fun. I wish I could witness what I read on one website:

> *Partners are observed going on what can only be described*
> *as joy flights, tumbling and soaring, even locking toes and*
> *somersaulting in mid-air. They balance wild dates with*
> *down time, caressing beaks, preening one another, and*
> *cooing soothing comfort sounds to the other.*

Listening to their wild vocabulary, I realize how it has enriched my winter days, when most of the other birds have gone. I discover that the sheer diversity of their vocalizations, which can extend to imitating human or human-made sounds, might not have an evolutionary purpose. It may be to show their prowess to other larger birds, or just because they can. Or it may be purely for the joy of it.

I cannot see them simply as birds now. They are teachers, companions, paradoxes; complex emotional beings who know how to spin intellect, light-heartedness, curiosity and death into knowledge.

It is true that in some cultures, including my own, corvids are thought of as harbingers of death. But could this reputation have co-evolved with the destructive forces of civilization, as these dark birds were seen to court gallows and battlefields eating eyes from the corpses of the defeated? In older mythologies, Raven is revered for his intelligence: as world-maker, trickster, mediator, one who moves between worlds. Bjarni has told me that in Norse mythology ravens were both – and all – these things. And they were familiars of Óðinn the Allfather, Hrafnaguð – 'raven god' – god of wisdom, death, poetry and prophecy, who exchanged one eye, and even hanged himself, for knowledge. Óðinn (commonly known in the West as Odin) had two raven companions, who were essentially parts of his mind: Huginn – 'Thought'; and Muninn – 'Memory'. They sat on his shoulders and he trained them to speak. Each day he sent them out to fly around the world gathering news and knowledge to whisper into his ears on their return. Óðinn was especially anxious that Muninn would not come back. After all, what is thought without memory?

I continue up the valley, across the cattle grid and into the zone where the houses disappear, leaving only snow-blanketed fields and the trace of the river snaking down its length. A stream flows beside me in a muffled gurgling below the thick snow layer and I make a point of sticking to the track, where I know that what is below my feet is solid. Snow melts first around rocks, whose dark colour absorbs any light there is, turning it into heat. Walking off track is a dangerous business.

Above me, the colour is golden and azure. The sun's light creeps down the mountain. The tall journeys of fallen scree etched into the snow are thrown into sharp relief. I hear them: rocks tumbling – the freeze-thaw-freeze-thaw coming to its inevitable conclusion. It is a cacophony while it lasts; a sound like the first moments of the world tearing apart, or a tree being felled. But I cannot see any rocks falling.

How can something invisible be so loud? Like the mechanics of the raven's *plokking*, the action itself eludes me. All I experience are its echoes and its traces. Echo: *bergmál* – 'the language of the mountain'.

I turn back towards home to feed Krummi. I walk now towards the village, towards the sea. Finally, as I near the cattle grid, I hear rockfall again. I look up and glimpse a golden spray of snow on the side of the mountain like sparks from a welding iron, as if the world is being made again even as it tears apart. The spray closely follows a rock which scribbles an unsteady vertical line down to the valley floor. All it took was a change of position, and a change of light, to see what was happening.

Svartfuglsegg – 'Black-bird's-egg'

23 June 2012

Jónsmessunótt – Midsummer's Night. We are on the shore at my in-laws' summerhouse, newly husband and wife. It is still light at midnight, but clouds block the sun. The fjord is calm, as the wind holds its breath between night and day. I walk with Bjarni along the black-sand beach back to our wedding party. Behind us the evening blue distance of Snæfjallaströnd is a delicate wash of colour. Ahead: laughter, music, the glow of paper lanterns floating skywards.

We are returning from an unexpected sea swim. I'd told our guests earlier that it is tradition to roll naked in the dew at midnight on this night, for good health in the year to come. Some – mostly Icelanders – have taken it further. How could I not join them? We pass heaps of clothes dotted along the shoreline. Splashes and squeals from naked bodies rupture the sea's glassy surface. Bjarni's friend Hákon has missed out this step and waded straight in in his suit, waving his walking stick and spouting drunken enthusiasms. The water is frigid, but it's invigorating, and I stayed in longer than I expected my body to handle. The bonfires are ablaze to warm us, and the dancing continues. It is time to cut the wedding cake. I am wearing only a towel, but nobody seems to care.

On top of the cake are three hollow guillemot eggs: one for me, one for Bjarni, and one for our union. They have been placed delicately in a nest of birch twigs, crafted by my aunty. As she arrived for the proceedings this afternoon, I tasked her with decorating the cake using whatever she could find. All I gave her were the guillemot eggs. Of the many things we have had to think of, and do, to make a wedding in this place possible, decorating the cake in advance was not one of them.

Building the infrastructure for an outdoor wedding in an almost uninhabited fjord two hours' drive from where we live has been a major undertaking. There are 150 guests, 100 of whom are Bjarni's family and friends, mostly Icelandic. Mine have come from Kenya, France, England, Oman, Germany, Spain, the US and an international crowd from Ísafjörður. With little money to throw at it, we engaged in a dance with time, care and resourcefulness. It is imperative to leave no trace on the land around Haukur and Gyða's precious place: that was the condition for being able to use it. And what we built had to be resilient to unpredictable weather, even in June. We've pulled it off through teamwork: family, friends, foraging for materials and the harvesting of seeds planted long ago.

The marquee is homemade, a huge white tarpaulin rolled onto long wooden posts which once were pine trees. Any wind would billow the tarp like a sail, putting huge tension on the posts. We secured them by digging deep slots into the ground and sinking them in. We had to wait for the ground to thaw in mid-May to start construction, coming here every weekend from then on with helpers. Trees to make posts tall enough to sit 1 metre underground and protrude 3 metres above ground are not easily found. I had clocked these ones lying readymade outside the scout hut in Ísafjörður when I worked at Húsasmiðjan. Dreaming up the shape of the day, designing our marquee to scale with sketches and matchsticks at the kitchen table, became possible because of our knowledge of their existence. Without sturdy shelter, there could be no wedding.

The tallest tree, for the central pole, arrived around that time as an unprecedented act of love and foresight from Bjarni's father. The gesture made me think differently of him. Ever since I had first come here he had taken it upon himself to challenge me, make fun of me, refuse to speak English. In fact, he went as far as to claim that he didn't speak any English, which I only found out after a year or so was untrue. There was a kind of fondness but it felt as if I had to win his love. Perhaps from his perspective the kindest thing was to make me learn Icelandic as quickly as possible through immersion.

We were round at their house for dinner. 'Got something for you,' he said, and we followed him out to the garden. He peeled off a tarp against the stone wall at the back, revealing the 6-metre-long trunk of a tree, the branches lopped off. 'Town Christmas tree,' was all he said.

Doing the maths, I realized he must have thought further ahead than we had. On 6 January – Þrettándinn ('the thirteenth day' or Epiphany) – the last of the *jól* celebrations takes place outside the town library's ornate three-storey building, which was once the hospital.

On this day, the religious festivities are entwined with something more folkloric. A torchlit parade of elves and beings called the Yule Lads surrounds the enormous tree, resplendent with lights and decorations. Icelandic tradition has no Santa Claus. Instead, the Yule Lads are the thirteen mischievous sons of Grýla, a mountain troll, and her lazy husband Leppalúði. They have names like Gáttaþefur (Door Sniffer), Skyrgámur (Skyr Gobbler) and Þvörusleikir (Spoon Licker). Each night between 12 and 24 December, they take it in turns to visit homes to place a gift in a shoe left for them on a windowsill. Grýla also has a black cat which eats children who have not been given new clothes for Christmas. This might explain the persistence of a keen handknitting culture in almost every household. In the glow of a bonfire, songs are sung, fireworks are let off, and revellers pile into the community hall for a disco.

Not long after that, the tree is taken down. Haukur, imagining what we might need come summer, had acquired Ísafjörður's Christmas tree from the council and kept it in his garden for almost six months. As the 'keystone' to a structure that would shelter all our guests, this was no small detail.

In spring, I had a Viking-style brooch made by a blacksmith as Bjarni's 'wedding ring'. He doesn't like the constraint of a band around his finger. In fact, he doesn't like to wear jewellery at all. Instead, at our Ásatrú (Norse pagan) ceremony on the headland overlooking the beach, as we made our vows witnessed by a circle of family and friends gathered around us, I draped an embroidered shawl around Bjarni's shoulders and fastened it with the brooch.

It is a wrought-iron Jörmungandur, the cosmic serpent of Norse mythology which surrounds the whole Earth, gripping its tail in its mouth. It is said that if it lets go, this would trigger the world's ending. What is love? A nurturing cloak held close by an ouroboros – a symbol of eternal renewal. What is longevity? Bjarni made my ring himself from an old silver spoon curled around a teardrop-shaped piece of labradorite. The stone had fallen from the ring I was wearing years ago when we first met. Unbeknownst to me, he had found it and kept it for this day.

We have built compost toilets, a covered stage for the band, and three bonfires. We have turned the roofless stone walls of the ruined boathouse into a chill-out space for an all-night Ethiopian coffee ceremony served by Azeb. I had wanted something of East Africa at our wedding, but never dreamed it could be possible here. It was a happy surprise then to have stumbled upon Azeb's Ethiopian restaurant last winter, tucked between the geothermal greenhouses in the southern flatlands. As we chatted, it emerged she wanted to travel beyond the region where she lived with her Icelandic husband, so it was a good fit. We invited them to cater the coffee. With the smoke of frankincense unfurling into the bright night, she roasts coffee beans in a skillet over a small fire until they are dark. She grinds them with pestle and mortar, adding the grounds to a clay-spouted coffeepot full of boiling water and brews the coffee on glowing embers. The coffee is poured into small china cups, and popcorn is served from a brightly coloured wicker plate. Though strong, Ethiopian coffee is much gentler than the Icelandic staple. It is an unfolding soft alertness: no peaks, no troughs. A good companion for a wedding party that will have no cue for its ending, as one day spills into the next and the sun never sets.

Valdi, a boat-building and Viking enthusiast from Þingeyri, has lent us a 3-metre-long barbecue from the 'Viking village' there. He brought it by sea from several fjords away in a replica Viking ship which he built in his evenings over several months, but never uses much. It sits down by the shore, picturesque, sturdy, but longing for the waves. Earlier in the year, I asked if he might like to put his boat to use as my bridal transport. He and his wife were more than happy to make the two-day sail here, which is fortunate because the barbecue is far too large for a car.

We have sourced all the food from friends, family, land and sea: lamb, monkfish, lake trout, goose; salads of dandelion leaves, sheep sorrel, home-grown potatoes and chives. Our wedding present from Haukur's best friend was three whole sheep carcasses for the feast. The problem was that he had forgotten exactly where in the municipal cold store he had put them after the slaughter last October. But he didn't mention this detail until a few days ago. It became a race against the clock to find them in time for them to thaw, so that we could butcher them into usable cuts for the wedding chef. We stepped through the rubber fringe of the cold store entrance into a vast concrete room filled with towers of identical beige plastic tubs a metre squared, stacked five high – one of which was his gift to us. We scaled these tubs like climbers, reading their labels, stepping over seal flippers, fish, meat, until we found his name and something that looked like frozen sheep. A few days later, thawed, we drove them to a friend's farm to use their electric saw. We came away with sacks of lamb pieces ready to marinate.

But for all our effort and seamless teamwork for the wedding's infrastructure, something is not right within the core team – us as a couple. I first noticed it when he returned from sea. We were sitting on a hillside in the sun brainstorming the ceremony and he reacted angrily to my suggestion that a friend read a poem: *Desiderata* by Max Ehrmann.

We had already been talked through the format of the *Ásatrú* ceremony by our priestess. It involved, among other things, hailing the four directions; all three of us holding a large ring of copper as Bjarni and I made our vows; and us, the priestess and every single guest toasting the future with a cow horn full of mead passed round the circle.

'Why make it complicated? What's wrong with it as it is?' he snapped.

I was taken aback. I found it a bizarre question, and put his reaction down to general nerves. But something else was niggling at me.

Then four days ago, his favourite aunt, Yrsa, passed away. She had been ill for a long time, but we had hoped she'd make it through. It was a kick in the teeth, and it has meant that neither she, nor any of her children – Bjarni's cousins – can be here today. One of them, a chef, was going to do the feast, and we've had to find a last-minute replacement. Bjarni is shaken, and holding it together. There has been no time for grieving or space to unravel.

Each time he was at sea, I perceived our relationship to be on hold, paused. Not in the sense that our love or our own selves were not developing. But paused like a freeze frame in a film: the quotidian gestures that build a love could not happen for days, or weeks, at a time. As soon as he went to the boat, we were not together, not able to speak on the phone. Everything would remain as we left it, so we better leave it well – or so I thought. I did not account for another kind of alchemy doing its work, with the elements that also shape us. A kind in which he was dissolved in darkness, stirred by the waves, bottled up in his struggle to express emotion, and rolled around by time. Each time he came home, we could not simply pick up where we left off. There was trust to be re-established, catching up to do: with each other, and with ourselves in relationship. Each time, we had both slightly changed. He was always exhausted. This delicate process of renewal, like snow settling, required time and calm. But it was often gusted by other commitments: a visit from or to his parents, or friends, or the many things on the 'to do' list. And we were always on borrowed time, until his phone bleeped him back to the boat.

We have now been together nearly four years – long enough to be looking in the same direction, as his grandmother once promised we would. But in doing so, we have perhaps not remembered, or been able, to look at each other often enough.

Two days ago, our guests began arriving from all over the world and all over Iceland. We hosted my people at our house and in our garden, and transported them by coach the two-hour journey to the summerhouse and Haukur's birthplace a short distance away.

All our guests converged there, and this empty farm soon became a sea of tents and campervans, the farmhouse bustling with life. This morning, serenaded by an accordionist, the guests walked together across the fields to arrive here, at the black-sand beach, the Christmas tree wedding tent, the tables set with wildflowers from the meadow around our house. And the wedding cake, topped with three guillemot eggs.

My aunty has done an amazing job with the cake, especially considering it is actually three different cakes, arranged on a three-tiered stand. Together, they are meant to echo Yggdrasill – the sacred Life Tree of Norse mythology, an ash, around which the nine worlds of the cosmos are arranged, encircling its roots, trunk and branches. And it is the tree upon which, in his never-ending quest for knowledge, Oðinn is said to have sacrificed himself to discover the runes – their forms and their magic – which gave him his power.

Two of Bjarni's many aunties made the cakes, proudly bringing us samples to taste until they had got it right. We were quite happy with the first iterations, but as baking seems to be a sign of prowess for people like Bjarni's aunties, they continued until satisfied themselves. The lowest cake – beetroot and chocolate – symbolizes the roots of the Life Tree. My aunty has decorated it with deep-pink flowers, made from peels of beetroot centred around a wild blueberry dusted with bloom. The middle cake symbolizes the fruits. It is a Black Forest gateau scattered with berries and shards of chocolate and oozing with cream. The topmost cake symbolizes the leaves: a polenta sponge doused in birch leaf syrup. Here the nest of eggs sits. I admit it is a conflation of worlds to put guillemot eggs in a symbolic tree, but no more than the conflation of worlds that our marriage is. It seems to have been evident to my aunty that the eggs need protection. She knows that they are special to me.

I wonder if she knows that these are the eggs of seabirds, laid on narrow cliff edges without a nest, among thousands of other similar eggs. I wonder if she knows what I learned, faced with a cliff full of guillemots in Vestmannaeyjar, the Westman Islands – those islands off the south coast of this island: that because of their habitat, the mother lays her eggs in a clutch of only one, with a pattern specific to her throughout her fertile life. When she lays her egg, before incubating it, she stares at it to remember that particular pattern, or to remind herself of it if she has bred before. Once she has incorporated it into her visual lexicon, she may easily recognize her egg among the myriad others when she returns to the cliff, after searching for food. When I learned this, I fell in love with them all over again, in the way that one admires a great teacher.

My first encounter was with the shell. I have had one of them since the beginning of my story here. I remember spotting the eggs as I waited at Salvar and Natalía's front door, before I had even met them. Their windowsill was curated with a display made up mostly of reds and oranges, which seemed to be the aesthetic ambassadors of Natalía's Russian nationality, and likely provided some much-needed warm hues during the long blue-grey winter. In among these warm tones was this inclusion of turquoise eggs – some dark, some light, some almost ivory-coloured, all splattered with markings.

They were one of the first things I asked about. I had held them, photographed them. *Svart-fugls-egg*, they told me they were called. 'Black-bird's-egg'. I have seen all of these *svartfuglar* now, these black birds – the common guillemot, Brünnich's guillemot and razorbill – as they cluster together on steep cliffs, their black backs to the wind and, once, to the seafarers who would have named them. Salvar and Natalía told me that the egg's long pointed end and rounded base allow for a tight turning circle, should it accidentally roll from the parent's incubating stance. On my departure from their home, I drew one in their guestbook as a signal of the certainty of my own imminent return. Natalía gave me one from her jar as I left, green-blue, the colour of raw turquoise. It has faded now, but the shell is still speckled and scrawled with an intricate patterning of burnt umber. To me, then, they were as precious and novel as a dinosaur's egg.

When I came to live here two years later, in this place of fjords and mountains and seabird cliffs, the eggs came into my life again, and differently – the next layer in: yolk and albumen. Once a year in early June, they begin to appear in supermarkets – an other-worldly and carnal apparition in an otherwise plasticky branded visual landscape. They are expensive, at least £3 each, because of the hazards faced in acquiring them. To gather them, egg hunters must scale the vertical cacophony of cliff faces, mostly in the Westfjords, where each year these councils of seabirds – guillemots and razorbills, puffins, Northern fulmar and kittiwakes – come to dwell for the summer and reproduce. Underneath them, the Arctic Ocean continues to probe the cliffs' integrity, sometimes gently, sometimes with force. These days, the gatherers use safety equipment. *Í gamla daga* – in the old days – they did not have much more than a length of thick rope and took thousands of eggs. These days, they have learned, officially at least, that it is not good to take too many. They take them early in the season so that the birds have the chance to lay again, although the second round are weaker and paler in colour, the young less resilient. This seems a poor deal for the guillemots.

One June evening last summer, Gyða and Haukur invited me and Bjarni for dinner: a regular occurrence. It always amused (and bemused) me that Bjarni would ask his mother what was on offer before taking up the invitation. '*Svartfuglsegg*,' came the reply. This was a first for me, and not a regular event for him. Haukur had been working away on a construction job in the south of the Westfjords – near to Látrabjarg, one of the largest seabird colonies in Europe. He had come back with a box of *svartfuglsegg*. He is notoriously resourceful and generally does not believe in buying food that exists in the wild. But there are no guillemot colonies where he grew up so he didn't develop the skills in belaying and egg gathering. And besides, his hips are not what they used to be. There's no way he'd attempt gathering them himself. He had bought them directly from an egg hunter and that was the next best thing.

We arrived to find Gyða boiling a pan of water ready for four blue eggs. Motherly, full-bodied with a face like the sun, she ran the household and her life with a warm generosity and uncompromising firmness. There was nothing else on the table. This would be the meal.

I could not imagine breaking the perfection of that pear-shaped shell to scoop out the insides. Instead, I asked if I could drain out the contents, so that at least I would have another shell for my collection; another genealogical map to admire. Gyða set me up on the work surface with a narrow-necked jar. I carefully made two holes: one for the contents to come out, and another to release air locks.

I hoped desperately that these weren't the embryo eggs. I remembered my friend Svetlana describing, in disgust, her Icelandic mother-in-law purring about how much she enjoyed eating guillemot eggs in which the chick had started to form. 'Krranchy. Can you facking believe it? She said she likes them because they're krranchy.'

'*Nei nei.* We don't eat them like that,' breezed Gyða with conviction of her moral position, yet somehow without judgement.

'*Matur!*' – 'Food!' – she shouted as she scooped them out of the boiling water with a spoon. Haukur and Bjarni gathered around the grey formica table: three eggs, three spoons. The Arctic summer light streamed in through all the windows. My draining operation was lengthy. The yolk and white were viscous and strong and I had tried to keep the holes discreet. The others were not going to wait for me. Suddenly, I felt self-conscious about being the sentimental foreigner, doing things differently – *again*.

Rás 1 burbled softly behind Haukur's shoulder. It had the same soporific quality as the British Shipping Forecast. Haukur was a radio addict as well as a TV addict and was as loath to part from its waves as some fishermen are to part with the sea. Normally, dinner was a radio-free zone – a compromise he must have struck with his long-suffering wife years ago, as he knowingly clicked off the dial before each meal began. But this would be a quiet meal and it was tacitly agreed that it was alright to have it on low.

They ate mostly in silence, punctuated with small talk, like a dandelion clock catching on a blade of grass, its tender white hairs quivered by the breeze, then blown on again. Gyða clutched her egg elegantly, pointed end down, in her thumb and forefinger, and scooped the white flesh into her mouth with a slow pleasure approaching sensuousness. Haukur usually mashed together his meals – fish and potatoes, lamb and potatoes, or sometimes horse and potatoes – with a fork, or sliced more solid foods straight into his mouth with his pocketknife. He could do neither here. These eggs commanded delicate handling. Bjarni, a nature lover and a food lover, quietly alternated between inspecting the egg with the curiosity of a child scientist and indulging his tongue.

Finally, I gave up on my attempts to eat a drained egg, conceding that there is usually a good reason why things are done a certain way for centuries. I left gravity to work its slow process on an upturned shell, and asked to have a taste of Bjarni's. My sense of anticipation was conflicted. Something about this felt taboo, like eating a pet.

The egg white was more rubbery than a hen's egg and the yolk's flavour more wild. It tasted good – I could appreciate that much. But I felt immune to the layers of appreciation that must be tied up with having experienced the gathering of these eggs, or having had one's forefathers tell of it: the risks, the excitement; the short-lived bounty of the Arctic summer annually punctuating centuries of hardship. Nine months of the year spent barely getting by, freezing in turf-roofed huts and eating fermented, smoked and pickled foods. This *svartfuglsegg* was one of the first fruits of summer, and the eating of it was a ritual not to be sullied by any other food. And so we ate, in silence, until only the shell was left – theirs broken and mine whole. This one also now sits in the birch twig nest on top of my wedding cake.

I bought the third egg less than a month ago, from Kári the fishmonger. I wasn't expecting to see them in the shop when I went to ask about seafood for wedding canapés, but Kári trades also in unexpected extras. Sitting on top of the glass display cabinets, next to some bow-ties made of fish skin, the eggs' colours and flawless natural design tugged at me again. They are like globes stretched into a point at the North Pole. I wanted to make a better job of draining one than I had last time. At Gyða and Haukur's, I had made the hole too big as I was embarrassed about the time it was taking to empty. This time I took it home to my kitchen, made two small holes and blew. This one glows the brightest of the three on our wedding cake, years of blue receding.

*   *   *

Three years later, Bjarni and I are separated, and I am living in England. I ask him over Skype, '*Hvað er að frétta?*' – 'What's the news?'

His response makes me feel physically sick, giddy: 'Apparently *svartfuglsegg* contain ten times the "safe" limit of toxins, whatever that means... things like PCBs. They've advised people to stop eating them, especially women of child-bearing age, because toxins accumulate in the body and pass to the foetus.'

I think back to that time at Salvar and Natalía's house when I first took in the eggshells' perfect adaptation to their environment; their beauty; their colours. I think back to the time in the Westman Islands when I began to learn just how intelligent these birds and the design of their eggs were. And to that meal where I tasted their wild inside, not knowing that this precious oval of potential life was already poisoned, a consequence of the cascade effect of our polluting ways.

My fascination with guillemot eggs would not loosen its grip, long after I left Iceland. From a book, *The Most Perfect Thing: Inside (and Outside) a Bird's Egg* by ornithologist Tim Birkhead, I would learn, finally, that the eggs' pear shape is not primarily for the tight turning circle. Some eggs *do* roll off the cliff. He believes it is to keep the egg clean. The eggs are laid among thousands of others, and parents vie for space on narrow cliff edges. Their guano is everywhere, and the eggs become covered in it. The surface microstructure of the shell repels water, and the shape ensures the guano is washed down to the pointed end by wind and sea spray. This cleansing is essential for two reasons. The first is so that the pattern remains recognizable to the parents. The second is that the air cell is at the round end, which is also where the chick's head is when it punctures through to the air cell thirty-five hours before hatching: life's vestibule. Some hours later, still inside the egg, the chick makes its first distinct peep and the parents respond with their distinct call. Guillemots live in such close proximity that not only must they recognize their eggs but also their chicks before they hatch. Later Birkhead would discover that the shape also helps the eggs stay upright on a slope, which broadens the possibilities for nesting sites on the crowded cliffs. The chick takes a leap of faith before it can fly. Neither chick nor parents will return to the cliff before the following spring.

It is for all these features – beauty, strength, fragility, intelligence, adaptation and wildness – that I wanted them to crown my wedding cake; a symbol of the ingredients for a good marriage, a good life. Had I known they were toxic, would I have chosen differently? Had I known that being able to breathe when covered in shit was more important than occasionally rolling off the edge, would I have chosen differently? Probably not, because the outcome is still beautiful. Something in me must have known this marriage would not be forever, or accepted that I cannot impose my designs onto life. I can intend, and remain open. My vows promised 'for this cycle of time that has been given to us'. What more can one ever promise? When we are entangled with so many threads in the world, we are not the sole authors of our story.

Hvalurinn – The Whale

October 2012

'*Góðan daginn*,' I mumble, shuffling into the dark kitchen at 6.30 a.m. 'Good morning.'

'*Daginn*,' chorus the small group around the table, clasping their steaming mugs of coffee, barely looking up as they gaze out of the window the way that farmers seem to do. It is evidently not worth lighting the paraffin lamps before the sun rises, and I am relieved to have some respite from the oily odour of last night.

We are here at Kálfavík, Haukur's birthplace, for the yearly sheep gathering. The kitchen is spartan, not cosy, but I like it. Gyða and Haukur have renovated this farmhouse with a significant nod to its past, or rather maintaining its original state. For the most part, it sits empty but it is used by the extended family during the summer, and for autumn gatherings requiring a large group of people like the sheep round-up. It remains off grid as it always has been. Water comes from a stream running down the cliffs behind the former farm, and electricity is done without. Above the door of each room is a curling yellowed paper sign, hand-written in black marker pen, to show its previous function – *Búr* ('pantry'), *Stofa* ('living room'), and

264

more curiously up in the attic, *Híramíuherbergi* ('Híramía's room'). Híramíuherbergi is kept locked and through the keyhole you can make out an old loom almost filling the space, wooden parts poking awkwardly at angles, long since disused. The house has the feel of a family museum, which, thanks to my in-laws' hard work, can still be used for gatherings like these.

Gyða gets up from her chair and crosses the deep-red concrete floor, newly painted using leftovers donated by Bjarni and me from our bathroom renovation. It is still a little tacky and her peeling footsteps are unexpectedly loud in this dawn silence. She goes to the small annexe whose sign reads 'Búr'. She brings out the stack of homemade blueberry jam pancakes left over from the feast last night, for me and the other gatherers to pick at as they arrive. Haukur spreads butter thickly onto his rye bread as usual.

The cast-iron diesel range rumbles in the corner. On top of it an aluminium kettle billows steam from its spout. '*Kaffi?*' Gyða offers.

'*Já takk.*' 'Yes please.' I am annoyed at myself for having left my tea bags at home, but coffee will have to do. Once I commit to one cup I will have to keep drinking it all day to avoid the slumps. Things need to get a lot more desperate before I'll drink Melrose's tea though – the brand that every farmer in Iceland knows, and seems to keep in their cupboard for curiosities such as myself. It is as if there has been no evolution in choice or quality since Melrose's was introduced to Iceland in the 1940s, or as if the arrival of consumerism on these shores has largely passed the rural populations by.

The mist on Aðalsteinn's glasses evaporates as he withdraws his mug of coffee from his lips. He reaches over to the thermos of brewed coffee and places it in front of me, revealing a large hole in the armpit of his woollen jumper.

'*Gjörðu svo vel*' – 'Here you go' – he smiles shyly through his grey beard.

As the head of this weekend's sheep gathering, Aðalsteinn is the first of those not sleeping here to arrive this morning, on time. After yesterday's drawn-out and coffee-punctuated start we cannot know when the others will turn up, or when we will finally begin. The gatherers are a motley crew of folk whose dedication to the task is wavering. Since the last time I helped with a gathering, Hallgarður, the *aðalbóndi*, has died, and his wife – Bjarni's aunt, Yrsa – followed him a few months ago. Her flock at Ögur, the farm neighbouring Aðalsteinn's, has been sold off and the sheep we are gathering today are not connected to Bjarni's family. This is something many of Yrsa's children no longer want to be doing, especially the younger ones who have moved away to Reykjavík. Now it is mostly Aðalsteinn's flock, with a small number of sheep belonging to a woman who is far too old to gather. But Aðalsteinn is no leader, not the keystone that his name suggests. He is shy and pensive and has the air of an intellectual. He has never married and, aged fifty, still lives with his mother. It seems that he is a farmer by happenstance. But a generations-old guiding principle of reciprocity brings the gatherers back. Everybody knows in their gut, even if they have forgotten it in their mind, that it is because of helping each other that we are still here on this rock in the Atlantic.

'No ghosts to report,' I interject into the silence, pouring myself a cup of coffee.

'*Núúú?* Híramía didn't pay you a visit?' Haukur enquires with a half-smile. He slurps at his mug of *silfurté* – 'silver tea': a mixture of milk and hot water.

I remember the first time I came here Haukur proudly showed me, with a gap-toothed half-smile, the bedroom upstairs in which he was conceived, and born. The bedroom in which, he told me, the ghost of a criminal named Marius appeared at the end of his mother's bed and threatened to haunt her if she did not name her child after him. Haukur Marius Guðmundsson.

He grew up in this house and Híramía was a farm hand who lived and died here. How she died nobody has told me. There is a beguiling black and white photograph of her upstairs: a beautiful young woman perched playfully on a dry-stone wall. She is wrapped in a woollen shawl, her infinite dark braid hanging over her right shoulder like a ladder between earth and sky. She is said to haunt this house. Last night I slept in the room next to Híramíuherbergi to see what would happen. I wonder whether the door of her room in the attic is locked to keep people out or her ghost in.

'I had a dream though,' I say, reaching for a pancake.

Aðalsteinn's eyebrows lift above his glasses. '*Nú.* What happened?'

'We were sheep gathering. But in the sea, in shallow waters.'

'*Núúú!*' Gyða chuckles from her perch beside the range. It is an exclamation that always strikes me as the sound that eider ducks make as they bob around on the wavelets, especially the way she says it.

'The seabed was lined with newspaper pages in black and white. Haukur was telling us to pick up all the pages that had pictures on them and cut them out.'

Haukur chuckles and gets up to go to the bathroom.

'Then Bjarni and I were lying in deeper water, on our backs. And behind him a little distance away, I saw a whale breach. I thought, "If that jumps there's going to be a *huge* swell where we are." Suddenly, Bjarni froze and told me there was a massive whale's eye right behind my head. Then I woke up.'

'*Nú, jæja,*' Aðalsteinn chirps, stroking his moustache into place with his thumb and forefinger.

I don't usually remember dreams but this one was particularly vivid. We *are* on a sheep-gathering mission, and yesterday we *were* accompanied up the fjord by the exhalations of a humpback whale, so it might seem an obvious set of solid images for my subconscious to dissolve into a dreamscape. But I wonder about the newspapers, and the foregrounded nature of the whale's eye.

Aðalsteinn leans forward onto his elbows with interlocked fingers, circling his thumbs around each other – a characteristic tic that others impersonate in jest. His dark grey eyebrows furrow into serious reflection. 'The newspaper pages indicate that something of historical significance is happening. And water means trouble.'

I sit down in front of him, delighted. Not only is he a farmer-poet, he's a dream interpreter as well.

'And the large eye means something is watching over you, looking out for your mistakes. Probably your father-in-law.'

It is a relief to have such a connection made by a third party. Nobody can argue with an allegory.

'*Haaaa?*' Haukur bellows, striding back into the kitchen. 'Are you talking about *me?*'

Haukur is characterized by a kind of shyness that prevents him ever revealing his feelings explicitly or engaging readily in conversation with people he does not know extremely well – of whom I am one and will remain so until we have a shared history. Despite this shyness, I have found that Haukur loves being the centre of attention within his own element. It was made startlingly clear yesterday. I have waited two years – two farming cycles – to film the sheep gathering in which Bjarni and his family participate. I have wanted to learn Icelandic, to build relationships with those involved and to participate fully as a gatherer myself, before attempting to document it. The main character was supposed to be Aðalsteinn – the owner of the majority of the flock. But Haukur has seen to it that he is the star of the show, striding into the frame with entertaining antics and wry jokes which eclipse Aðalsteinn's gangling and introspective demeanour.

I don't mind. A character is a character after all, but it has left me wondering, as I often have, what story I am telling; whose story I am telling. Aðalsteinn is someone to be quiet with, who slowly reveals himself through his thoughts and movements. Haukur is the storyteller, the joker, the player, who saunters into situations like a man who thinks he knows best. Even though I am behind the camera and not a 'character', my involvement with this place and with these people does not allow me to be an invisible observer.

I am embedded in their dynamics. As I filmed Aðalsteinn arriving yesterday, removing his wellies lined with carrier bags, of course he greeted me and congratulated me on our wedding. Of course, I responded. Haukur knows me well enough not to need words to draw me into his narrative. I am beginning to realize I still need to know who *I* am before I know which story I am telling.

Am I talking about Haukur?

'No,' I smile inwardly. 'We're talking about a whale.'

Seljavallalaug –
'Shieling-plains-pool'

May 2013

I cup my hands around the warm ceramic curve of a mug of tea, the steam settling on the wisps of hair around my forehead. I am sitting at a laminate table across from my mum and dad, supported by the firm angular sponge of the campervan sofa. Horizontal rain nails at the large Perspex window, which frames a view of fog swirling within a black-sand valley, blurring its lines, reducing it to the very barest of details: black, grey, white. Nothing out there is solid, or still, or whole. A dark angle of a slope appears suspended in blankness, then disappears again. Light momentarily flashes off a river. The large metal box that has been our home and transport for a week is buffeted by gusts of wind that make clear the superficiality of its shelter.

'Landscape' is an insufficient term for places and moments like these: the land seems to have less weight than the sky, and can it even be called 'sky' when wrapped in a restless fog? What the window frames is a constant reconfiguration of matter and wind direction. It is a reduction, like a well-made broth, rather than an erasure: a concentration of ingredients, each distinguishable and foregrounding itself at different moments. The whole is more than the sum of its parts, but at the same time it obliterates itself. The reduction of landscape to an emotional palette: unbridled, unmediated, wild. It is an antidote to the ordered plasticity of the camper's interior and I want to be out in it. My parents look tired. I ponder the next move.

It is 30 May, my mother's 65th birthday. For whatever reason, she has decided to celebrate it by coming with Dad from their home in Kenya to visit me. I know my parents are only in Iceland because I am. This is not how Mum would choose to spend any day, let alone a landmark birthday. They said they wanted to spend some time exploring a different part of the country from the Westfjords where they have visited me twice now.

Bjarni cannot be with us. He has started a new job at the harbour from which his trawler *Valbjörn* used to depart; still departs – but without him on it. Now he is a weighmaster, logging and weighing all the landed catch from a control tower on the pier. Still working with fish, still not home much, but at least I know where he is and that he is safe.

Two years ago, I didn't imagine I would still be here by now. I don't know what I imagined. But by last autumn I had reached my limit, knowing the sluggishness that Arctic winter brings, and Bjarni was up for new horizons. Trying to balance both our needs after getting married, we are experimenting with a pattern of spending the winter in England and summers in Iceland, doing as the birds do. It is not uncommon for Icelanders to spend winters abroad. So we went. It was a challenge. He did not find his groove: he does not thrive as an individual trying to make a life from scratch. There, it came home to me even more just how much he is stitched into this place, buoyed by a reputation already known – both his own and his family's. Picked apart from this fabric, he began to lose himself and an old depression only recently acknowledged to me and his parents reared its sometimes brutal head. I am relieved that he is back in his domain, feeling competent, with some sort of a rhythm to stick to, even if his shifts can sometimes be 48 hours long as he waits for all the boats to land. His rhythm is mostly work and sleep. In both, the objective is clear. He seems to need that simplicity to stay the course. There is no real need, when weighing fish or sleeping, to deal with decisions, emotions, memories or ambitions. No creative meandering, no tomfoolery. I am having to get to know a quite different man from the one I fell in love with.

My tour guiding will not start until mid-June when the cruise ships begin to appear, so I have a week or so left of freedom. I met my parents in Reykjavík and hired a campervan. Now we are attempting to travel along the south coast as far as Jökulsárlón – a glacial lagoon that seems to epitomize the convergence of matter that makes Iceland – or at least its cliché: ice, lava, sea. *This* moment is as Icelandic as it gets – fog, sand and strong wind – but it is not what many people come for. I know it is a lot for them to do this kind of journey, and I am touched by their effort. But they know they chose to move to the other side of the world when I was young. They cannot challenge me for having a life that takes me to far-flung places. I know I must embrace their apparent enthusiasm to explore, while it lasts.

At this time in late May, the summer has not yet quite arrived. No amount of words can persuade those who have not experienced it, how late and how suddenly it comes. Even when it arrives in a couple of weeks, the weather will still remain changeable, especially in the mountains. Temperatures in summer can range from around freezing to 29 degrees Celsius. But the daylight lengthening into totality, and the abundant life that comes with it, seem to balance out the extreme weather. The verdant growth and the arrival and nesting of migratory birds anchors this island in the familiar reality that life is established and ongoing. In this moment, however, the scene out of the window is undeniably primeval and colourless.

We have only made it a little way along the coast road from the campsite where we parked up last night. As we turned from the campsite track onto the main road, we were soon stopped in our tracks by a German tourist in a similar vehicle. He was obviously a seasoned Hymer traveller.

'*You cannot drive today in zis van. It is too tall for ze vind speed,*' he insisted, hanging out of his window briefly as he continued driving slowly on, presumably looking for a park-up himself.

I have only ever travelled around the country in our old Toyota HiAce van which seems to be able to go anywhere in any weather. I am not used to such mundanities as strong winds limiting my range. But with the German's emphatic protests I wondered if we were being reckless.

There is only one thing to do in weather like this if you do not have a house to retreat to: sit in hot water. Fortunately, I knew that a short way along the road was one of the most strikingly located hot springs in the country – a small concrete swimming pool suspended part way up a mountainside, in a valley at the foot of a volcano. Eyjafjallajökull: that volcano which so many people outside of Iceland remember – not for the thick layers of ash that covered the area and forced farmers and their sheep to evacuate; not for the *jökulhlaup*, the catastrophic glacial flooding; not for the toxic gases; not for the visibly disappearing wooden fence posts blasted to oblivion by volcanic ash and high winds; not for the eruption's remarkable beauty and magnitude. These were not the foci of the international news narratives. Those people remember it because, perhaps for the first time, they realized that natural events could greatly disrupt their well-made travel plans. This fact was irritating, and then forgotten, and life went on as normal.

We are here now, and we can either sit here all day in a rocking campervan, or we can step out into the brooding alchemy of this place. I feel at once responsible for my parents' enjoyment, and aware that it is entirely beyond my control. We decide to go.

'Button up,' I say. 'It'll be worth it.'

I last came here four years ago with Bjarni on our long and ambling campervan trip around Iceland. It is one of the most astonishing places I have ever been. I carry a vivid distillation of the elements which so moved me in my imagination. Although I can barely see 5 metres in front of me, and the wind carries rain, express, to our downward-angled faces, my mind feels sure the destination will be as it was on that still September evening. It is as if we only need step through this veil of fog to get there: a steep-sided bowl-shaped hanging valley, lined with dazzling green moss and grasses, glowing with a golden light. In my mind's image, every detail is clearer than the naked eye could see – a paradox that only makes sense from inside of it: meltwater from the glacier above etches its jagged white cascades all around the curve of the bowl, as if it is leaking from the outside. Outcrops of sand-coloured stone, rounded by time, play with the light and shadow. They assume expressions, becoming faces or statues. Steaming hot water trickles in glistening sheets down a black cliff. Reality is a magnifying lens held up to itself.

I felt, back then, that I had entered a place that was not for mortals; or at least that I should have to strive harder, or be a better person, to be granted permission to access this place. It amused me then, to come across a patch of earthly decrepitude – the charmingly dilapidated concrete swimming pool snuggled up to a cliff and lined with algae, with its even more dilapidated changing rooms at one end. The hut smiled like an old man, missing a few teeth. The holes for windows were still there, but the windows themselves were long gone. A small placard explained that it was built in 1923 by the local Youth Association; that the local council was the first in Iceland to make swimming a part of the school curriculum – safety at sea would be integral to the growing importance of the fishing industry. It stated that this is the oldest operational pool in Iceland. Suddenly the place became rooted in the history of a nation, in a time not so long ago. Places like these rendered the landscapes no less wild or magical, but knitted them into everyday life and a history of dwelling.

The pool is not signposted but I am sure I can follow my nose; navigate by my memories. I remember it being a short hike upstream beside a river, then up a mountain path a kilometre or so into this bowl-shaped dreamscape. We tramp alongside the river, facing upstream. I am going slowly but my parents are going slower. My sense of time and distance is amorphous. Everything feels eternal, or outside of time, on days like these.

'Nearly there,' I shout through the rain, not quite believing it.

We continue alongside the river, but I cannot make out a trail going up the mountainside. I don't remember it being far. The map we have doesn't show this place in any detail so there is nothing to check. Usually, you pass a few others when going to a place like this – hot water, relatively close to the main ring road, Route 1. We seem to be alone today – nobody with whom to cross-reference my memories. Suddenly, a figure emerges out of the fog. She is anoraked and clutching a rolled-up towel under her arm. All the signs are good.

'Excuse me. Do you know where the mountain path up to the pool begins? Have I passed it already?'

'Just follow the river – you'll hit it.'

'I don't go uphill? I've been before, and I remember climbing *up* to it.'

She shrugs her shoulders, smiles and walks on.

What can I say? She has just come from the pool. I wonder about the reliability of memories, but at the same time I am certain. On my previous visit, I know that I was perched high on a slope, looking down at a river valley.

Sooner than I expect, we reach the pool. It has been spruced up a bit. The old man has had a face lift, a lick of paint. The pool is much the same. *But the river is level with the pool.*

Suddenly, the explanation dawns on me: both my memory *and* my present reality are correct, dramatically different as they are. During that eruption, which kept people stranded on the wrong side of the world, sleeping at airports, which forced local farmers to flee with their sheep and later dig their lives back into order, this valley filled with volcanic ash. My eyes are looking on a scene and a change which belongs to geological time.

Herring Adventure

May 2013

The following day, it is better weather, and time to hit the road. Mum and Dad seem happier now the sun is out. With the campervan we begin to make our way together slowly north, towards my home, towards my summer self. There are things to do that are tugging at me, and I do not enjoy the feeling of my mind being elsewhere at this hinge of the year. I want to watch the ground waking up in my place, from my front step, as I have watched it in all its lights and weathers through winter. The waking is so brief, the shift from melt-sodden death to coursing, fecund life so rapid, that I feel I would have to watch many of these start-of-summer hours to piece together some sense of it as a whole reality. I imagine a mother feels similarly being away from her child who is about to take its first steps, no matter how many children she has had before. These are the first steps of *this* year's life, and they will have their own stories in them.

This trip with my parents is my 'summer' holiday, before I dive into my summer persona. This brief period in late May/early June comprises a rare combination of elements conducive to travel: it is a time of relative calm when there is much light in the sky, the roads are clear of snow, and blizzards are far less likely. It is a time when, in the south of the country at least, some of the restaurants and museums have opened their doors for the season.

A strange kind of anticipation precedes the arrival of summer. With experience, I can now foresee the activities, responsibilities and ideas that the return of light makes possible. At the same time, I know they will not *all* be possible to enact unless I never sleep. The fullness of life and the ever-presence of light do nothing to make sleep feel like a priority. And so, in these days just before I begin to brim over my own edges, I am on an upswing and it is exciting. But I know that I must work hard to manage it, to circumvent a crash. This is not my light, my land, or my rhythm, and I am continually adapting.

Both Bjarni and I are continually adapting, it seems – to one another, and to new territory; to new lights and new darknesses. Naively, we thought our wedding would simply celebrate something already made. But we have learned that this 'we' is a constant state of becoming and unravelling at once. What kind of creature must I be, in what kind of vessel, to feel at home in a world where everything is in motion?

Once I am home and the tourist season starts properly in June, I will become a guide again – two to three coachloads of fifty cruise-ship tourists every couple of days, the tour company has told me. I will come to feel the impact it has, both on me, and on the place. The number of passengers on cruise ships docking at Ísafjörður has more than doubled in three years, as 'remote', 'wild' Iceland becomes a hot destination for those wanting to escape a busy, degraded world – the

Arctic a place to see before *it* dies. I've seen it in black and white. The tour company sends us the ship lists in spring so we can make a rota: 2009 – 28 ships, 15,220 passengers; 2012 – 32 ships, 31,385 passengers. This in a town with a population of about 2,600. My job requires switching between three different languages and telling stories of this place in different ways. I try to weave the impact of tourism into the stories I tell them, and to answer their questions honestly. I do this in an attempt to keep it interesting for myself, and to resist the commodification of a landscape and culture for which I have so much admiration.

I do not love this work. By last September, it was already starting to wear thin. One seemingly innocent gesture made me shudder: at the end of one of the last tours of the season I am standing at the door to the coach saying my farewells to each guest, making small talk: *goodbye… thanks so much… goodbye.* Some slip a note into my palm – dollars, pounds, euros – as they shake my hand, smiling. One lady, smelling strongly of perfume, places in my palm a mint from the ship. It is small and round and has a blue cellophane wrapper. A stylized image of a polar bear peeks out from behind large white letters. They spell *BYE POLAR.* I wonder, as the Greenland Ice Sheet melts and the health of our minds is so clearly entangled with the health of the planet, how such an inappropriate thing could ever have made the market, let alone a cruise ship to the Arctic. It troubled me to think that perhaps nobody on that coach had noticed.

But my employment options are limited: the potential filming gigs in this region seem to be mostly the preserve of one man who has been doing it for years. Guiding is one of the only jobs available that uses some of my skills. The income will tide me over a little into the unknown of winter.

After the day job is over, I shall continue work on renovating our house and garden while the weather is calm and dry. This persona – and it is a persona: one who performs to the world – welcomes the friends and visitors who come and stay at this time of year; shows them the places she loves. Between it all she tries to be herself, snatching time to give attention to, to be inside of, what the light brings: the cheeping of eider nurseries riding the wavelets like a molten brown island; the sublime stillness of bright nights; the unsetting sun backlighting lupine buds at the point of blooming, their downy coating glowing like a halo. There will be no time to go inward; only to catch the scent of this summer moment before it goes to seed. There is much to prepare to make such outwardness and such stillness possible.

Once my parents and I get out west onto the Snæfellsnes Peninsula, I feel I am back in my home range. We are still far from my house, but this landscape is familiar. I have travelled through Snæfellsnes before and spent time in it in different seasons. It interests me to see how it unfolds now into late May. We park up for the night in a cove whose cliffs explode in dark-grey basalt roses – a kaleidoscope of striations and joints all arced like a dancer's limbs reaching for the unfathomable. Seabirds wheel around in lemniscates of white and grey, each time bringing food back to their high-perched nests. The teal-blue sea heaves through an arch and booms, and booms, through the bright-fogged evening.

We have nothing much that will make supper in the campervan mini-fridge, so I go to the tiny café which clings to the slope above. I step into its warmth through a sturdy door which hushes the sea sounds. Diners huddle quietly over their meals, clinking cutlery and drinking coffee from dainty china cups. The tongue-and-groove panelled walls are hung with embroideries, appearing twee from a distance but, on closer inspection, revealing themselves to be satirical cross-stitch. Lace curtains frame and contain the dynamism of summer's beginning in domestic constancy. I ask the owner if I might buy a fish, if they have one to spare. Yes, just a fish; not a meal. She smiles and gives me a cod from the freezer; asks me what I'm going to make with it. Something with tomato and olives, I think – with rice. Delicious, she says.

She won't take any money for it. It is still May, the tourist season proper has not yet started, and I have spoken to her in Icelandic. These facts affect this moment and her willingness in it. There is still time to be Icelandic – a mode of being in which transactions are not necessarily monetized or simultaneous. Help is given if possible now and may be asked for in return later – most likely from another source. Right now, her personal resources are plentiful. She can be generous, and she can know that I am part of a network of exchange on this island. Come mid-June, albeit awkwardly for some, a more capitalist mentality will likely creep in. Or perhaps that is just an Arctic mentality – grabbing the bounty while it is here, because you don't know how long it will last – and I am as much a part of it as anyone. There is a word for it: *hvalreki*, a windfall or unexpected stroke of luck. Literally, a 'beached whale' – a welcome source of food in the *gamla daga*. But can it be called a *hvalreki* when it goes on for several summers and shows no sign of abating? Is a different response required when it does? Come September, we shall all be exhausted by it, and need time to breathe again.

The next day, we continue along the north coast road, driving beyond the end of the tarmac and onto a part that is still a dirt track, as all roads in Iceland used to be. I can see the distant blue mountains of the Westfjords from here: I know well where I am heading. At Kolgrafafjörður – 'coal-digging fjord' – new road-building has brought a causeway to cross this narrow, shallow fjord. It makes the journey quicker. Unfortunately, it also makes the sea's breathing slower and more laboured. The structure of the short bridge in the middle of the causeway leaves a much smaller gap for the tide to sigh in and out of; for the same amount of sea and its inhabitants to move through.

As we approach the fjord, our eyes are drawn to the bullets falling out of the sky, silhouetted against the cloud: cross-shaped, then suddenly straight. We pull over behind several other cars whose drivers are out clutching their cameras, staring and smiling at the sky. A flock of northern gannets perhaps numbering more than a thousand is plunging from the sky in darts travelling at 60 miles per hour. The sea thuds and splashes in eccentric percussion as they pierce the surface of the water, diving deep down to retrieve their bounty. I feel, not for the first time, as if I am standing in a time before modernity, when the world teemed with life, and humans were sparse. I wonder if this sight is commonplace here or whether a special story is unfolding. My parents are delighted, and our spirits are lifted. We are sharing that thrill of being witness to a natural wonder – something we last shared in Kenya many years ago, watching the annual migration of wildebeest.

When I return home, I wax lyrical about the sight to my in-laws.

'Kolgrafafjörður? That's where the herring deaths happened last winter. *Thousands* of them,' Gyða responds.

I read up about it and find out that this fjord had been the site of two mass herring deaths in the past year, the cause of which remains a mystery. The fish were found to be neither infected nor under-nourished. It is not known what drove hundreds of thousands of herring into its shallow waters – perhaps a killer whale, perhaps a quest for warmer water. What is known is that the two incidents resulted in the death of around 55,000 tonnes of herring. Apparently, the majority of the herring asphyxiated. The shore was littered with silver carcasses and more sank to the seabed. The bridge we had driven across was mooted as being at least partially responsible: its small opening prevented the herring from escaping fast enough into the open sea when oxygen levels became too low. They were forced to use up all the dissolved oxygen in the seawater contained behind the bridge, as the fjord was frozen over. As the national fishing quota for summer-spawning herring is around 67,000 tonnes, the articles I read frame these events as a great loss for an economy still built foremost on fishing, though tourism is rapidly taking over.

The seabirds, whales and seals had a field day at least. Then the rotting began. Local residents had to pull together and bury them to stifle the stench.

I scroll down a news article from December last year:

> 'People are leaning towards the theory of a sudden cooling.
> It's not the least likely explanation,' Róbert commented,
> adding he hoped the Marine Research Institute's research
> would lead to a definite conclusion.
> The condition of the herring in the fjord was examined
> from a boat last weekend. According to www.skessuhorn.is,
> an immense amount of dead herring was found on the ocean
> floor but no sign of life.

A photograph of a beached killer whale catches my eye in another article dated a couple of months later:

> A local man Vilmundur Þorgrímsson contacted Skessuhorn
> after seeing photographs of the carcass. 'It is obvious from the
> photographs that the whale had bad teeth. When the teeth
> are damaged, they can become infected, and the infection
> can then spread into the jawbone, where the nerve leading to
> the ears is located. This whale was probably in excruciating
> pain, which led him into trouble.'
> He speculates that the whale could have been feeding
> on dead herring which had sunk to the bottom of
> Kolgrafafjörður, where he was located. In the process,

however, the whales wear down their teeth as they are
digging in the rocky bottom of the fjord.

I think about the difference between passing through and dwelling; how when one knows and is part of a bigger narrative web – which includes the weather, climate change, species movement, economics and human progress as protagonists – one cannot help but become implicated; one cannot help but care. That moment in which the tourists, my parents and I had stood on the causeway beguiled by thousands of plunging gannets will be captured on their cameras as evidence of Iceland's natural health – an image that Iceland believes it needs to perpetuate in order to attract tourists. But looking at my photos, now, it is a much more complicated story.

There is another story in which herring are the main protagonists, or victims. The so-called 'herring adventure' is a time in Icelandic history from 1867 to 1968 that Icelanders like my father-in-law speak of fondly. It is synonymous with economic success – a time of plenty. It is also hailed as a shaper of destiny; a period of 101 years that allowed Iceland's modern society to develop. I have seen sepia photographs of boat after boat *filled* with herring – the gunwales almost level with the sea; smiling fishermen aboard, pipes hanging from their bearded mouths. By late 1960, herring accounted for more than half of the country's export income. However, the herring adventure narrative does not dwell upon the fact that, after years of abundance, in 1969 the herring failed to appear and did not return for decades.

The tourism boom is the new herring adventure. It is being treated as a temporary glut, a *hvalreki*, rather than a new status quo requiring investment in an infrastructure to welcome visitors sustainably. I wonder if it will be addressed before it happens: when the numbers of economy-boosting tourists damage the very image they are coming to capture, and then go elsewhere, leaving the damage they caused behind them. There is not enough oxygen behind the bridge.

To Hell and Back

September 2013

We cruise along the infinity line of a carless road. It is simple: linear, without obstacle – everything that our relationship is not. We are two bodies in the same metal shell which is moving us in the same direction, but our cells have been reconfigured by this summer. We are not moving in the same direction, nor at the same speed.

The road cuts its hard asphalt course through a vast carpet of autumnal shrubs, which stretch to the horizon in all directions. The afternoon sun dazzles the windscreen and suspends us in the kind of reverie that thrives on long journeys.

I wonder why Bjarni is asking me nothing about my summer. I have just been on the most incredible journey: two months alone on foot around Britain, writing a much-read blog for a major publisher. He was so supportive of me doing it, and helped me make it a reality. In the event, it was an opportunity to hear myself; to get closer to remembering where I begin, and he ends. His depression overwhelmed our lives last winter and I felt wholly alone in keeping us afloat – materially and emotionally. His parents did not seem to want to acknowledge it was happening. If they did, they did not seem very supportive. It left me spent. On this summer journey of mine, safe in the knowledge he was back in the embrace of his extended family and his landscape, the thousands of footsteps worked on me like a slow transfusion. I have asked him about his summer, but he is taciturn. Perhaps there is only so much he can say when he has spent it in a harbour control tower doing 24-hour shifts weighing fish catch. Perhaps he doesn't know what to say at all.

My journey on foot was a shift in our planned pattern – at least my part of it. I won the blog contract in June, only a month after I'd made my seasonal migration to Iceland. As the job required me to walk around Britain, I returned there, and it meant we spent the summer apart. I have relished the space more than I am comfortable to accept.

Bjarni's mobile rings, jolting us into the present.

'*Sæll og blessaður Faðir vor!*' Bjarni greets his father, changing gear, steering onto the roadside and slowing to a halt all with a deft one-handed movement, the other hand pressing the phone to his ear.

It makes me smile every time Bjarni calls his father *Faðir vor* ('Our Father'). It is one of many family in-jokes made at the expense of the church, the state, or people's characters, but never with any unkindness. It seems to be an integral part of their not taking life, or themselves, too seriously. I have followed suit by calling him *Tengdafaðir vor* ('Our Father-in-law').

'Listen, Bjarni. Are you still looking for a wood burner?' Haukur crackles down the phone. He seems to believe mobile phones work like walkie-talkies and his crowing can be heard within a metre radius of the handset. I can picture him at home 700 kilometres west, lying on his corner sofa in front of the TV, in his stained blue work trousers and chequered flannel shirt that smells of oil and ageing man, proud of the knowledge he is about to impart.

Bjarni looks at me, eyebrows raised, reiterating the question with his face. 'Sarah, are we still looking for a wood burner?'

'Maybe,' I concede. I have always wanted a crackling fire in our living room – much more alive a presence than electric heat. This is an unlikely possibility in Iceland, though, there being so few trees. But we own one of the handful of remaining houses with a functioning chimney. And as Haukur is able to provide us with a constant supply of offcuts from his joinery workshop, it is a real possibility.

The detail is that we are not planning to be living in the house in winter anymore. The unspoken detail is that our marriage is unravelling.

The sun blazes through the dense jungle of wiry ginger hair that is his beard. It glows orange. He claims it is the Celt in him, while his dark blond hair is the Norwegian bloodline. He is still handsome, but changed. He, like all Icelanders, is from many places. Yet, that one winter away from his country and back in mine, dealing with his long-held darknesses, has scarred him. It has scarred me too. Perhaps it is also the venturing out of his comfort zone – marriage, compromise, having to prove who he is in a new terrain, rather than being born of it. Something of his fire has gone out, and yet he is as volatile as magma. I do not know how to be with him.

'*Kannski*,' Bjarni relays. 'Maybe.'

'There was one outside Péturskirkja last time we went there, just inside the ruined enclosure. You'll see it.'

Péturskirkja: I only know this to be the Icelandic name for St Peter's Basilica in the Vatican.

'Péturskirkja?' Bjarni enquires.

'Yes. It's not actually a church. It's a white house on the lava on the road towards Askja, not far from the turn-off from Route 1.'

We are at the northern edge of the vast expanse of rocky desert, wind and water which makes up the uninhabited heart of Iceland. We are heading to Askja anyway – a caldera – to visit a warm opaque turquoise crater lake that pools at the bottom of it. It is named Víti – 'Hell'. Our marriage teeters on an edge, paradoxes existing inside us that we can barely contain, nor know how to navigate. After what we've been through recently, a little road trip to Hell and back seems a fitting way to mark our reunion.

* * *

'What, so we're just going to go and take it?' I query, as we continue on.

'If it looks like nobody is going to do anything with it, and it's been there for a while, then, maybe yeah,' Bjarni defends, although I need no persuasion.

His father is notorious for being constantly on the prowl for free treasure, particularly things from 'the old days' that are no longer valued by many Icelanders. In Ísafjörður the municipal refuse centre sometimes even calls him up if someone dumps something they think he could use. Bjarni and I are of the same ilk: it feels like a moral obligation to rescue these relics from potential obscurity. Our house is now filled with furniture, paintings and fittings gleaned from the municipal skips, charity shops and flea markets, and Haukur's garage is equally full of scavenged objects. I am particularly impressed, though, at his knowledge of a potential haul many hundreds of kilometres from where he lives. Our journey has suddenly taken on the delicious taste of a mission.

We have spent the best part of the day crawling around on soft moss on our hands and knees, inspecting small pockets of the vast tundra which is ablaze with the colours of autumn; awed by the diminutive beauty of the plant life. Each hour of sunlight cast by summer saturates the hues of the landscape, drop by drop. Swathes of luminescent red blueberry ling jostle for space with the jagged yolk-yellow leaves of dwarf birch. Up close, each fingernail-sized blood-red blueberry leaf, backlit by the glow of afternoon, is traced with yellow veins. It is like looking through closed eyelids at the sun. At their feet, lush green forests of moss, open fans of alpine lady's mantle and purple blooms of wild creeping thyme are knitted into a carpet, ready to catch the leaf-confetti as the temperature drops into winter. Anyone who believes that Iceland lacks colour would be forced to eat their words in autumn, if they ever managed to close their awestruck mouths again.

Autumn is by far my favourite season, infused with the accumulated energy of summer and tinged with the melancholy of the turning in – the acceptance of the long hard journey of winter ahead. It is a time to go home, to nest and create. Instead, we are on a knife edge: together or not, England or not. Either way, with no idea of whether we can find happiness any time soon. And now, we are on a detour into No Man's Land, a last jaunt on our way home to pack up our things, to try living in England together for one more winter. Or not.

I love this landscape as much as I love Bjarni, though each seems as indifferent as the other. Bjarni's indifference hurts me much more deeply. No matter how much I try to rationalize it – 'he is ill, he is hurting, he is emotionally impotent right now'– I am hurting. I have found my fire again and I do not want to let him put it out. Nor do I want to feel I have not tried everything I am able to before giving this up.

For now, we turn inland, towards Askja, towards the desert: the interior where nobody can live. It is accessible by normal vehicles only in summer – that momentary suspension of elemental extremes, replaced by a rapid transformation of matter: snow melts; meltwater gushes and drains; rivers fill and flow. There is not time for much growth to take hold on the dark lava sand, except the occasional miraculous pink mound of moss campion, and tussocks of lyme grass whose delicate network of roots attempts to hold this fragile terrain together. The crowds of tourists come – curious to penetrate it, to feel they have been to the furthest corner of the Earth – and leave again soon after. Now in September few tourists will be left. Autumn's chest is fully inflated, ready to breathe out the winter at any moment.

Quite soon, we notice a single white house with a bright red roof, perched on the lip of a lava field. Péturskirkja. It is an extraordinary juxtaposition: a microcosm of domesticity in the vastness of this raw terrain. We draw close. Propped against the house is a ladder; one old man at the top and another at the bottom. They are giving the building a lick of paint before the winter comes. The house is little more than a concrete room with a roof – a shelter probably used during sheep gatherings. Certainly, nobody lives in it. Given that we have come on a 'foraging' mission, the men's presence is slightly inconvenient.

We pull up in front of the house, which now stands above us on a low cliff – the edge of a lava field. One of the men saunters over to the edge in paint-spattered overalls, brush in hand. He looks down at us, his woollen hat askew on top of his bright white hair. His broad shoulders give him an air of guardianship of this place, like a priest at a pulpit.

'Welcome to Péturskirkja.'

'*Góðan daginn*,' we greet him, searching our minds for a different reason to be here than what could be deemed as potential thieving. 'So... you're painting?' Bjarni stalls. I know that, as a rule, they will chat about the weather and where we are heading, which will give me more time to think of an excuse. A radio burbles in the distance.

'Yes, we are. A freshen-up. Before the weather turns bad. Although that may happen sooner than we expected.' The man squints into the sun as he turns to gaze into the far distance, as if he might spy a clue as to its ETA.

'*Núúú*.' says Bjarni. 'What's the forecast?'

'There's a storm coming tomorrow morning or possibly sooner, and they're advising people to leave the area.'

We have talked about doing this trip for years. It is painful how close we are to the lake: we cannot turn back now. Though I also don't want to be one of *those* people, who at least once a year makes the headlines by getting into trouble ignoring safety advice and putting the lives of those who attempt to rescue them at risk.

'We're heading to Askja. We *really* want to make it. Do you think it's OK to continue?' I ask, slightly rhetorically.

If we, or Icelanders in general, were risk-averse, they would say 'absolutely not'. But they and we are not. In this moment the storm has not yet come and may not come for some time. So he answers with the classic response that at once throws responsibility back to the questioner and to the gods:

'*Já. Er það ekki?*' ('Yes. Isn't it?')

Bjarni and I look at each other and smile, then look again at the man. When this is said, it is implicit that you are both agreed *in that moment* but aware that the situation might change to make all involved review the judgement call – although nobody will be considered responsible. It is a phrase that is as good as any at summing up an Icelandic approach to decision-making, and one that I learned early on.

'Would you like to come in?' he invites us.

'Actually, that would be great. Would you mind if we eat our picnic inside?' It is already past three o'clock and we have been too absorbed in the worlds of vegetation underfoot to think about lunch. And it gives us a 'reason' to be here that is not foraging wood burners.

'Help yourself.'

He tells us Péturskirkja was built by a farmer, Pétur Jónsson, in 1925, the name 'St Peter's' revealing the man's sense of humour. This humble shelter in the middle of a lava desert has been a godsend for many. It is a *sæluhús* (a 'house of well-being'): built to be used as a gathering hut during the annual sheep round-up. But shelter is shelter and over the years it has acted as a refuge for travellers, and an emergency rescue hut.

'I need to carry on here but make yourselves at home.' The white-haired man strolls over to join his colleague.

We climb up some steps chipped into the cliff and greet the man who is up the ladder. Stepping across the threshold into the hut, we experience this feeling of refuge instantly. The thick walls hush the wind, and we begin to unwind. We lay out our picnic on the long table: rye bread, Gouda, and lettuce and tomatoes grown in geothermal greenhouses in the south. The small, whitewashed room is lined on three sides by bunk beds. A new wood-burning stove, which probably replaced the one we've come looking for, stands in the corner beside an opening onto a tiny kitchen. We sit in the pool of sunlight streaming through the window, able suddenly to feel its warmth now that we are sheltered from the well-travelled wind of the plains. We might have thought it a good idea to press on, having learned of the imminent weather change. But there is something perverse that seems to happen to time in Iceland. When needed – *really* needed – speed, efficiency and stamina can be mustered, almost as if by magic. But until that point, a laid-back approach is the status quo. In this moment, the weather is good, we are hungry and there are still five hours of light left.

We enquire about the wood burner on our way out. We are glad to hear it has been taken away to be restored and will be used. Haukur will also be pleased and accept it as a valid reason for us to come home empty-handed. I am touched to have been able to spend a while in this insertion of colour, shelter and humanity, in the everyday of some residents of the sparsely populated north, before we head back out in our van into the grey desert.

The flat horizon of charcoal-grey lava sand is stuccoed with rock of the same colour; hewn, chiselled, sculpted and smoothed by wind and lava fragments – a rasping tongue which licks protrusions of rock into shapes of its own imagination.

We journey across the surface of the Earth, its curve almost perceptible; the only measure of distance covered being a single volcanic cone moving slowly closer, then passing us. The wind picks up and sands the paintwork on our van a little more with each kilometre. It is a beat-up old thing anyway. Ahead of us, the clouds gather and darken their underbellies. A light rain starts to fall. Mercifully, it settles the dust and makes the rocks glisten in the lowering light.

At last we reach a river. The water and the green ribbon of vegetation that follows its course is like an apparition. Globed stems of mature angelica poke this way and that, and shrubs of willow tumble around their feet. The river is clear and steady now, not mixed with snowmelt and turbulence as it would have been

earlier in the summer. Its name is what it is: Jökulsá á Fjöllum –
'the glacial river in the mountains'.

We stop the van and climb out to listen to the river's gurgling, to
relish this sudden band of life. Bjarni skims stones. I harvest angelica
seeds. We are well practised at silently, together, knowing when the
point comes that it is time to move on. We climb back into the van,
and Bjarni expertly fords the river as he always does – slow and steady
– the water reaching part way up the doors. He switches on the radio
for an update. It whines and crackles a little now that we are some
way into the interior, but we can make out some words – Bjarni more
than I.

'Oh,' he says.

'What?'

'The storm might come as early as midnight. I think we're going
to have to go to the lake this evening, so that we can leave first thing
tomorrow.'

When you are in a hurry and know that you will have to retrace
the very same route only hours later, time passes very slowly. We
drive on, in silence, my heart starting to race a little. Bjarni doesn't
do turning back, and in this scenario, nor do I.

Finally, we arrive at Hell's campsite where there are two wooden
huts and a campground empty of tents. A triangular metal toilet hut
lies on its side, and nobody is to be seen. There are a few four-wheel
drives parked along the track. We make our way to the warden's hut.
He has seen us coming and opens the door to his warm, sheltered
space – his home for the summer months.

'Good evening,' he says. He is wholesome-looking, his blue eyes clear and glad. He is wearing a grey Icelandic jumper and smoking a pipe, as if he is enjoying his country persona for the last days of the tourist season before returning, as most do, to his Reykjavík winter life. 'Are you staying the night?'

'Yes, in our van,' I chip in.

'That's easy then. I've asked all the campers to stay in the huts tonight because there's a storm coming.'

'Yes. We've heard.'

'Coffee?'

'Thanks… Think we're going to walk to Askja before dark, so we can leave first thing if needed.'

'Not a bad idea. You've got about an hour and a half before it gets properly dark.'

It is only recently that real darkness has become a possibility – true night finally becoming part of the daily cycle as the sun arcs southwards in autumn. Summers in Iceland are spent looking forward to this darkness, and when we least need it, it comes.

'There are some yellow markers on the trail, so you should be able to find your way in the dim.' He raises his pipe in farewell and steps back into the warmth of his hut, closing the door. The sweet scent of pipe tobacco lingers for a moment.

We make off up the path leading from the campsite, hoping it will not be too far to the lake, and knowing in the back of our minds that this is probably not the right time to think about swimming in it, although a bathe in a hot lake is exactly what we need. I am

300

cocooned in my usual attire for any activity outside, which seems to be most activities at one point or another: thermal underwear, jeans, an Icelandic jumper, a big down jacket, a woolly hat, woolly gloves and thermal welly boots. Bjarni usually wears a slightly less practical version of the same outfit, and has been known to hike up a mountain wearing a suit. This time, at least he has a coat, although his charity shop trainers are not the most appropriate footwear for the task.

My wellies thud purposefully. We are not used to walking this fast on an adventure. Our walks usually take the form of a meander with a loose destination, and the possibility of losing ourselves in small details on the way – like the bright lichens creeping across a rock face, or the crystalline sulphur tracery around a geothermal vent. At first, our steps are a solid crunch on crumbs of metallic black lava, like a sea of very burnt toast. As we round a hill the landscape opens up into a bowl that scoops down towards the caldera's edge. Gravity and urgency pull us faster. Suddenly I feel as if I am bouncing. Each footstep rings in a way that my ears and brain struggle to fathom. The ground beneath my feet seems to be hollow. Are we in fact walking on a fragile crust thinly veiling a massive dormant magma chamber?

As the warden said, there are yellow plastic markers with fluorescent strips – the same kind that mark the edges of the roads: double strips for the left edge and single for the right, in case there is so much snow or fog that the road itself becomes invisible. They seem conspicuous here, but they are useful for getting us quickly to our destination. We begin to run. The wind picks up a little. My thick-soled rubber boots spring on the rubber earth. The black ground becomes darker than the sky, although it is the sky that is darkening. We are running towards something that we should be running away from. Everything is surreal: I feel as if I am inside a dream in which I have died. Is this what Hell is like and is that where I am going?

We reach the upward slope of the bowl and run up it, bent forwards into the wind. We stop on the ridge and are almost instantly knocked over by the strength of the gust. We cling to each other in glee at the sheer force of it, our bodies suddenly as unstable as feathers. Our eyes squint against the wind and its cargo. Through the sand gathering on our eyelashes we can make out the oval form of the lake, bright in the dim. We hold hands and turn our backs on the wind, leaning into it at forty-five degrees. *This* is being alive. *This* is why we are still together.

Clambering down the other side of the ridge towards the lake gives us some shelter, and the calm to drink in this scene. Víti: a still, oval pool the colour of opal at the bottom of Askja, a black rock bowl; like a gemstone in a raku-fired chalice. Beyond the bowl is a much bigger lake of darker teal blue, choppy as the storm mounts. It is the tipping point of evening. As the darkening sky soaks into the blackness of the sand, Víti appears to luminesce. It is as if *this* is the place on Earth that is light's own home; the place to which it returns at evening time, draining from the hillsides in a daily migration. I wonder if many people have ever seen Víti at this time of day, in this

302

season. Were it not for the coming storm, we also would not have witnessed this miracle.

The time comes where we know the window to return is as small as it can be. Again we run, bouncing across the hollow earth, making out each yellow marker from the one before, until the path to the campsite comes into view.

*   *   *

During the night, I hold Bjarni tight as the wind rocks the side of our van violently. Occasionally, he lifts himself onto his elbow, and looks out of the window, as if it will narrow our chances of being blown over. We have parked in the most sheltered spot we can, so all there is to do is hope. I imagine I am at sea, so that I might find the movements of the van more relaxing. Sleep, like the wind, comes in gusts.

*   *   *

In the morning, people in brightly coloured anoraks emerge from the main hut, one at a time, running to their cars with luggage and straight back to the hut again. The bed is empty – Bjarni must have braved the toilet. One man comes to put some bags in the jeep next to our van. I see him open the vertically hinged door to his boot and run off to get more luggage.

'Idiot!' I curse.

It is a ground rule I learned early on: hold onto doors in strong wind, or just keep them closed. When he returns I knock on the window to get his attention. I am worried for him, but also for our van. We are in the line of fire. I knock and gesticulate wildly at the window, but he cannot hear me. Finally, I take the plunge and get out. It is not the weather for pleasantries.

'Excuse me,' I shout from within my hood, having to tap him on the shoulder to be heard. 'You mustn't leave the door open. It might rip off.' He looks at me, bemused. He must think I am vastly exaggerating. 'This is a really strong wind. A loose door is bad for everyone.'

Admittedly, you never hear of such stories on the continent, and this is still Europe after all. But he probably hasn't lived in a village where cars have been moved around by the wind. Besides, the evidence for my caution blows around us. He slams the door shut and runs back to the hut.

Though it is wild, the wind does not feel as fearsome once I am standing on solid ground. Bjarni strides across the car park. 'That was fun,' he smiles.

'What, the toilet?'

'Well, yeah, but also there's a gorgeous gorge just behind the campground. It looks most int*rrr*iguing.' Bjarni rolls his 'r's more than anyone I know, and can make anything sound intriguing because of it. 'Shall we have a little walk?'

I consent with a smile. I love this about him also: his ability to hold a calamity at bay and focus instead on something wonderful right in front of us. Again, the apparent urgency of our departure is postponed because of a more urgent tug in the present: our shared inability to turn down opportunities for moments with the sublime.

'I think we need to protect our eyes. There's loads of pumice blowing around in there,' he adds.

And so it is that, like the mad creatures we are, we make our way up the gorge wrapped in jackets and scarves and with our eyes protected by Speedo swimming goggles – mine a blue-tinted plastic, as if the scene was not surreal enough already.

It feels like borrowed time, as if we have been turned away from Hell and asked to come back later; invited to explore its waiting room in the meantime. The gorge is an intimate topography of jagged steep sides; nooks and crevices that arrange themselves into expressions on the faces of trolls. The wind funnels through it. Flying specks of pumice sting my face, and I can hardly convince my brain that, with goggles on, I do not need to squint. A river courses through a pebbly riverbed perhaps 6 metres wide, pausing here and there in sheltered pools where it whirls in eddies, not wanting to stop, like a jogger at traffic lights.

'*Sko!*' beams Bjarni, pointing at one of them. 'Look.'

I crouch for a closer inspection. On the surface of the eddy, floating crumbs of pumice ride this perpetual spiral. They look like Rice Krispies swimming in milk. The crumbs line up flank to flank, buoyed by the flow, until they hit a patch of confusion, then find their way onwards again. It mirrors the course of our marriage, and I long for the 'onwards': our eddy has lasted just about as long as I can manage. Tugged by Bjarni's playful curiosity, I flit between my adult internalizations and a present state of mind like a child with her playmate.

To Bjarni, it looks like an enormous flock of sheep being rounded up, as seen from the sky. We imagine that we are giants looking down on this sheep gathering of his. It is a tiny happening in a foot-square pocket of this Earth. We have decided not to run from our impending chaos, but to stay and witness it; to find space within it. We shall return to England for the winter, together.

The Raven's Nest

Bjarni and I have overwintered in England again, living in a rented house and finding jobs: a last-ditch attempt at finding a shape and rhythm of life that fits both of us; at saving our marriage. It did not go well. He finally moved back to the Westfjords in May, to his family. Now I'm back here too, briefly, to figure out how to deconstruct this life we shared; how to weave together these fragments of places and relationships into something that might serve me now. Our home sits frozen in time, full of our things as we left them last summer, but with neither of us living in it. I am safe now, staying in the house alone, unhitched from the centre of the mess we were in. But I am in pieces; adrift.

What am I to this place, these people, Bjarni's family? Am I a tourist now? What do I do with this experience when it has changed my shape?

Bjarni lets me borrow his car. I take a drive through the mountain tunnel to Bolungarvík, without any particular agenda. This journey is body memory: the route I drove for more than a year, back and forth through the tunnel, to drop Bjarni off and pick him up from his fishing tours. For the moment, it represents to me my enabling of a situation I did not want. I'd like to recast this memory, these memories, into something new or revelatory.

I realize this is a very Icelandic thing I am doing: going for a drive for no particular reason. It is called a *rúntur* (a 'round') and kids start doing it as soon as they get their driving licence. A more extended version of this which might come a little later in life is called an *óvissuferð* – one of my favourite words – an 'unknown journey'.

I emerge from the tunnel into the daylight. I feel like going to the top of the mountain, Bolafjall, which fills my windscreen. The view from there is astonishing: the kind of view that puts things in perspective. You can see across to the intricate fjords and mountains of Hornstrandir – one of Europe's 'last wildernesses' – and out into the open sea. You can imagine, but not quite see, the abandoned villages. People say you can see Greenland on a clear day, but I never have. You can watch the trawlers and small fishing boats cruise slowly across the broad blue vista of Ísafjarðardjúp, humming like bumblebees drunk on nectar.

At the top, there is a signboard that I translated into English for the Sheriff of Bolungarvík, Jónas, a couple of years ago. It is about the history of the NATO radar tracking station that sits, also abandoned, like a giant golf ball on the wildest of courses. I remember being struck by the text's opening, not least because it was my first introduction to Fata Morgana, a complex mirage that appears to float landmasses in the sky:

> *You are on Bolafjall at 625 metres above sea level.*
> *The earth you stand on is a part of the Westfjords high*

plateau, which came into existence more than 14 million
years ago.
It is commonly stated that Greenland is visible from here in
clear weather. In fact that is not possible unless a strong Fata
Morgana lifts the glacier's image above the horizon.
Around 25 million years ago Iceland and Greenland were
connected. When the continents drifted apart, their edges sank
bit by bit into the ocean and Iceland became an island.

Bolafjall has a lazy summit: because of this radar station there is a four-wheel drive track, though I'm not too sure about risking it with Bjarni's car. Perhaps I'll see if Jónas fancies a jaunt. He'll have a jeep – most people do. I'll try and find him later.

For now, I pass the expanse of gravel where the Arctic terns nest and brood all summer. It is several years since the shrimp factory dumped a mass of shrimp shell there, knowing it would work well as a fertilizer. Vegetation is beginning to take hold now. The hundreds of terns – *kría* – hover, swoop, *kriiiiiii* and click, ferociously guarding their young. They are preparing to leave for their epic southward journey.

Bolungarvík looks just the same as the day I left. Life goes on in this small fishing village of 933 inhabitants, clustered around the outermost tendril of the national road network. The gutting sheds, the wholesale fish market and the weighing ramp curve around the harbour, where the trawler *Valbjörn* is unloading its catch, which Bjarni will weigh and record. I wave as I pass Arngeir, Bjarni's father's best friend – the one who towed their summerhouse, floating, across the sea. He is smoking a pipe outside one of the gutting sheds, clad in bright orange rubber dungarees and a plastic hair net. The few wide streets lined with concrete houses extend behind the harbour until abruptly the wild, treeless valley begins. Not many people are out and about, though it is summer.

My car draws alongside a golf buggy which is humming along the cycle track, travelling faster than I am. A shaft of sunlight cascades between two mountain peaks onto the golf course where a man tees up a shot, dwarfed by his surroundings.

I hang a left to where I think I'll find Jónas.

Náttúrustofa – the Natural Science Institute of the Westfjords – and the Natural History Museum are housed in a characterless pebbledash block upstairs from the tiny, cramped Samkaup supermarket, which I have frequented many times. I smile as I recall how the shopping trolleys are provided but ill advised. In the narrow aisles the villagers briefly cross paths with, and crash into, docking fishermen coming to stock up with Coca-Cola, meat and a few withering vegetables for their next tour. Once upon a time, Bjarni was one of them and I was one of the 'villagers'. His stocking-up shopping trip was sometimes the only time I saw him in days. On Bjarni's boat, they never ate the fish they caught. Every day and every night: trawl, haul, gut, pack. 'How can we eat it too?' he said.

Upstairs in the Náttúrustofa, it is the inverse of downstairs. The end of August is already the end of the tourist season. It is clearly not worth paying someone to be on the museum entrance desk: I am probably the first visitor of the day. The door buzzes as I enter, which prompts a man behind a glass partition to come through into the one-room museum. I can see it's Giorgio.

I know Giorgio, a little bit. He is one of the other foreigners here who became entangled first with the place, and then with an Icelander. He, more than some, has found his groove – a career even – working here at the Náttúrustofa.

'*Hæ, Hæ*. Is... Jónas in?' I ask him hesitatingly. There are few enough people in villages like this one that it mostly suffices to mention a first name for anyone to know who you are referring to.

The coordinates for Jónas on my mental map of people and institutions that I may one day need have placed him here, but I cannot recall their source. I have found that things are never made particularly obvious or accessible: it is the incomer's job to ask the questions and to know which questions to ask. Signage is discreet. It is assumed that everybody just *knows*. Locals *do* know. My map has had to be created, and constantly revised, from snippets of information gleaned and linked up – as I've learned Icelandic and met more people, paid attention to details in their conversation and learned what questions to ask. It has felt like discovering and recording an archipelago of sense, island by island. Sometimes an island turns out to be a mirage.

Giorgio saunters towards me.

'*Sæl og blessuð!*'

He is handsome and full-bodied; Italian but with a round, dark-stubbled face, more Latin American-looking somehow. His eyes are warm when he smiles: the creases around them break into a volley of arrows pointing towards the kindness in their dark-brown depths.

I feel bad for not having greeted him properly first, instead furthering my new-found agenda to find the Sheriff to take me up the mountain. I know my omission is a response to an Icelandic peculiarity that I have never got my head around. Approaches to greeting have always struck me as fickle: one moment I might be treated like a long-lost friend; another I might be ignored in the street. The result is that I never know quite where I stand with people. When it happens, the greeting '*Sæl og blessuð*' for women or '*Sæll og blessaður*' for men means '[May you be] Happy and blessed', which is no small wish for someone. Currently I feel anything but. I've learned not to take the blanking personally, not to read into it: everyone has their story and their norms. But it means that sometimes I am less friendly than I might be, in a bizarre attempt to fit in by being similarly closed. It feels even more unnatural having spent more time in England recently, surrounded by mannerisms I only noticed when I left them. Today is a 'long-lost friend' day, it seems. I am relieved: I need it.

'*Sæll og blessaður*,' I reply, remembering to accentuate the '*ll*' for the masculine. I was surprised by how my Icelandic began to flow as soon as I landed, eleven months since I last spoke it. It was as if a pause button had been pressed since last summer and the words had been waiting to come out. But what will I do with them now, all these words in my body that only make sense here? Where will I put them in England?

As much as I enjoy this flow, it feels slightly forced that we two foreigners are communicating in Icelandic when we can both speak much better English, so I am glad when he continues: 'Jónas? His office is across the road, by the bank. It's open 1.30 to 3.30, Tuesdays and Thursdays. So, no luck today.'

'Hah! He's in work for *that* long?' I jest.

Once I stopped being irritated by the opening times here, I was amused and touched by them. Their complexity took up a lot of brain power when I was first trying to establish myself. Like the weather, no timings seemed constant or consistent. And in trying to look them up online, I quickly discovered Icelandic Google only cooperates if you have the word for the thing you are searching for grammatically correct. As every noun changes depending on what is happening to it, this is a tall order for a language learner.

This is even the case with names. About a year after I met Bjarni, he gave me a rock into which he had sculpted the profile of a face – my face. He has a talent for animating the natural forms of rock, wood or bone; transforming it into something or someone. In this rock he had seen the beginnings of me, and I remember being deeply moved by the gesture. On one edge, he had carved '*Til Söru*'. I had to ask what it meant: 'For Sarah,' he said, as if it was obvious. 'You can't change my *name!*' I said jokingly, though admittedly feeling a subtle threat to something, a part of my identity that had never been challenged before. I realized I would not only have to accept the spelling of my name being changed, Icelandicized, but also the very sound of it too. I realized too that his family might have mentioned my name many times without me being aware because I didn't recognize the sound.

The result of Icelandic Google's idiosyncrasies was that I could not research opening times without going to the place anyway. But I came to appreciate what these 'irregular' opening times demonstrated: that work is not everything, or at least that everybody does several jobs. They cannot give themselves to only one thing: Iceland does not function like that. An existence is forged out of multiple improvised solutions. That is how existence should be; I have learned that much. That is the shape of resilience.

'The Natural History Museum': it is a grand title for a yellowing collection of birds' eggs, ageing taxidermy, and the enormous disintegrating jawbone of a blue whale. The cases full of birds are reflected in the polished grey lino, rippling slightly like a boat reflected in almost still water.

'Why are you looking for Jónas? Are you getting a divorce?'

No doubt word will have spread about me and Bjarni and it is true that the Sheriff deals with the bureaucracy of major life events. Yet I am caught unawares by such a forward question from someone who is ultimately not much more than an acquaintance.

'Actually I am.' I realize this is the first time I've said the words publicly. 'But that's not why I'm looking for Jónas.'

My throat tightens, then snaps and my eyes pool with tears.

'*Oii* sorry. I didn't realize. I mean, I thought you and Bjarni split up ages ago. It's still fresh, huh?'

All I can do is nod. I feel like a little girl.

My heart has clanged like a cracked bell since the day I didn't recognize him, since the patterns we had carefully established – those

intricate dances and gestures of a loving relationship – suddenly
stopped working.

'Ages ago'. Does he mean May this year when Bjarni left England to
come here alone, which no doubt the community would have noticed?
Or a year ago when I committed to giving it one last push but found
my shoulder up against a mountain, and learned that pushing is not
the way to go. Or even two years ago when the extent of Bjarni's
depression became apparent to me and Bjarni (though I've no idea
how to Giorgio). When does a relationship end? In this moment,
Giorgio and I do not have the same relationship with time. And time
does not have a linear relationship with pain, or grief, or love.

'I'm so *insensible*. What's the problem, then? Are you pregnant?'

At this point, I have to laugh as well as cry.

'No. I've just put on a bit of weight, maybe.'

'God, I really should shut up… You want some coffee?'

'That would be nice actually, thanks.'

His shoes squeak across the floor as he disappears behind the glass
door to the Bureau kitchenette. I stand alone among the stuffed
svartfuglar and the *svartfuglsegg* admiring their variegated colours and
perfect shape – rounded at the base and pointed at the top: this shape
that has come to mean so much. I read the curling label:

> Guillemots and Razorbill only lay one egg at a time
> (except for the Black Guillemot that lays 1–2). None of the
> Guillemots build nests but lay the eggs on the bare rock and
> don't try to hide their eggs. The Common and the Brünnich's

*Guillemot lay their eggs on defined ledges or recesses, but the
Razorbill prefers cracks or other more sheltered places.*

The last time I saw Giorgio we were both helping to return a replica
nineteenth-century wooden fishing boat to its winter storage. Was it
last summer, or the one before? I forget: the summers and the winters
look mostly the same in my memories. Differences between years are
marked by major events that have some impact on the rhythm; or a trip
abroad. In the summer, this boat is housed just up the road from here at
Ósvör, a collection of replica stone fishermen's huts built as a museum.

The boat is part of the display at Ósvör, and I cannot count the
number of times I have stood beside it with one of the bearded
museum staff dressed in lambskin trousers, smock and sou'wester,
amusing tourists with his rope 'G-string': the pre-modern-era safety
equipment for a man overboard. I would tell them how the boat was
used to catch Greenlandic shark, which was in demand for its liver oil
– shipped to Europe by the barrel-load for street lighting. I would tell
them that a crew of six men with a captain rowed and sailed for three
days into Greenlandic waters to find these sharks. I would tell them
that a woman stayed at the hut preparing food, fixing clothes and lines,
and darning the men's woollen socks and their two-thumbed mittens:
a vernacular bit of kit designed to be turned around as a hole wore in
one joint, so the wearer could continue rowing. A bit of kit made to
continue working even once it was damaged.

One September evening on the pebble beach, I had happened upon
a team of men, which included Giorgio, the G-string man and Bjarni's

father's friend Arngeir, smoking his pipe as ever. They were sliding the boat onto a series of whale ribs, placing the rib released from the back to the front, and repeating, all the way to the water. This is how it was always done, they said. I took over with the rib shifting as they pushed, until the boat had made it into the sea. I accepted their invitation for a short trip across the bay, which consisted of one word: 'Coming?'

In four years, I had never made it to the Natural History Museum, even out of curiosity over how notoriously tired the displays were: aesthetically powerful enough to be used as set for a scene in the film *Nói Albinói*. Thanks to Giorgio, my first visit is turning out to be quite memorable. I think I'll stay here for a while.

I am still not clear about the responsibilities that Jónas's Sheriff title confers. What I do know is that he has given me work, entrusting me with the translation of several tourist signboards without any initial evidence of my ability, and it has continued since I've moved away. He is always very happy with my translations. Once, he paid me double what I'd asked for because he was late paying. Perhaps he thinks I am a genius learning Icelandic so fast. What he doesn't know is that I have a nepotistic pact with Bjarni's uncle Salvar who pre-translates the passages for me in his charming and slightly too literal way. I then work them into more flowing English. Salvar also works for Jónas designing the artwork for these signboards.

Earlier, I passed a signboard that I'd translated for Jónas a couple of years ago. It is a special one made of driftwood logs on a patch of grass down by the harbour. A brazier stands in front of it, and

Salvar's design is a patchwork of parchment and runes. The signboard celebrates Bolungarvík as being a possible place of origin of the *Völuspá* – The Prophecy of the Seeress – a part of the *Poetic Edda* detailing the creation of the world and its imminent destruction, thought to have been authored by Bolungarvík's female settler and her son around AD 940. Legend has it that this settler was named Þuríður sundafyllir – 'Þuríður the channel-filler' – because she used her magic to attract myriad fish to the region as she had done in her native Norway. The fishing village of Bolungarvík was born as a result. Once, stone fishermen's huts, like the ones at Ósvör museum, lined the beach. Still now the trawlers catch millions of fish, and many families have someone at sea. To think that the actions of a sorceress more than a thousand years ago precipitated the end of my marriage.

What am I now; now that I am gladly not a fisherman's wife?

Recently, I completed a signboard translation for Jónas's most recent brainchild – a project to formalize hitchhiking as a mode of public transport in the region, by having signposted pick-up points, listing guidelines for behaviour. Through this, I learned the beautiful Icelandic word-concoction for hitchhiker, which I could easily deduce by knowing the parts. *Putta-ferða-maður*: 'thumb-journey-human'. I enjoy still being asked to do this work. It feels like a part of me still lives here, and if I wish to I can visit my words dotted around the landscape whenever I return. Perhaps this is what I am now: a thumb-journey-human.

Giorgio returns with coffee and chocolate-coated raisins – '*nammi*' – the word for any sweet treats.

He leads me over to the whale jawbone which is in two identical halves. Each is at least 3 metres long, slightly tapering at the end. The brittle structure – full of air holes for buoyancy – is clearly disintegrating. It is wrapped in cling film for now, to keep the fragments from falling to the floor.

'This is the one that used to be at Skrúður, remember?'

I remember it well. Skrúður is a miraculous botanical garden, an oasis in the rugged coastal terrain at Núpur, 50 kilometres from here, created by one Reverend Sigtryggur Guðlaugsson in 1909. It was one of the stops on my guiding trips. The Reverend had been headmaster of the neighbouring school, which these days is a hotel. With the garden, he wished to show his pupils that hard work and the right materials could make an Eden out of any corner of this Earth. The long white reaches of this jawbone were once placed symmetrically at the entrance to the garden, touching at their high tips to form an archway. I must have taken more than a thousand cruise-ship passengers under it in the three summers I worked as a guide.

'It got in a bad condition, so we had to take it down. It doesn't look so beautiful like this but what can we do?'

After coffee and chat, Giorgio leaves me to browse the collection. Ironically, much of it you can see alive and well not far from here. I'm not sure why tourists would come to see these birds and mammals in a museum, but their expensive trips don't allow the luxury of time. Perhaps they'd rather see them dead than not at all. The effort made here is charming if you let go of expectations, but it is clearly an effort made a couple of decades ago.

Am I a tourist now? No. I will never be. Not here. I have gathered too much that is now a part of me. And I have left too much of myself around this place. But what am I now, to this place and these people, to Bjarni's family? And what are they to me? What can I build with this experience?

A cluster of sticks in a cubic glass case catches my eye. It is both chaotic and coherent. I stroll over and look at it from above – a circular nest perhaps a metre in diameter. The perimeter, which makes up most of it, is a rough entanglement of twigs, driftwood, mussel shells, a strip of yellowing plastic container, a sheep's shoulder blade, a wooden knife handle, a TV aerial, and the rusted head of a rake with four missing tines. It is perfect for its purpose – a hotchpotch of plant, human-made and animal detritus holding it together, weighing it down against the high winds. There are no big trees here for a large bird to nest in: the nest must be resilient alone on a cliff. Its centre is a small, intimate hemisphere – less than a third of the whole: a bed of intricately woven fine grasses and frayed green plastic rope threads, lined with down. Inside this centre lie four small eggs, almost lost in the flotsam. The label reads: *Raven's Nest*. The nest is 'safe' now, sealed in this moment against the high winds. It is safe, though these eggs will never hatch. How might it live again, contain life, out in the unknowable wilds of the future?

Sjóndeildarhringur – Horizon
(*sjón* – sight; *deild* – partition; *hringur* – circle)

August 2014

I am going back to England in the midst of a tremor swarm. I am going back to England, unable to get divorced because of a telephone and internet drop-out.

In Reykjavík, with an afternoon to spare before my flight, I decide to check out some of my old haunts. After a bowl of *momos* at a new Tibetan café on the harbour front, I walk across to the Museum of Photography. It is housed on the top floor of the unexpectedly stylish Municipal Library. Rows of books, magazines, DVDs and music are shelved among clusters of white designer bucket chairs, which sit in the middle of bright rooms encircled by windows, allowing you always to get a glimpse of the mountains and the sea; to constantly remind you as you delve into the rest of the world, that we are Here on this rock.

I am happy to find that there is a retrospective exhibition of an Icelandic press photographer, Ragnar Axelsson, whose work has captured my imagination since early on in my relationship with

Iceland. For the past thirty years, he has documented the disappearing ways of life in the Arctic with complete devotion. His extensive journeying around Iceland, Greenland and the Faroes has yielded an unparalleled body of work featuring humans and animals and their ongoing conversations with their changing landscapes. Through his eyes, and with his instinct, his index finger on the shutter release is as a stethoscope to a heartbeat. He catches in black and white those intimate and fleeting moments that distil many lives lived across many decades, shown through one person, one horse, or one mountain. The viewer participates as much as Axelsson does in those moments – we hear and smell the scenes he portrays.

There are perhaps fifteen darkroom-printed images in this show, all at least a metre and a half wide and a metre tall, mounted spaciously on white walls. They are large enough that you can get inside them. The labels are brief: there is nothing to say. The images say it all and you are silenced by it. My eyes scan the whisking textures of a horse's mane; the tension of the rope reins on a dog sled; the tones from the darkest black of an Inuit hunter's pupil to the burning white of an ice field, through flecks of grey resolution clustering like midge swarms in summer.

One image roots my feet to the ground and makes my stomach thud. My focus zooms out and I see it as a whole. It is a grey sea at a tilt. In the foreground, a small white wooden boat captained by a solitary old man ploughs towards some near-distant dark mountains, its frothy wake spilling off the margins. I *know* those mountains. I know their profile like I know Bjarni's neck. That is *my* valley;

my village. I check the label to make sure. *Fisherman Guðmundur Eyjólfur, in Ísafjarðardjúp, the West Fjords.*

I am right. It *is* my valley and my village, seen from the sea, from the northwest; from an angle I have never seen it until now, but from which Bjarni saw it many times: every time he left me and every time he returned. From here, if he had a telescope, he would have seen me filming one of the saddest video clips I have ever made. He would have seen me standing at our living-room window watching as his bright-orange trawler slowly sailed across the fjord from the right of the frame to the left, moving imperceptibly slowly in the vastness of the darkening blue evening. I had tried to call him. The phone rang and rang but was never answered. He was probably doing something important with the nets. I did not know when I would next get to speak to him, or when he would be back. Nor did he. It was not the first time that had happened, not at all. But that time I had nearly reached my limit, and the only thing I could think of doing to cope was to video that moment; to attempt to make it abstract; to turn it into 'material'.

The photograph in front of me is both sad and uplifting because of what it portrays: a lone ageing fisherman, buffered from the coming weather by his woollen jumper and rubber dungarees. The small boat means he is a day-fisherman, who comes home each evening. He is nearly home now. There is a bucketful of fish, caught by his single line. His wife will be happy with the catch, and their house will be immaculate when he returns, as it was when he left that morning. He will scale and gut the fish, then have a shower. She will boil one fish and some potatoes for their dinner and put the rest in the freezer for later. Then they will watch the news to see what is happening in the rest of the world.

Few people fish like this now. The quota that was once allocated to all fishermen has mostly been bought up by huge fishing companies. That was the problem: the quota's saleability. For many small-scale fishermen, the temptation to have a lot of money up front rather than toiling for years in cruel weathers was too great. They did not realize that, in just twenty years, selling off their quota would kill a way of life that has been part of Icelandic identity for centuries; that it would cause whole villages to have almost no livelihood. Back when proposals were being budgeted for Vestfjarðargöng, the tunnel which now links Ísafjörður with the fjords beyond, Davíð Oddsson, then-Governor of the Central Bank of Iceland, claimed the state coffers would be better off if they put the whole population of Suðureyri – one such village – in an apartment block in the capital and let it return to wilderness. But this man is a stoic Westfjordian, still out on the sea, not prepared to sell his quota and regret it; to bemoan his loss in an old people's home in Reykjavík.

For me this image is also so much more. If that is my village that must be my *house*. Here, on a sheet of photographic paper at the top of a tower block, I am looking at the corrugated-iron-clad house in which all of this life of mine happened in sharp focus and full colour – this joy, this loneliness, this love, this creation, this attempting to belong – reduced to an indistinct white rectangle nestled among leaden grey buttresses of basalt. It is a speck of background in another story that is different from my own yet so much the same: the end of one way of life and the beginning of another.

Acknowledgements

Many miles, years, encounters and relationships have gone into this story playing out and finding its way to the page. I am indebted to more people and places than I can mention, but I hope the appreciation woven through these pages is evident. My gratitude goes foremost to Iceland and those I met there – human and other – for their elemental truths; in particular, to my ex-husband and his family for all they taught me – lessons which are still reverberating years later. And to the Icelandic language for inspiring in me evolving ways to be in and with the world, and for showing me what richness there is in silence.

My deepest gratitude to: Janni Howker for believing I had a book in me, for giving me the tools to start and for seeing what was needed. Sharon Blackie and David Knowles at the now defunct *Earthlines* magazine, the team at *Dark Mountain* and Robert Macfarlane for being early champions of my work and giving me the confidence to continue. Dr David Borthwick and Professor Alison Phipps for being profoundly insightful and supportive midwives and mentors for this book. The College of Social Sciences at the University of Glasgow for the PhD scholarship which made it possible, and to Professor Margaret Elphinstone and Professor Hayden Lorimer for their generosity as examiners.

Profound thanks to Olga Bloemen, Nancy Campbell, and Emily Lethbridge for their heartfelt and diligent feedback on my manuscript at various stages and to the places in which we met to discuss it. I am grateful beyond words for the chance encounter on the Faroese schooner Norðlýsið, which introduced me to Pétur Einarsson. For answering my thousands of tiny questions over many years, for keeping me connected across the distance and for helping me look back from the sea: þúsund þakkir.

For their unstinting emotional support and encouragement through good times and bad, I owe particular thanks to my parents Jean and Barrie, and to Jonny, Ben and Annabelle. Also to dear friends Maia & Hugh, Claire & Matt, Eva & Liam, Mary, Hans & Eva, Sam, Ezra, Alyssa & Zac, Ally & Ed, Laura, Kate, Beryl, Aitan, Olga, Pavlos, Lisa, Hannah, Sue, Lucy and Georgia for being hands at my back at various stages of this book's journey.

John Nicoll's incredible generosity provided an inspiring place to write for several months in a time of need and Dave and Sharon Wilkinson offered a nourishing space for the final touches. Colleagues and fellow artists Abi Andrews, Jo Blake, Nancy Campbell, Claire Dean, Tim Dee, Charlotte Du Cann, Jay Griffiths, Jill Hopper, Nick Hunt, Sarah Hymas, Natalie Marr, Autumn Richardson, Lucy Neal, Richard Skelton, and Em and Dougie Strang have all offered stimulating ideas and insight on writing and the creative life. I am grateful for all of it. Special thanks go to Cal Flynn for her incredibly generous and astute mentorship, and to Caroline Clarke and the Nan Shepherd Prize team and Jacques Testard at Fitzcarraldo Editions for their support and guidance on the journey to publication. Thanks also to the Kairos Collective, to the Body Breath and Story circle and to Rebecca Darbishire for helping me to stay in my body in among the desk-bound days.

I had the good fortune to meet filmmakers Bela Tarr and Kim Longinotto while living in Iceland and I am grateful for the impact of their words and their films. Ólöf Arnalds and Ólafur Arnalds are two inspiring artists among many whose music particularly has been a soundtrack and companion to the writing of this book. I treasure the alchemy they brought about.

Innilegar þakkir til Ásthildar og Juan, Önnsku og Úlfars, Benediktu og Inga Hrafns, Emiliano, Emily og Garðars, Jelena og Jóa, Mörtu, Smára og Nínu og Póe for their hospitality, humour, sound-boarding and fact-checking on my comings and goings to Iceland and from afar. Thanks also to Heimir Hanson at the Westfjords Tourist Information Office, the late Dick Phillips and his amazing Iceland library at Fljótsdalur, Dr Hugh Tuffen at Lancaster University, Dr Lizanne Henderson at the University of Glasgow, Þorsteinn Sigurðsson at the Marine and Freshwater Research Institute, Reykjavík, Cristian Gallo at the Natural Science Institute of the Westfjords and to Dr Emily Lethbridge and the staff at the Árni Magnússon Institute for providing place-related literature, images, data and statistics.

Huge thanks to Ed and Lucy at The Old Mill Palnackie, to Dougald Hine, Anna Björkman and The Assembly at A School Called Home, and Jo Blake and our storytelling circle, who all held space for me to fulfil my ambition to read *The Raven's Nest* aloud in its entirety before it found a publisher. These readings took place in a weekly candlelit *kvöldvaka* – first in a room, then on Zoom – in that strange winter of 2019/20. Much appreciation to Alice Campbell for darning so many of my socks as she listened!

To my wonderful agent Matthew Marland at Rogers, Coleridge & White, to my sensitive editors James Pulford and Sarah Chatwin, to Karen Duffy and the amazing team at Atlantic Books, my gratitude for handling this book with such care and curiosity.

To all the natural bodies of water – hot and cold – in which I sat or swam, or walked alongside while living and writing this story; to the quartz which sparks in the dark; to the glaciers which are in retreat; to the birches which pave the way for the rest, and the boletes which appear at their feet; and to Raven, companion and eternal inspiration – my gratitude and love. May you continue to speak to one another and to me, and may I continue to listen.